CAMBRIDGE LIBRARY COLLECTION

Books of enduring scholarly value

Printing and publishing history

The interface between authors and their readers is a fascinating subject in its own right, revealing a great deal about social attitudes, technological progress, aesthetic values, fashionable interests, political positions, economic constraints, and individual personalities. This part of the Cambridge Library Collection reissues classic studies in the area of printing and publishing history that shed light on developments in typography and book design, printing and binding, the rise and fall of publishing houses and periodicals, and the roles of authors and illustrators. It documents the ebb and flow of the book trade supplying a wide range of customers with products from almanacs to novels, bibles to erotica, and poetry to statistics.

Treatise on the Laws of Literary Property

Originally published in 1828, Robert Maugham's Treatise on the Laws of Literary Property was the first comprehensive examination of copyright laws in Britain. Maugham was writing at a time when the rights of the 'scholar' and the 'artist' were under great debate, themes paralleled in the increasingly 'digital' literary climate of the 21st century. Dedicated to protecting the rights of the author, Maugham branded the introduction of copyright laws, and the debate surrounding the subject, a 'great literary controversy'. His Treatise served to inspire changes in copyright law and provides an accessible, detailed, and thorough discussion of the statutes that governed British authors and publishers in the nineteenth century.

Cambridge University Press has long been a pioneer in the reissuing of out-of-print titles from its own backlist, producing digital reprints of books that are still sought after by scholars and students but could not be reprinted economically using traditional technology. The Cambridge Library Collection extends this activity to a wider range of books which are still of importance to researchers and professionals, either for the source material they contain, or as landmarks in the history of their academic discipline.

Drawing from the world-renowned collections in the Cambridge University Library, and guided by the advice of experts in each subject area, Cambridge University Press is using state-of-the-art scanning machines in its own Printing House to capture the content of each book selected for inclusion. The files are processed to give a consistently clear, crisp image, and the books finished to the high quality standard for which the Press is recognised around the world. The latest print-on-demand technology ensures that the books will remain available indefinitely, and that orders for single or multiple copies can quickly be supplied.

The Cambridge Library Collection will bring back to life books of enduring scholarly value (including out-of-copyright works originally issued by other publishers) across a wide range of disciplines in the humanities and social sciences and in science and technology.

Treatise on the Laws of Literary Property

Comprising the statutes and cases relating to books, manuscripts, lectures ; dramatic and musical compositions

ROBERT MAUGHAM

CAMBRIDGE UNIVERSITY PRESS

Cambridge, New York, Melbourne, Madrid, Cape Town, Singapore,
São Paolo, Delhi, Dubai, Tokyo

Published in the United States of America by Cambridge University Press, New York

www.cambridge.org
Information on this title: www.cambridge.org/9781108009454

© in this compilation Cambridge University Press 2009

This edition first published 1828
This digitally printed version 2009

ISBN 978-1-108-00945-4 Paperback

A

TREATISE

ON THE

LAWS OF LITERARY PROPERTY,

COMPRISING

THE STATUTES AND CASES

RELATING TO

BOOKS, MANUSCRIPTS, LECTURES; DRAMATIC AND MUSICAL
COMPOSITIONS; ENGRAVINGS, SCULPTURE, MAPS, &c.

INCLUDING THE

PIRACY AND TRANSFER OF COPYRIGHT;

WITH A

HISTORICAL VIEW,

AND

DISQUISITIONS ON THE PRINCIPLES AND EFFECTS OF THE LAWS.

By ROBERT MAUGHAM,

SECRETARY TO THE LAW INSTITUTION,
Author of the " Law of Attornies," &c.

" I have entered into a work touching Laws, in a middle term, between the speculative and reverend discourses of Philosophers, and the writings of Lawyers."—BACON.

LONDON:

PUBLISHED BY LONGMAN, REES, ORME, BROWN, AND
GREEN, PATERNOSTER ROW ;
HENRY DIXON, 19, CAREY STREET, LINCOLN'S INN ;
ADAM BLACK, EDINBURGH.

1828.

My Lord,

Having composed a Treatise on the progress and present state of the Laws of Literary Property, with some Disquisitions on their Principles, and an examination of their effect on the interests of Literature, I was naturally desirous to dedicate my labors to the distinguished Chief of that Court where those laws are the most appropriately administered---where they have ever received the most liberal construction---and where the most effectual remedy is afforded for the injuries of authors, and the proprietors of their copyright.

A work thus devoted to the investigation of the rights and interests of the *Scholar* and the *Artist*, it is no small privilege to be permitted to dignify with the name of a Nobleman, alike distinguished by his profound knowledge of the law, and his taste for the elegant arts, and the pursuits of literature.

It was not long ago observed by your Lordship, during a debate in the Senate, " That it would be wise not to over-" whelm the Judges with business ; making them, in too " many instances, slaves to the *technical* part of their profession " —that they should have the opportunity of *cultivating general*

" *literature,* and be allowed the leisure to return to the pleasant " pursuits of early years, which, it was to be lamented, too " many of the Bar (greatly to the injury of the profession) " were obliged to suspend."

Since the expression of these enlightened sentiments, your Lordship has been elevated to those seats of Legislation and Justice, where the influence of such opinions will embellish Wisdom with the grace of Refinement.

To the friends of literature it must be peculiarly gratifying that your Lordship has spared, from the weighty duties of your high office, some moments to the encouragement of genius, and bestowed your presiding sanction at assemblies convened for its stimulus and reward.

Encouraged by the noble interest which your Lordship has thus evinced in the cause of letters, and grateful for the permission with which I have been distinguished, I beg to dedicate this work to ONE, who, by a rare combination of excellence, has attained the highest judicial station in this great Empire.

I have the honor to be,

MY LORD,

With the deepest respect,

Your Lordship's

Much obliged and very humble Servant,

ROBERT MAUGHAM.

Great James Street,
October 24th, 1828.

LAWS OF LITERARY PROPERTY.

Introductory Dissertation.

THE promotion of learning seems, at the earliest periods of
our history, to have been a favorite object, not only of our
ancestors in their individual capacity, but of our system of
jurisprudence. Thus schools and colleges were established
and endowed in all parts of the kingdom, by the munificence
even of private men. Scarcely a town existed, where an edifice
of splendour or utility (now too often crumbling to ruins)
was not devoted, like the halls of classic instruction, to the
purposes of intellectual improvement. It was not beneath
the dignity of the law to co-operate, in a noble spirit of protection, with this general feeling towards the cultivation of
letters. It was not deemed inconsistent with the policy of
our legal system (however objectionable it may now appear
to the legislative philosopher) to grant to the *scholar* a partial
immunity in the administration of its criminal code, which
was denied to the uneducated offender. Justice relaxed its
severity in favor of Learning; and, in veneration for those rare
attainments of the mind by which the world has been human-
ized, Mercy interposed its hand, and saved the "learned
clerk" from an ignominious fate. Still further,—the prompt
and efficacious remedy with which the lords of the soil had
armed themselves, in the form of distress for rent, for suit,
or services, was superseded, not only in favor of the need-
ful implements of husbandry and trade, but the *books of a*

scholar were also respected as sacred property, devoted to the service of mankind.

The contrast is singular between the favor which was thus shown to literature in times comparatively savage, and the discouragement it encountered during the refinement of the last century. In the ages of semi-barbarism we perceive every inducement presented to the ingenious student for the improvement of his faculties, and the cultivation of letters. In the era of boasted enlightenment, we witness the curtail. ment of rights, and the imposition of burthens !

The dawning of a better day seems, however, of late to have appeared in our system of jurisprudence. The legisla- ture, moved by the enlightened spirit of some of its members, has indicated a liberality of feeling, on many recent occa- sions, towards the interests of science, literature, and art, which may reasonably encourage the expectation, that the claims of justice will, in future, be more favorably consi- dered than on former occasions, and the injury diminished, if not entirely removed.

The principles which now prevail on the Law of Copy- right, it is well known, are totally at variance with the opinions of many distinguished judges, and especially of Lord MANSFIELD and Mr. Justice BLACKSTONE. It has, there- fore, been remarked by Professor CHRISTIAN, that every person may still be permitted to indulge his own opinion upon the propriety of the law, without incurring the impu- tation of arrogance.

We shall accordingly avail ourselves of the privilege thus conceded, and discuss the several statutes by which the in- terests of literature are affected, trace their successive stages, and examine the principles on which they are founded.

In this preliminary part of the Treatise, the disquisition will be brief and general ; but we deem it necessary to advert to some of the leading points in this great literary contro- versy, before we enter on the details of the subject ; the more especially as some of them must necessarily be of a technical nature, and we are desirous of engaging the atten-tion, not of the professional student alone, but of every one who is interested in the progress of learning and science.

Although the view which we must take of this subject will be unpalatable to many, there are, happily, several encouragements to the undertaking, which in no slight degree lead us to expect a favorable reception, as well with the public in general, as the liberal of all classes, and the learned in particular.

" Indeed, all arguments in support of the rights of learned men in their works must ever be heard, said Lord KENYON, with great favor, by men of liberal minds, to whom they are addressed(')."

The enlightened spirit in which this feeling was expressed, was entertained in an equal degree by Lord HARDWICKE. The Attorney-General of his time had argued that the Copy-right Act, being a monopoly, ought to receive a strict con-struction. " I am quite of a different opinion," said his lordship ; " it ought to receive a *liberal* construction. It is very far from being a monopoly. It is intended to secure the property of books in the authors themselves, or the pur-chasers of the copy, as some recompense for their pains and labor in composing works useful to the learned world(²)."

Fortified by these high authorities, we may venture to arraign the present code, under which we think that literary property is oppressed with severer restrictions and greater burthens than any other production of human industry.

Not only is its *duration* limited to the short period of twenty-eight years, but it is *taxed* for the benefit of wealthy corporations, to an amount always burthensome, and fre-quently destructive of all the remuneration it would other-wise afford. Indeed, the impolicy, as well as the injustice,

(1) 7 T. R. 627.   (2) 2 Atk. 143.

of the existing laws, must be admitted by every one who is in
the least degree acquainted with the subject, and possessed
of the smallest share of impartiality. Even the Universities
acknowledge (as well they may) that the limitation of the
term is grossly unjust; and all classes must pronounce the
imposition of eleven copies of all kinds of publications, to be
contrary to every principle of equity.

That it may not be supposed we enter on this critical
part of our task with a feeling drawn only from the complaints
of disappointed authors, or that we are disposed to put a
forced and unmerited construction on the acts of the legislature, it may be remarked, that Sir *John Dalrymple,* one of
the counsel (in the cause of Donaldson v. Beckett) who
opposed the perpetuity of copyright, expressly urges that
"this Act of Queen Anne, which was ushered in under the idea
of encouraging literature, was very far from having such a
tendency. What (he demanded) did the authors and booksellers gain? Why, a perpetuity was changed to a term of
fourteen years only. A price was fixed, and a clause inserted,
to force them to send copies to public libraries. What
encouragements are these? They, on the contrary, were
discouragements."

The history of these statutes regarding literary property,
and the construction which they have received, present a
striking proof of the injustice of their nature.

Nothing, in the first place, could be worse than their
origin; and they have consistently continued in a state of
undeviating oppression and severity. They were established
in the most despotic periods of our political annals, and were
designed for the express purpose of suppressing all free
inquiry, and the diffusion of all kind of knowledge, in any
way relating to the affairs of the church and state.

But although no book of any kind whatever could then
be published without the license of the constituted authorities, and though (compared with the present laws) *the
moderate number of three copies* were required to be delivered to

the King's librarian and the Vice-Chancellors of the two Universities, still there was *no restraint* on the *duration* of an author's rights. So long as the press could be held in sufficient subjection, it was not the intention, even during the most arbitrary administration of the affairs of Government, to curtail the property of inoffensive writers, or burthen them with exactions unknown to other classes of the community. Barring the sacred ground of theology and politics, the learned and ingenious of those times were allowed to exercise their talents, and reap the fruits of their intellectual labor, like every other subject of the realm, liable only to the tax, which, although obnoxious enough in *principle,* was comparatively mild in *amount.*

" When," to use the language of MILTON, " books were as freely admitted into the world as any other birth ; when the issue of the brain was no more stifled than the issue of the womb ; when no envious junto sat cross-legged over the nativity of any man's intellectual offspring,"—when the licensing system ceased, and men were permitted to publish their works on their own responsibility,---this exaction of three copies soon ceased altogether.

It was reserved for the " Augustan age of English literature,"—for the days of Pope, Swift, and Addison,—to revive this odious impost, and to increase it in a *threefold* degree ! To the same enlightened era we are indebted for the reduction of the *perpetual* right, which the justice of the ancient law of the land had previously protected, down to a space, often briefer than that which was occupied in the composition of the work !

Still, it seems that a remnant continued of the juster feeling of the olden time ; for though the *language* of the statute limited the administration of justice to fourteen years, (as modern ingenuity construed it) its *spirit* was understood to apply only to the penal enactments against piracy,---leaving untouched the ancient remedy for the recovery of actual damages. This, it seems, was an *honest blunder,* into which even the marauders on literary property had fallen; and in future they were enlightened by the expounders of the law, and permitted to rove at large over the legalized spoil.

We reserve to another part of the Treatise the investigation of the reasoning or sophistry by which it was thus established, to the satisfaction of *five* out of *eight* judges, that the Act of Anne,—in its preamble expressly professing "to prevent injury to authors, and to encourage learned men to write useful books,"—really reduced the perpetuity in copyright (which existed, according to a majority of the judges, at common law) to fourteen years! yet, such had been the plain interpretation by the common sense of all parties, that not one of the graduates or students of any of the Universities, nor even the lower order of publishers, however piratically inclined,—no one, from the 8th of Anne, in 1710, until 1774, ever dreamt of such a construction. After no less, however, than sixty-four years, some one, with more technical ingenuity than love of literature, enjoyed "the bad eminence" of overthrowing the evident spirit and intention of the act, by the supposed ambiguity of its language.

We have seen thus far, that whenever the rights of authors were brought before Parliament, they were generally abridged, or their burthens increased. Even the favorable construction which the legislature itself put upon the statute of Anne, with regard to those books which (requiring not the aid of penalties to protect them) were not registered, their interpretation was so inefficiently expressed, that it was held by the judges not to control the literal meaning of the previous statute. Hence, in the year 1812, it was decided that the eleven copies of every book, whether it sought the protection of the statute or not, must be delivered according to its provisions.

It was soon after the infliction of this last blow to the interests of literature, that the injuries of authors were again introduced to Parliament. Some mitigation of the library tax was requested. The Committee to which the subject was referred, recommended that *one* copy should be delivered to the British Museum *only*, or at all events that the number should be restricted to *five* copies. The House, however, was inexorable. The whole eleven copies were persisted in, and the only advantage which the proprietors of copyright obtained—wrung, it seems, with a " slow consent," but which for very shame could not be refused,—was the extension of the term to twenty-eight years *certain*, which had previously depended on the life of the author, and a further term in case he lingered beyond that time, until the close of his existence, leaving his family to be provided for by precarious benevolence, or the stinted relief of parochial charity.

Although the advocates of the Universities were thus inflexible in exacting the full penalty of their " bond ;" it must be allowed they liberally and strongly enforced the rights of authors in some other important respects.

Professor Christian stated, with considerable ability, the hardship and absurdity of the law as it then existed. " If an author when he is advanced in age offer a valuable work for sale, as the production of the labor of a long life, he will have the mortification to be told, that the price of his work must necessarily be much lower, than if he had completed it twenty or thirty years sooner at an earlier period of life. Thus, (said he) when the work is more valuable to the rest of the world, it becomes less profitable to the author and his family."

Whilst the learned Professor thus does justice, with good feeling and eloquence to the cause of letters, on a topic in which his *alma mater* was unprejudiced, it may be useful to notice what has been done on this important part of the subject by the legislature, in reference to the same kind of rights, when *in the hands of a powerful corporate body*, instead of a helpless individual.

The decision which the House of Lords, in its judicial capacity, pronounced in the year 1774, upon the construction of the statute of Anne, equally affected the Universities as the public in general; and as there was no exception in the statute in favor of copyrights held by the Universities, their duration was brought down, like those of individuals, to twenty-eight years; and the clause in favor of surviving authors could not apply to a corporate body. The Universities therefore applied to Parliament to restore, in their collective case, the right which had been taken from individual authors, and they succeeded in their application. A legal anomaly, somewhat curious, must follow this enactment.— The copyrights held by the Universities consist of works, which of course are not composed by a body of men appointed by the Universities, or paid out of their funds. They have been either purchased of individual authors (which we may conjecture is not often the case), or bequeathed by them. Now the author can convey or bequeath that only which by law he possesses, namely, a short lease in the property; yet the corporate purchasers or legatees receive, as it were, the freehold inheritance to themselves and their successors for ever! Such is the measure of equal justice, and legal consistency, which is manifested on the face of these statutes.

The state of the law in other countries affords not only a strong and additional argument in favor of the policy of extending the rights of authors, and diminishing the burthens of literature; but indicates the sentence of other nations on the injustice of our regulations.

In the NETHERLANDS, *three* copies only are required to be deposited in the public libraries.—In AUSTRIA, *two.*—In FRANCE, before the revolution, four copies, but since that event, *two* only are required for the national library. In AMERICA, PRUSSIA, SAXONY, and BAVARIA, only *one* copy can be demanded.

It is remarkable, also, that in all these instances the copies are not required unless the exclusive copyright is reserved. And whilst such is the state of the law over all Christendom, (except in this part of it) in regard to the imposition of the library copies, it is observable that there, too, the *duration of the right* is either perpetual, or considerably more extensive than the term allowed in this country.

Thus, in *France*, the term of copyright is twenty years after the decease of the author. In most, if not all, of the *German* states, it is perpetual.

If the comparative superiority of the practice on the continent were not well authenticated, we should have anticipated the contrary to be the case. We have been too much accustomed, amidst the conflicts with our neighbours, to laud our own laws and institutions, and utterly to condemn every thing belonging to those by whom we were opposed. We suspect, that besides the evident improvement which might be effected by imitating this better code of literary jurisprudence, there may yet be made other discoveries, by which it will appear that we have not altogether monopolized the maxims of wisdom and justice.

There can indeed be no subject which ought to engage the attention of the friends of literature, and the reading public, in a higher degree than the rights of authors and publishers, and the means by which the literature of Great Britain may be enabled to *compete* with, if it cannot surpass, the excellence and cheapness of the continental press.

It may fairly be asked, what is the consequence to literature in general, and the community at large, of this juster system of literary protection, which thus prevails amongst the other nations of Europe? Following the objections which have been raised by the adversaries of improvement, it may be demanded, Do the continental writers and their publishers *abuse* the power which the laws afford them? Do they (as it has been idly imagined would be the case here) *suppress* valuable works, or limit their diffusion and usefulness by *exorbitant prices?* No!

In France, as Dr. Johnson observed, they have a book on every subject. In Germany, the abundance of literary works is still more extensive. In both countries, the price of books is beyond all proportion lower than in Great Britain. Compare, also, the literature of France and Germany, where the one is limited (though not to the contracted period of twenty-eight years), and the other is free. Does the perpetuity of German copyright render the writers of that country less original or profound than those of France? Does it tend to a superficial manner of writing? No! we believe there are of late years more great and original works of enduring excellence published' by the German press, than by that of any other country.

Let it be recollected, also, that the limited and stinted protection which is here allowed to intellectual labor, was not declared to be the law of the land until the year 1774. Anterior to that time, a more liberal rule was *understood*, if not expressed ; and it seems not that the wider latitude of literary rights which then prevailed, was productive of the mischiefs that have been anticipated.

Many of the great and lasting works, which constitute the glory of English literature, and shed a bright lustre upon the age in which they arose, were composed before this exposition of the law was announced. True it is, that, in spite of that interpretation, numerous accessions of a standard nature have been made to the treasures of national learning; but these have been encouraged by other means than Acts of Parliament---they have been produced, in spite of them, by the irrepressible energy of a few of our distinguished countrymen.

It cannot be urged that we have no EXPERIENCE to guide us in the melioration of the law. It was not, as we have seen, until about fifty-three years ago, that the construction now put upon the old statutes was attempted ; so that in all time, since the first book was published in this country, until the reign of Queen Anne, did a perpetuity in copyright exist,---not only without prejudice, but with benefit to the public; and since the passing of the statute in question

until the year 1774, no evil was imagined to arise by extending to literary property the common protection afforded to all
other. Nay more, to show that the chain of experience has
been unbroken,---before the lapse of a single year, the Universities obtained the restoration of *their* rights, and have
enjoyed them to the present time. No disadvantage has
arisen to the interests of literature, or the public, by allowing
to the Universities that privilege which has been denied
to the authors of the very works they possess. If an experiment were necessary before justice could be done to
literary men, it has therefore been sufficiently made; and the
time, we should presume, has now arrived, when this deep
stain on our statute-book may be for ever erased, and
even-handed justice dealt alike to all.

It cannot be denied that private interest should yield to
the public good ; but in this instance, the community, so far
from being benefited by the united evils of unequal restraint
and anomalous taxation, evidently sustains an injury.

If, however, there be a reasonable doubt on the policy
of administering just and equal laws, surely those who devote
their lives to the interests of literature and philosophy, are
entitled to the " benefit of the doubt." Surely no man of
honorable spirit,---not to say of a liberal one,---can hesitate
on the propriety of giving unlimited copyright, at least, a
fair trial.

If, contrary to all reason, as well as all experience,
mischief should arise, then, but *not till then,* let the fetters be
new riveted, and let the yoke and the burthen be replaced
on the shoulders of the ingenious and the intelligent.

We have thus given a brief sketch of the condition in
which literary property is situated, and the circumstances
which have attended it. We trust that the wrongs at which
we have taken a hasty glance, are calculated to excite some
degree of attention, even in the minds of those whom they do
not personally affect, and that a full examination of the subject will be patiently encountered. The public have an equally

strong interest, and a positive duty, in promoting the general adoption of just principles—each man being individually concerned in enforcing and upholding that which is right and just; since the mischief that is done to his neighbour to-day, may be perpetrated on himself to-morrow.

In arranging the PLAN AND GENERAL DIVISIONS OF THE WORK, it has beenthought most desirable in the *first* book—after defining the nature oliterary property, and considering its claims to protection under the comprehensive provisions of the common law—to take a historical view of the origin and progress of the legislative regulations—subdivided under the general heads, of the *duration* of copyright, and the *tax* imposed upon the publication of books. We shall thus be enabled fully to trace thesubject from the memorable invention of printing, through the interesting periods in our history which immediately succeeded. And we shall also have an opportunity of shewing the interest which many celebrated works have attained in the annals of the law, as well as of literature.

This course indeed appeared necessary as well as interesting; for although the last Act of Parliament on the copyright of books has incorporated the provisions of the former statutes, the *past* require to be referred to for the purpose of assisting the construction of the *present*. The old statutes, however, will be printed in the smallest type, and appended to their analysis by way of notes.

The various classes who are interested in literary undertakings —in securing them from invasion, or avoiding the consequences of violating the law—in the mode of transferring copyright and the contingent interests of authors—must naturally be desirous to ascertain the decisions which have occurred in the courts of justice regarding these subjects. And although in some respects the law remains imperfectly defined, still it appears highly important to collect, and appropriately arrange, the legal doctrines which have been pronounced, and the facts and principles on which they are grounded. In the *second* book, therefore, besides treating of the duration and extent of copyright, of the library tax, and the registry at Stationers' Hall, it has been deemed necessary to devote a considerable portion of the treatise to the details of *pirating copyright*, its *transfer*, &c. These, it is presumed, will be found of great practical utility, both to authors and publishers.

The *third* book, and the notes which follow it, contain the disquisitions on the principles of the laws and their effect on literature.

ANALYTICAL TABLE OF CONTENTS.

Introductory Dissertation.

HISTORICAL VIEW.

Duration
of
Copyright.

Definition and Nature of Literary Property.
Its perpetuity by the Common Law.

Its Recognition { in Acts of { State, Parliament, by ancient Customs.

Origin of the Statute 8 Anne.
Intention of the Legislature.

Construction of the Act prior to 1775, { in Equity, at Law.

The Statutes, { 12 Geo. II. 15 } Geo. III. 41 }

Library
Tax.

Origin of the Tax,

Grounds of the Library Claim by { Cambridge, Oxford, Scotland and Ireland.

The several Statutes,
Their Interpretation.
Legal Decisions on unregistered Books.

THE PRESENT STATE OF THE LAW.

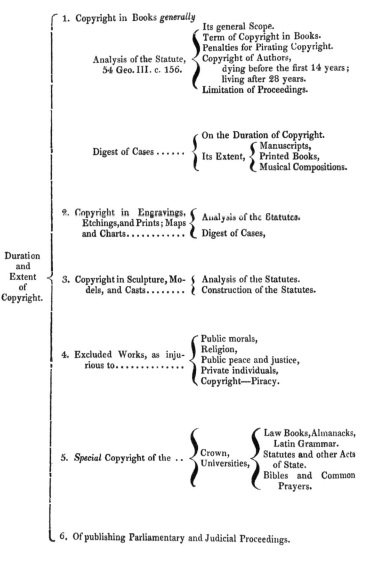

1. Copyright in Books *generally*

Analysis of the Statute, 54 Geo. III. c. 156.
- Its general Scope.
- Term of Copyright in Books.
- Penalties for Pirating Copyright.
- Copyright of Authors,
  - dying before the first 14 years;
  - living after 28 years.
- Limitation of Proceedings.

Digest of Cases ......
- On the Duration of Copyright.
- Its Extent,
  - Manuscripts,
  - Printed Books,
  - Musical Compositions.

2. Copyright in Engravings, Etchings, and Prints; Maps and Charts............
- Analysis of the Statutes.
- Digest of Cases,

Duration and Extent of Copyright.

3. Copyright in Sculpture, Models, and Casts........
- Analysis of the Statutes.
- Construction of the Statutes.

4. Excluded Works, as injurious to..............
- Public morals,
- Religion,
- Public peace and justice,
- Private individuals,
- Copyright—Piracy.

5. *Special* Copyright of the ..
- Crown, Universities,
  - Law Books, Almanacks, Latin Grammar.
  - Statutes and other Acts of State.
  - Bibles and Common Prayers.

6. Of publishing Parliamentary and Judicial Proceedings.

THE PRESENT STATE OF THE LAW, *continued.*

Library Tax and Registry at Stationers' Hall.

1. Analysis of the Statute, 54 Geo. III. c. 156.
   - The tax on original Works,
   - 2d. and subsequent Editions.
   - periodical Publications.
   - Maps and Prints.
   - The Quality of the Paper.
   - The places of delivering the Books.
   - The Penalties for Non-delivery.
   - Registry of Books at Stationers' Hall.
   - Duty of the Warehouse-keeper.
   - Penalties for Non-registration.

2. Construction of the Act ..
   - Works included,
   - excluded.

Pirating Copyright.

1. Printed Books ....
   - Original Works.
   - Notes and Additions
   - Abridgments.
   - Compilations.
   - Translations.

2. Manuscripts ....
   - Unpublished MSS. in general.
   - MSS. of deceased Persons.
   - Private Letters, literary and general.

3. Lectures ....
   - written.
   - oral.

4. Dramatic Works ....
   - Unpublished Plays.
   - Representing published Plays.

5. Unregistered Works.

6. Fine Arts ·············
   - Engravings and Prints.
   - Sculpture.
   - Maps, Charts, and Plans.
   - Musical Compositions.

7. Remedies ....
   - By Damages at Law.
   - Penalties under the Statutes.
   - Injunction in Equity.

BOOK I.

HISTORICAL VIEW

OF

THE LAW.

LAWS OF LITERARY PROPERTY.

BOOK I.

𝕳istorical 𝕍iew.

FIRST PART.

OF THE DURATION OF COPYRIGHT.

CHAP. I.——FROM THE INVENTION OF PRINTING, TO THE
STATUTE 8 ANNE, 1710.

SECT. 1.——*Of the definition and nature of Literary Property.*

LITERARY PROPERTY, or COPYRIGHT, may be defined to be the ownership or rightful possession to which an author, or the person to whom he assigns it, is entitled in the *copy*([1]) or original manuscript of his literary works; and it comprises the exclusive right of printing and publishing copies of any literary performance, including engravings, musical compositions, maps, &c.([2])

Lord MANSFIELD adopted the word " copy " in the *technical sense* in which, he said, that name or term had been used for ages, to signify an *incorporeal right* to the *sole* printing and publishing of something intellectual, communicated by letters([3]).

Mr. Justice ASTON also observed, that " the copy of a book seemed to have been not familiarly only, but *legally*, used as a technical expression of the author's sole right to print and publish: and that these expressions in a variety of instruments were not to be considered as the creators or origin of that right or property, but as speaking the language of a known and acknowledged right; and, as far as they were active, operating in its protection([4]).

The right of an author to the exclusive use and publi-

---

(1) " Copy," the autograph, the original, the archetype; that from which any thing is copied. *Johnson.*——" The first of them I have forgotten, and cannot easily retrieve, because the *copy* is at the press. *Dryden.*
(2) Tomlin's Law Dict. Articles " Literary Property " and " Copyright."
(3) 4 Burr. 2396.
(4) Ib. 2346. " *Copy* of a book," was likewise described by Mr. Justice *Willes* as the term which had been used for ages to signify the sole right of printing, publishing, and selling copies thereof. 4 Burr. 2311.

cation of his own literary compositions, is classed by Sir W.
BLACKSTONE amongst the species of property acquired by
occupancy, being grounded on labor and invention([1]).

When a man, says the learned Commentator, by the exertion of
his rational powers has produced an original work, he seems to have
clearly a right to dispose of that *identical* work as he pleases ; and
any attempt to vary the disposition he has made of it, appears to be
an invasion of the right. Now the identity, says he, of a literary
composition, consists entirely in the *sentiment* and the *language.* The
same conceptions, clothed in the same words, must necessarily be the
same composition ; and whatever method be taken of exhibiting that
composition to the ear or the eye of another, by recital, by writing, or
by printing in any number of copies, or at any period of time, it is
always the identical work of the author which is so exhibited ; and no
other man, it hath been thought, can have a right to exhibit it, especially for profit, without the author's consent([2]).

It will not be necessary to enter into any elaborate consideration of the arguments on the origin of property. There
seems no rational ground for creating a distinction between
literary and any other species of property. The rights of
each are equally entitled to protection. Such a distinction
cannot be founded upon the degree of *labor* bestowed in the
acquisition of other objects of property. Even the right to
the possession of land has been acquired as often by good
fortune as by merit, and is frequently retained without the
bestowment of labor. The property in a literary work may
be acquired in the same way. The first thought may have
been accidental, which labor has enlarged and improved.
The descendants of those who have produced intellectual
treasures, are as well entitled to inherit them, as the posterity
of the accumulators of land or money. To say, that the
definition of property in the old legal authorities does not
include the property in question, can be nothing to the
purposes of justice. If it does not include it, the definition
is a bad one, because it is not sufficiently comprehensive.
Besides, if literary works possess none of the usual charac-
teristics of property, according to its present technical de-

(1) 2 Blac. Com. 405.
(2) Ib. 406. The Roman law adjudged, that if one man wrote any thing on the
paper or parchment of another, the writing should belong to the owner of the blank
materials ; meaning thereby the *mechanical* operation of writing, for which it directed
the *scribe* to receive satisfaction; for, in works of *genius and invention,* as in painting on
another man's canvas, the same law gave the canvas to the painter. As to any other
property in the works of the understanding, the law is silent; though the sale of literary
copies, for the purposes of recital or multiplication, is certainly as ancient as the times of
Terence(a), Martial(b), and Statius(c).
(a) Prol. in Eunuch, 20.   (b) Epigr. i. 67, iv. 72, xiii. 3, xiv. 194.
(c) Juv. vii. 83.

scription, let them form a class of themselves. Injustice should not be done for the sake of preserving consistency in verbal or metaphysical distinctions, which have nothing but their antiquity to support them.

It is held by all the law authorities, that an author possesses a strictly legal property in his literary labors, whilst they remain in manuscript. There can be no real distinction in the nature of the property, in the sentiments or ideas and language, before and after publication. The law which prohibits the publication of his *manuscript* without his consent, should also protect the *printed copy*, and prevent the appropriation of the profit of publication by any other person than the author.

The definitions adduced by those who argue that there is a *want of " property"* in literary works, are evidently very inadequate to the objects of property in the present advanced state of society. They are adapted to things in a *primitive*, not to say imaginary, state; when all things were in common; when that common right was to be divested by some act to render the thing privately and exclusively a man's own, which, before it was so separated and distinguished, was as much the property of another.

These definitions also, it has been justly observed([1]), will be found principally to apply to the *necessaries of life*, and the grosser objects of dominion, which the immediate natural occasions of men called for ; and therefore the property so acquired by occupancy, was required to be an object *useful* to men, and capable of being *fastened on*. Enough was to be left for others. As much as any one could use to the advantage of life before it spoiled, in so much he could fix a property. Whatever was beyond this, was more than his share, and belonged to others.

These definitions give a sort of property little superior to the legal idea of a beast-common ; the bit of mouth snatched, or taken for necessary consumption to support life. Thus ruminating back to the *origin* of things, men lose sight of the *present* state of the world, and *end* their enquiries at that point where they should *begin* their improvements.

But distinct properties, says Pufendorf([2]), were not settled at the same time, nor by one single act, but by successive degrees, nor in all places alike ; but property was gradually introduced, according as either the condition of things, the number and genius of men required, or as it appeared requisite to the common peace.

Since those supposed times of universal communion, the objects of property have been much enlarged by discovery, invention, and arts. The mode of obtaining property by occupancy has been abridged ; and the precept of abstaining

(1) Millar v. Taylor, 4 Burrow, 2339.   (2) B. 4, c. 4, sec. 6.

from what is another's, enforced by laws. The rules attending
property must therefore keep pace with its increase and
improvement, and must be adapted to every case.

A DISTINGUISHABLE EXISTENCE in the thing claimed
as property, *an actual value* in that thing to the true owners,
are its essentials ; and these are not less evident in the case
of literary property, than in the immediate objects of those
definitions which relate to the primitive condition of things.

There is a material difference greatly in favor of this
sort of property, from that gained by *occupancy*, which before
its occupation was common to every one ; because a literary
work is *originally* the *author's;* and therefore unless clearly
rendered common by his own act, and full consent(1), it
ought still to remain his property.

The *utility* of the thing to man required by the definition
in Pufendorf(2) to make it an object of property, has been
long exploded, as appears from Barbeyrac's note on this very
passage, where it is held an unnecessary and superfluous
condition(3).

The best rule both of reason and justice seems to be, to
assign to every thing *capable of ownership* a legal and deter-
minate owner.

For the capacity to " fasten on," as a thing of corporeal nature,
being requisite in every kind of property, plainly partakes of the
narrow and confined sense in which property has been defined by
authors in the *original* state of things. A capacity to be *distinguished,*
answers every end of reason and certainty, which is the great favorite
of the law, and is all that wisdom requires to secure their possessions
and profits to men, and to preserve the peace(4).

" Nothing," says Professor Christian, " is more erroneous than
the practice of referring the origin of moral rights, and the system of
natural equity, to that savage state which is supposed to have preceded
civilized establishments, in which literary composition, and of consequence the right to it, could have no existence. But the true mode of
ascertaining a moral right, is to inquire whether it is such as the reason,
the cultivated reason, of mankind must necessarily assent to. No
proposition seems more conformable to that criterion, than that every
one should enjoy the reward of his labor, the harvest where he has
sown, or the fruit of the tree which he has planted." Whether literary property is *sui generis,* or under whatever denomination of rights

(1) The *constructive* consent, deduced from the act of publication to the world,
will be discussed in the next section.
(2) Lib. 4, cap. 5.
(3) Things of fancy, pleasure, or convenience are objects of property, and so considered by the common law: even so insignificant a thing as a popinjay, a monkey, a
parrot, or the like; in short, any thing merchandizable and valuable. 12 H. s. 3. a. b.
&c. ; Bro. Abr. Tit. " Property," pl. 44 ; 1 Comyn's Digest. 602.
(4) 4 Burr. 2340.

it may be classed, it seems founded upon the same principle of general utility to society, which is the basis of all other moral rights and obligations. Thus considered, an author's copyright ought to be esteemed an invaluable right, established in sound reason and abstract morality(¹).

The consideration of the *objections* advanced against these definitions of the nature of literary property, we defer to that part of the work in which the *justice* of the laws are discussed. The Legislature has thought proper to deal with literary works as "property," and we have deemed it sufficient for the present purpose to state, from the authorities to which we have referred, the general principles by which the question ought to be regulated. We proceed, in the next place, to consider the subject as it stood at the common law, prior to the existence of any statute, and independent of any recognition of the exclusive rights of literary property, either by the State or the Parliament.

SECTION II.
Of the perpetuity of Copyright by the Common Law.

It is a leading principle in the English Law, and forms a just ground of its praise, that it provides redress for every wrong and grievance which the subject may suffer from the invasion of his rights ; and the remedy, says COKE, varies and is adapted according to the variety of the right(²).

From the benefit of this general rule of extensive justice, *literary* men ought not to be excluded. The exertions of the mind deserve as much encouragement as those of the body. Whatever may be suggested by the subtilty of legal reasoning, drawn from the origin of property, it is clearly the interest of society to afford that protection to literary labor, which is readily extended to every other species. The reasoning which demonstrates the expediency of guarding the fruits of manual industry, must equally establish the adoption of the same protection to those of intellectual acquirement. Property will not be acquired if it be not protected. The very existence of society, and its best interests, depend on the encouragement of industry ; and as national wealth depends on labor, so does knowledge depend on mental exertion. Yet neither the corporeal nor the intellectual powers will be freely and fully exerted, unless they are permitted to enjoy their productions unshackled by restraint, and unencumbered

(1) 2 Comm. 407, note.   (2) 3 Coke 48, a.

by burthens, from which other classes of the community are exempt.

It being intended in this section to review the subject of literary property as it anciently stood, according to the common law, it will be necessary to notice the comprehensive character of this part of our system of jurisprudence: and without following the exact phraseology of the ordinary definitions, we may describe the COMMON LAW to be

The law of this kingdom, as it was generally holden before any statute was enacted in Parliament to alter it. It includes the laws of God and nature. It is grounded upon the general customs of the kingdom, and comprises the principles and maxims of the laws, which are founded upon reason, observation, and experience, acquired by long study, refined by learned men in all ages, and it is thus said to be the " perfection of reason." Its end and object is *justice*, in the most comprehensive sense. It is the common birth-right of the subjects of the realm, for the safeguard and defence, not only of their goods, lands, and revenues, but of their families, fame, property, and lives[1].

The common law is described by BRACTON[2] as *universally comprehensive.* There seems no reason for excluding from its protection any kind of property, however insignificant in its nature, or trifling in its value. The *rules* in regard to property, like the principles of the underwritten law, are of the highest antiquity, and must ever have been the same; but the *objects* to which they are applicable, were not all at once known, and many things have been disputed which were afterwards established as objects of property[3]. The claims of justice do not depend on antiquity.

There are many things, the uses of which were unknown in ignorant times, that have now become valuable; and it seems as unjust to shut out from legal protection the intellectual labors of ingenious men, as it would be to declare that the mariner's compass and gunpowder, which were inventions within the period of legal memory, cannot be included in the laws of property[4].

The absence of judicial authority can form no objection

(1) Co. Lit. 97, 142. Treatise of Laws, p. 2.   (2) Lib. 1, c. 3.

(3) There is a case reported in the *Year Book* of a blood-hound, where it was argued, that when out of possession, the property in it ceased---that felony could not be committed of it---that it was not titheable, would not pass by a grant of omnia bona, &c. Yet it was held, " that where any wrong or damage is done to a man, the law gives him a remedy." 12 H. 8, f. 3, a. b.   So of a grey-hound. 31 *Eliz. Owen* 93, *Cro. Eliz.* 125.

(4) It was held by Mr. Justice Willes, that the principles of private justice, moral fitness, and public convenience, when applied to a *new subject*, made common law without a precedent---much more when received and approved by usage. 4 Burr. 2312. *For the usage, see the next section.*

to the claim. It was not decided until within a century of
the present time that a title to literary property could be
maintained, even *prior* to publication ; and that according to
the principles of the common law, no distance of time,
however great, could authorize a publication without the
consent of the author : as in the cases of *Lord Clarendon's
History* and the *Letters of Pope.* Many other points of law
have also been decided in recent times, for which there is no
precedent. For instance, it is not many years since, for the
first time, it was held actionable at common law to give,
knowingly, a false character, on the faith of which credit had
been given, and loss sustained---a decision which was evidently founded on the general maxim, that " there is no
injury without a remedy."

Having thus shewn the state of the question upon the
general and comprehensive principles of the common law,
prior to any legislative enactment or recognition, and independently of any judicial authority, we come now to the
consideration of the reasonings which have been adduced,
and the judgments pronounced by many learned judges on
the question of perpetuity, the substance and principal
points of which we shall select, and endeavour to present in
the most condensed form.

Of all the judges before whom this question has been
discussed, the majority have always decided that, by the
common law, an author was entitled to the exclusive enjoyment of his copyright in perpetuity.

It is remarkable also, that amidst the many controversies
which have taken place on this important subject, it was
never in the slightest degree denied that the *manuscript* of an
author was protected by the common law, and that it was
illegal to take his manuscript, or in any way to use or publish
it, without the clear and express consent of the author. On
the contrary, in the several cases which have been argued on
the extent of the right since the several Acts of Parliament
on copyright were passed, it has been all along, even by the
advocates whose business and duty it was to contend that
under those statutes the term of exclusive copyright was
limited to fourteen years, expressly admitted,

That *by the common law,* an author is entitled to the copy of
his own work *until* it has been once printed and published by his
authority ; and it has been also conceded, that the several cases in
Chancery in which injunctions were granted to restrain the printing
and publishing of the copy, were agreeable to the common law, and
that the relief afforded in those cases was properly given in consequence
of the *legal right*(').

(1) 4 Burr. 2396.

8 HISTORICAL VIEW.

Now it seems impossible to shew that there is any sound distinction by the common law, between the exclusive right to the copy *after* publication, and the right *prior* to it. For, as Lord MANSFIELD observed(¹), the common law as to the copy before publication, could not be founded in custom.

Prior to 1732, the case of a piracy *before* publication never existed---it was never put or supposed. There is not a syllable about it to be met with any where. The regulations, the ordinances, the Acts of Parliament, the cases in Westminster Hall, all relate to *the copy* of books *after* publication by the authors.

From what source then, demands his Lordship, is the common law drawn, which is admitted to be so clear in respect of the copy before publication?

From this argument,---because it is *just* that an author should reap the pecuniary profits of his own ingenuity and labor, it is just that another should not use his name without his consent. It is *fit* that he should judge when to publish, or whether he ever will publish. It is fit he should not only choose the time, but the manner of publication, how many, what kind of volumes, what print. It is fit he should choose to whose care he will trust the accuracy and correctness of the impressions---in whose honesty he will confide not to foist in additions.

These, and other reasonings of the same effect, are sufficient to shew that it is agreeable to the principles of right, the fitness of things, convenience and policy, and *therefore* to the common law, to protect the copy before publication.

But the same reasons, said the learned judge, hold after the author has published his work. He can reap no pecuniary profit, if the next moment after it comes out it may be pirated upon worse paper, and in a worse print, and in a cheaper volume(²).

The author may not only be deprived of any profit, but lose the expence he has been at. He is no more master of the use of his own name. He has no control over the correctness of his own work. He cannot prevent additions. He cannot retract errors. He cannot amend or cancel a faulty edition. Any one may print, pirate, and perpetuate the imperfections, to the disgrace, and against the will, of the author ; may propagate sentiments under his name which he dis-

---

(1) 4 Burr. 2397.
(2) It is admitted, that if the literary compositions of an author be taken from him *before* publication, he may maintain an action of trover or trespass. But how are the *damages* to be estimated? Should the jury confine their consideration to the value of the ink and paper? Certainly not: it would be most reasonable to consider the known character and ability of the author, and the value which his work would produce by the publication and sale. And yet what could that value be, if it was true that the instant an author published his works, they were to be considered by the law as given to the public, and that his private property in them no longer existed ? ---- Per Mr. Justice *Aston,* 4 Burr. 2341.

approves, repents, and is ashamed of. He can exercise no discretion as to the manner in which, or the persons by whom, his work shall be published !

Such are the monstrous conclusions which would follow the admission of the doctrine, that an author loses by the act of publication his exclusive right to the productions of his literary labor.

The claim of the author to the exclusive right of printing and publishing his own work, is founded, says Mr. Justice ASTON[1], upon the original right to this work, as being the mental labor of the author, and that the effect and produce of the labor is *his*. It is a personal incorporeal property, saleable and profitable ; it has *indicia certa*, for though the sentiments and doctrine may be· called ideal, yet when the same are communicated to the sight and understanding of every man, by the medium of printing, the work becomes a *distinguishable* subject of property, and not destitute of corporeal qualities[2].

But it is said that the copy is necessarily made common after the book is once published.

Now without publication, it is useless to the owner, because without profit; and property without the power of use and disposal, is an empty sound. In that state, it is lost to society in point of improvement, as well as to the author in point of interest. Publication, therefore, is the necessary act, and the only means to render this confessed property useful to mankind, and profitable to the owner---in this, they are jointly concerned.

Now to construe this only and necessary act to make the work useful and profitable, to be destructive at once of the author's confessed original property, against his express will, seems to be quite harsh and unreasonable; nor is it at all warranted by the arguments derived from those writers who advance, that by the law of nature property ends when corporal possession ceases[3].

(1) 4 Burr. 2341.
(2) All the metaphysical subtilties from the nature of the thing may be equally objected to the property before publication. It is incorporeal---it relates to ideas detached from any physical existence. There are no *indicia*---another may have had the same thoughts, upon the same subject, and expressed them in the same language verbatim. At what time, and by what act, does the property commence? The same string of questions may be asked upon the copy before publication:---Is it real or personal? Does it go to the heir or to the executor? Being a right, which can only be defeated by action, is it as a chose in action assignable or not? Can it be forfeited? Can it be taken in execution? Can it be vested in the assignees under a Commission of Bankruptcy? ----Per Lord *Mansfield*, 4 Burr. 2397.

(3) *Barbeyrac* clearly observes, that the right acquired from taking possession, does not cease where there is no possession; that perpetual possession is impossible ; that the above hypothesis would reduce property to nothing; that the consent of the proprietor to the renunciation of the right, ought to appear, for as possession is nothing else but an indisputable mark of the will to retain what a man has seized, so to authorize us to look upon a thing as abandoned by him to whom it belonged, because he is not in possession, we ought to have some other reasons to believe he has renounced his personal right to it.

BARBEYRAC, in his notes on PUFENDORF, says, that though we may presume an abandonment in respect to those things which remain such as nature has produced them, yet as for other things which are the fruits of human industry, and which are done with great labor and contrivance, it cannot be doubted but every one would preserve his right to them till he makes an OPEN RENUNCIATION.

Now there is no *open* renunciation of literary property, but a *constructive* one only, deduced barely from the act of publication. Whether there be a " renunciation" or not, is a *fact* which ought not to be presumed ; wherever it exists, it should be distinctly proved. It is always capable of proof, where the abandonment has really taken place, and when it cannot be proved, the legal inference, as in all other kinds of property, ought to be in favor of the original owner.

But then it is contended, " if a man buys a book, it becomes his own."

What ! is there no difference (exclaimed Mr. Justice ASTON) betwixt selling the property in the work, and only one of the copies ? To say, " selling the book conveys all the right," begs the question. For if the law protects the book, the sale does not convey away the right from the nature of the thing, any more than the sale conveys it where the statute protects the book.

The proprietor's consent is not to be carried beyond his manifest intent. Would not such a construction extend the partial disposition of the true owner beyond his plain intent and meaning ? Can it be conceived that in purchasing a literary composition at a shop, the purchaser ever thought he bought the right to be the printer and seller of that specific work ? The improvement, knowledge, or amusement which he can derive from the performance, is all his own ; but the right to the work, the copyright, remains in him whose industry composed it. The buyer might as truly claim the merit of the composition by his purchase, as to the right of multiplying the copies and reaping the profits.

The invasion of this sort of property is as much against every man's sense of it, as it is against natural reason and moral rectitude. It is against the conviction of every man's own breast who attempts it. He knows it not to be his own —he knows he injures another, and he does not do it for the sake of the public, but *mala fide et animo lucrandi*.([1])

(1) 4 Burr. 2343.

SECTION III.

Of the recognition by the State and Parliament of Copyright in perpetuity, and the evidence of Ancient Customs.

It is only *since* the *invention of printing*, that any question of the extent or duration of copyright could be expected to occur in the courts of justice.   To take an author's manuscript without his consent, was, of course, either actionable for the trespass or trover, or indictable in proportion to the amount of the offence, according as the circumstances might constitute a fraud or theft.   A single copy was then of much more value than after printing had multiplied the number of copies. The great manual labor necessarily bestowed on each copy, and the few readers at that time, rendered the *publication* of insignificant importance, compared with what it has since become.

From the time of this splendid discovery, down to the year 1556, a period exceeding a century, we have no evidence of the recognition, in any public form, of the copyright of authors, or of the remedies by which its infraction might be redressed.   This silence, however, may be very rationally explained.   The exact period of its introduction to England has been the subject of much discussion.   According to some authorities, it was introduced at Oxford in the year 1468; the sounder opinion assigns the period of 1471 or 1472.   But whatever was the precise time, it is obvious that several years would naturally elapse, after its first establishment, before the invention could become generally adopted(1).

Its process was impeded by many difficulties and restraints.   It was imported during one of the most stormy periods of our history, amidst contests for the crown and domestic war.   The revival of letters was then in its commencement.   Books were comparatively few in number, and but little sought for.   The establishment of printing presses therefore took place by slow degrees; and it was not until the signal advantages of the art became known, and literature extended itself, that the property, or copyright, in books became an object of importance.

No sooner, however, did the press display the great purposes to which it might be applied, than the works which issued from it naturally became the immediate subject of state regulation.

(1) The art of printing was first discovered at Mentz in 1438.   It was introduced into England in 1471 ; into Scotland in 1508 ; into Ireland in 1551.

The earliest evidence which occurs on the subject is to be found in the charter of the Stationers' Company, and the decrees of the Star Chamber.

The evidence thus to be adduced, appears the more satisfactory, and the less liable to suspicion, inasmuch as it was indifferent to the views of the Government whether the copy of an innocent book, when licenced, was open or private property. It was certainly against the power of the crown to allow it as a private right, without being protected by any royal privilege. It could be done only on principles of private justice, moral fitness, and public convenience ; which, when applied to a new subject, make *common law* without a precedent ; much more when received and approved of by usage([1]).

Recognition of the Right by Acts of the State.

1556.---The original charter of the Stationers' Company was granted by Philip and Mary, in the year 1556.

It was the declared object of the Sovereign at that time to prevent the propagation of the Protestant Reformation ; and it seems to have been thought, that the most effectual means to do so, was to impose the severest restrictions on the press.

The charter recites, that several seditious and heretical books, both in rhymes and tracts, were daily printed, renewing and spreading great and detestable heresies against the catholic doctrine of the Holy Mother Church.

For the suppression of this evil, it constitutes ninety-seven persons (whom it names) an incorporated society of the art of a stationer ; and it orders that no person in England shall practise the art of printing unless he be one of this society.

And the master and wardens of this society were authorized to search, seize, and burn all prohibited books, and to imprison any one that should exercise the art of printing contrary to this direction([2]).

From this charter we proceed to the decrees of the Star Chamber, the authority of which we are quite willing should be estimated as low as possible ; but in adducing the authorities which support the right in question, we are justified in pointing out, that even that arbitrary tribunal respected the rights of authors, and prohibited the printing of works without the consent of their owners.

In 1556, by a decree of the Star Chamber, it was forbidden to print against the force and meaning of any ordinance, &c. in any of the statutes or *laws* of the realm.

By another decree in 1585, every book, &c. is to be *licenced :*

(1) 4 Burr. 2312.   (2) This charter was confirmed by Elizabeth.

" nor shall any one print any book, &c. against the form or meaning of any restraint contained in any statute or *laws* of the realm * * *, or contrary to any *allowed* ordinance set down for the good government of the Stationers' Company."

In 1623, by a proclamation reciting the above decree, and that the same had been evaded " by *printing beyond sea* such *allowed* books, &c. as have been imprinted within the realm by such to whom the *sole printing thereof*, by letters patent, or lawful ordinance or *authority*, doth appertain :" and then the proclamation enforces the decree.

Again in 1637, by another decree, no person is to *print* or *import* any book or copy which the Company of Stationers, or *any other person*, hath or shall by any letters patent, order or entrance in their register book, *or otherwise*, have the right, privilege, authority, or allowance SOLELY *to print*.

This decree evidently supposes a copyright to exist, " otherwise" than by patent, &c. which could be clearly by no other authority than the common law.

These appear to be all the acts of state relative to the matter. Most of the judicial proceedings of the Star Chamber being lost or destroyed, no case of prosecution for printing without licence, or pirating another man's copy, has been found. But it is certain that down to the year 1640, copies were protected and secured from piracy by a much speedier, and more effectual, remedy than actions at law, or bills in equity. No licence could be obtained " to print another man's copy." Not from any prohibition, but because the thing was immoral, dishonest, and unjust ; and he who printed without a licence, was liable to great penalties(').

Recognition of the Right in Acts of Parliament.

1641.---After the abolition of the Star Chamber, all regulations of the press, by proclamation or decrees, were deemed illegal. The alleged licentiousness of the press, however, induced the two Houses to make an ordinance(²), which prohibited printing, unless the book was first licenced, and entered in the register of the Stationers' Company. Copyrights, in their opinion, then, could only stand upon the common law — both Houses took it for granted. The ordinance, therefore, prohibits printing *without consent of the owner*, or importing (if printed abroad), upon pain of forfeiting the same to *the owner or owners* of the copies of the said books, &c. This provision necessarily supposes the property to exist---it is nugatory if there was no owner, and an owner could not at that time exist, but by the common law.

(1) 4 Burr. 2313.   (2) 29th of June, 1641.

According to the authority of Carte, the historian([1]), if ever there was a danger of the invasion of copyright, it was in 1641, when the licentiousness of the press was carried to the greatest height.

It appears, however, that several divines who were the favorites of the prevailing party, signed a declaration strongly in favor of authors, and on the justice of allowing them solely to print their copies; alleging that otherwise, scholars would be utterly deprived of any recompence for their studies or labor, and urging that if books were imported to the prejudice of those who bore the charge of impressions, the authors and buyers would be abused by vicious impressions, to the great discouragement of learned men, and extreme damage of all kinds of good learning.

1643.---These and other reasons had so much weight, that it appears both Houses of Parliament, on June 14, 1643, joined in an ORDINANCE, declaring,

" That no book, pamphlet, nor paper, nor part of such book, pamphlet, or paper, shall from henceforth be printed, bound, stitched, or put to sale by any person or persons whatsoever, unless the same be entered in the Register Book of the Company of Stationers, *according to ancient custom ;* and that no person or persons shall hereafter print, or cause to be reprinted, any book or books, or part of book or books, entered in the register of the said Company for any particular member thereof, *without the licence and consent of the owner and owners thereof ;* nor yet import any such book or books, or part of book or books, formerly printed here, from beyond the seas, upon pain of forfeiting the same to the respective *owner or owners* of the said copies, and such further punishment as shall be thought fit([2])."

1647.—There was also an ordinance of Parliament made the 28th of September, 1647([3]), relating to unlicenced printing.

1649.---And by another ordinance in September, 1649, cap. 60, it was enacted, that

No person whatever should *compose, write,* print, publish, sell, or utter, or cause to be made, written, printed, or uttered, any book or pamphlet, treatise, sheet or sheets of news, whatsoever, *unless licenced,* as thereafter mentioned.

And the same ordinance prohibited the use of any printing or rolling press, except in London and the two Universities, and also York and Finsbury.

It then enacts, that no person or persons whatsoever in this

(1) Carte's Letters, published 1735. Sir E. Brydges' " Reasons for further Amendment."

(2) In 1644, *Milton* published his famous speech for the liberty of unlicenced printing, against this ordinance; and among the glosses which he says were used to color this ordinance, and make it pass, he mentions " the just retaining of each man his several copy; *which,*" said he, " *God forbid should be gain-said.*"

(3) Scobel's Collection of Acts and Ordinances, p. 134.

Commonwealth shall hereafter print or reprint any book or books, or part of any book or books, legally granted to the said Company of Stationers for their maintenance of their poor, without the licence and consent of the Master, Wardens, and Assistants of the said Company; nor any book or books, or part of book or books, now entered in the register book for any *particular member* of the said Company, without the like consent of the *owner or owners* thereof; nor counterfeit the name, mark, or title of any book or books belonging to the said Company or particular persons; nor shall any person bind, stitch, or put to sale any such book or books, upon pain of forfeiting six shillings and eight pence for every book.

1662.---The Licencing Act of 13 and 14 Charles II. cap. 33, was framed chiefly to control the liberty of the press. But its object was disguised by blending it with a renewal of the general ordinances for the regulation of printing.

It enacts, that no person shall, within this kingdom or elsewhere, imprint, nor shall import from or out of any other of His Majesty's dominions, nor from any other parts beyond the seas, any copies or books printed beyond the seas, or elsewhere, which *any person* by force or virtue of any entry thereof duly made, or to be made in the Register Book of the Company of Stationers, have or shall have the *right*, privilege, authority, or allowance, solely to print, *without the consent of the owner or owners of such book or books, copy or copies*— nor shall bind, stitch, or put to sale, any such book or books, or part of any book or books, without the like consent, upon pain of loss or forfeiture of the same, and of being proceeded against as an offender against this present act,"---(the penalty whereof was, for the first offence, a disability for three years, and for the second offence a disability for ever, to exercise the art of printing, besides bodily punishment at the Judges' pleasure,) "and upon the further penalty and forfeiture of six shillings and eight pence for every such book or books, or part of such book or books, copy or copies, so imprinted, imported, bound, stitched, or put to sale," &c.

The act, therefore, supposes an ownership at common law; and the *right* itself is particularly recognized in the latter part of the third section of the act, where the Universities are forbid to meddle with " any book or books, the *right* appointing whereof doth *solely and properly belong to any particular person or persons.*"

The sole property of the owner is here acknowledged in express words, as a common law right; and the legislature who passed that act could never have entertained the most distant idea " that the productions of the brain were not a subject matter of property." To support an action on this statute, ownership must be proved, or the plaintiff could not recover, because the action is to be brought by the " owner," who is to have a moiety of the penalty.

The various provisions of this act effectually prevented piracies, without the necessity of actions at law, or bills in equity, by owners.

The Licencing Act of Charles II. was continued by several Acts of Parliament, but expired in 1679. It was revived by 1 James II. c. 7 ; and continued by 4 William and Mary, c. 24 ; and finally expired in 1694.

Such is the state of the evidence as deduced from the Acts of Government and the Legislature in the most despotic and unsettled times ; and the inference is obviously strong, that if at those periods the rights of literature were respected when (if ever) they were liable to abuse, how much more ought those rights to be regarded and protected in an age like the present, which owes its improvement to the diffusion of knowledge.

We have next to turn to the only other source from which any public testimonials can be derived of the ancient usages and regulations which bear on the question, viz. the charters and registry books of the Stationers' Company.

Evidence of Ancient Customs.

It appears that it was usual from the earliest times for authors to sell their copyright in perpetuity, and that the copies were made the subject of family settlements for the provision of wives and children. In the case of Millar v. Taylor, tried in 1769, this ancient custom was proved to the satisfaction of the jury, and by their special verdict they found as follows :

" That before the reign of her late Majesty, Queen Anne, it was usual to purchase from authors the perpetual copyright of their books, and to assign them from hand to hand for valuable considerations, and to make the same the subject of family settlements for the provision of wives and children."

The historian CARTE, after speaking of the exclusive property which ever existed in all books printed in England, observes,

" That for the *making of it known*, the better to prevent all invasion thereof, when the Stationers were incorporated([1]), all authors, and the proprietors to whom they sold their copies, constantly entered them in the register of that Company, as their property. The like method was taken with regard to foreign books, to which no subject of England could pretend an original right. To prevent the inconveniences of different persons engaging (perhaps unknown to one another) in printing of the same work (which might prove the ruin of both), the person who first resolved on it, and entered his

[1] In 1556

design in that register, became thereby the legal proprietor of such work, and had the sole right of printing it : so that there has scarce ever been a book published in England, but it belonged to some author or proprietor, exclusive of all other persons.. This is evident to every one that hath ever viewed the Stationers' Register, from the erection of that company, down to the year 1710, when the Act 8 *Annæ* was passed, which refers to this as an usual practice. It was indeed so customary, that I hardly think there ever was a book (unless of a seditious nature) printed till within *forty years* last past([1]), but, however inconsiderable it was for size or value, the property thereof was ascertained, and the sole right of printing it secured to the proprietor by such an entry. I was surprised on carefully examining one of the registers in Queen Elizabeth's time, from 1576 to 1595, to find, even in the infancy of English printing, above *two thousand copies of books* entered as the property of particular persons, either in the whole, or in shares ; and mentioned from time to time to descend, be sold, and be conveyed to others ; and the whole tenor of these registers is a clear proof of authors and proprietors having always enjoyed a sole and exclusive right of printing copies, and that no other person whatever was allowed to invade their right."

The following is a brief account of some of the early entries contained in these registry books.

In 1558, and down from that time, there are entries of copies for particular persons.

In 1559, and subsequently, there are persons *fined* for *printing other men's copies.*

In 1573, there are entries which take notice of the *sale of the copy,* and the *price.*

In 1582, there are entries with an express proviso, " that if it be found *any other* has right to any of the copies, then the licence, touching such of the copies *so belonging to another,* shall be void."

1684.---Charles II. in the year 1684 confirmed the former charters, and extended them by new provisions. The new charter recited—

That divers brethren and members of the Company have great part of their estates in books and copies, and that for upwards of a century before, they had a public register kept in their common hall for the entry and description of books and copies.

It proceeds as follows :

" We, willing and desiring to confirm and establish every member in their just rights and properties, do well approve of the aforesaid register ;" and declare, " that every member of the Company who should be the proprietor of any book, should have and enjoy the *sole right,* power, privilege, and authority of printing such book or copy, as in that case has been *usual* heretofore.

There is then added a prohibition against piracies.

(1) That is, from the year 1695.

C

A few years anterior to this second charter, the Stationers'
Company made a by-law, in which it is stated, that divers
members of the Company had great part of their estates in
copies; and that by the ancient usage of that Company,
when any books or copies were entered in their register to
any of the members of that Company, such persons were
always reputed the proprietors of them, and ought to have
the sole printing of them.

In another by-law in 1694, it is stated, that copies were
constantly bargained and sold amongst the members of the
Company as their property, and devised to their children and
others for legacies, and to their widows for maintenance; and
it was ordained, that if any member should, without consent
of the member by whom the entry was made, print or sell
the same, he should forfeit for every copy twelve pence(').

(1) The following comprises a complete statement of these by-laws, which were
proved in evidence on the trial of the cause " Millar v. Taylor."

And the said jurors upon their oath further say, that the Stationers' Company, to
secure the enjoyment of the said copyright as far as in them lay, made several by-laws,
particularly the two following.

> " At an assembly of the Masters and Keepers or Wardens and
> Commonalty of the mystery or art of Stationers of the City of
> London, held at their Common Hall, the 17th day of August, anno
> domini, 1681, for the well governing the members of this Company,
> the several laws and ordinances hereafter mentioned were then made,
> enacted, and ordained, &c.

And whereas several members of this Company have great part of their estates in
copies, and by ancient usage of this Company, when any copy or book is registered to
any member or members of this Company, such person to whom such entry is made, is,
and always hath been, reputed and taken to be *proprietor* of such book or copy, and
ought to have the sole printing thereof; which privilege and *interest is now of late often
violated and abused(a)*; it is, therefore, ordained, that where any entry or entries is or
are, or hereafter shall be, duly made of any book or copy in the said register book of
this Company, that in such case if any member or members of this Company shall then
after, without the licence or consent of such member or members of this Company for
whom such entry is duly made in the register book of this Company, or his or their
assignee or assigns, print, or cause to be printed, import, or cause to be imported, from
beyond the seas or elsewhere, any such copy or copies, book or books, or any part of
any such copy or copies, book or books, or shall sell, bind, stitch, or expose the same,
or any part or parts thereof, to sale, that then such member or members so offending
shall forfeit to the Master and Keepers or Wardens and Commonalty of the mystery or
art of Stationers of the City of London, the sum of *twelve pence(b)* for every such
copy or copies, book or books, or any part of such copy or copies, book or books, so
imprinted, imported, sold, bound, stitched, and exposed to sale, contrary hereunto."

> " At an assembly of the Masters, Keepers or Wardens, and Common-
> alty of the mystery or art of Stationers of the City of London, held
> the 14th day of May, 1694, the several laws, ordinances, and oath
> hereafter following, were then made, enacted, and ordained.

Whereas divers members of this Company have great part of their estates in copies
duly entered in the register book of this Company, which, by the ancient usage of this

(a) In substance, this is the same language as that which is used in the 8 Anne.
(b) It is evident that the intention of the Act of Anne was to make the penalty
general, which is here necessarily limited to the members of the Stationers' Company.

There are several cases reported in the time of Charles II. which arose out of disputed property in printed books. Some of them were between different *patentees* of the crown; some whether the right belonged to the *author* from his invention and labor, or to the *king* from the subject matter.

The first case (in the 18th Charles II.) was between the law patentee and some members of the Stationers' Company. It was argued on the footing of a prerogative copyright in the crown. It was urged that the king pays the judges who pronounced the law. The House of Lords determined " that the king had the right, and had granted it to the patentees(¹)."

The next case (in 24 Charles II.) was also that of a law patentee, in which it was decided, " that the plaintiff, by purchase from the executors of the author, was *owner of the property at common law*(²).

There is another case (in 29 Charles II.) in which the grantees of the crown of an almanac were the parties, and in which the court thought that almanacs might be prerogative copies ; and it was held that the additions of prognostications did not alter the case, " no more than if a man should claim a property in *another man's copy* by reason of some inconsiderable additions of his own(³).

In the 31 Charles II. an action on the case was brought(⁴) for printing the Pilgrim's Progress, of which it was averred, the plaintiff was " the true proprietor, whereby he lost the profit and benefit of his copy ;" but it does not appear that the action was proceeded in.

Company, is, are, or always hath and have been used, reputed, and taken to be the right and property of such person and persons (members of this Company) for whom or whose benefit such copy and copies are so duly entered in the register book of this Company, and constantly bargained and sold amongst the members of this Company as their property, and devised to children and others for legacies, and to their widows for their maintenance ; and that he and they to whom such copy and copies are so duly entered, purchased, or devised ought to have the sole printing thereof;

Wherefore, for the better preservation of the said ancient usage from being *invaded by evil-minded men, and to prevent the abuse of trade by violating the same*(a), it is ordained, that after any entry or entries is or are, or shall be, duly made of any copy or copies, book or books, in the register book of this Company, by or from any member or members of this Company, if any other member or members of this Company shall, without the licence or consent of such member or members of this Company for or by whom such entry is duly made, or of his assignee or assigns, print or cause to be printed, import or cause to be imported, from beyond the seas or elsewhere, any such copy or copies, book or books, or part of any such copy or copies, book or books, whereof such due entry hath been made in the register book of this Company to or for such other member of this Company, or shall sell, bind, stitch, or expose the same, or any part or parts thereof, to sale, without such licence,—that then such member and members so offending shall forfeit and pay to the Master and Keepers or Wardens and Commonalty of the mystery or art of Stationers of the City of London the sum of *twelve pence* for every such several copy or copies, book or books, part or parts of every such copy or copies, book or books, imprinted, imported, sold, bound, stitched, or exposed to sale, without such licence or consent as aforesaid.'"

(1) Carter, 89. 4 Burr. 2315.
(2) Skinner, 234. 1 Mod. 257. 4 Burr. 2316.
(3) 1 Mod. 256. 4 Burr. 2317.
(4) Lilly's Entries, Hil. Term. Ponder v. Bradyl, 4 Burr. 2317.

(a) This is expressed in very nearly the exact terms of the preamble of 8 Anne.

In these times the King's prerogative ran high; but still these cases prove that the *copyright* was at that time *a well-known claim,* though the overgrown rights of the crown were in some instances allowed and adjudged to over-rule them.

CHAP. II.

FROM THE STATUTE OF ANNE IN 1710, TO THE YEAR 1814.

SECT. 1.——*Of the origin and purport of the Act of Anne, and the intention of the Legislature.*

It appears that after the art of printing had been generally adopted, the taste for literary works very rapidly increased, and the demand for them naturally stimulated the exertions of the booksellers and publishers.

Some of the fraternity, however, did not confine themselves to their own productions ; but, to supply the wants of the public, committed depredations on the literary property of their contemporaries. The greater part, if not all, of these dishonorable transactions, were committed by the lowest class of publishers, who were incompetent to pay the damages that might be recovered against them in an ordinary action. The proof of the extent of the damage was also difficult ; and it was therefore desirable that penalties and forfeitures should be inflicted to protect the growing importance of literary property.

Hence it appears that the proprietors of copies frequently applied to Parliament to assist them in maintaining their rights. In the years 1703, 1706, and 1709, they petitioned for a bill to protect their copyrights, which had thus been invaded, and "to secure their properties." They had so long been secured by penalties under the acts for licencing books, that they thought an action at law an inadequate remedy, and had no idea that a bill in equity could be entertained except on letters patent.

In one of the cases given to the members in 1709 in support of their application for a bill, the last reason or paragraph is as follows:

" The liberty now set on foot of breaking through this ancient and reasonable usage, is no way to be effectually restrained but by an Act of Parliament. For, by common law a bookseller can recover no more costs than he can prove damage ; but it is impossible for him to prove the tenth, nay, perhaps the hundredth part of the damage he suffers, because a thousand counterfeit copies may be dispersed into as many different hands all over the kingdom, and he not able to prove the sale of ten. Besides, the defendant is always a pauper, and so the plaintiff must lose his costs of suit. Therefore, the only remedy by the common law is to confine a beggar to the rules of the King's Bench or Fleet, and there he will continue the evil practice with impunity. We therefore pray, that confiscation of counterfeit copies be one of the penalties inflicted on offenders(¹)."

On the 11th of January, 1709, pursuant to an order made on the booksellers' petition, a bill was brought in for securing the property of copies of books to the *rightful owners, &c.* On the 16th of February, 1709, the bill was referred to a committee of the whole House, and reported, with amendments, on the 21st of February, 1709.

It is evident from the preamble of the act, which was passed in 1710(²), that it was not introduced on the part of

(1) 4 Burr. 2318.

(2) 8 Anne, cap. 19, *An act for the encouragement of learning, by vesting the copies of printed books in the authors or purchasers of such copies, during the times therein mentioned.*

" Whereas printers, booksellers, and other persons have *of late frequently taken the liberty of printing,* reprinting, and publishing, or causing to be printed, reprinted, and published, books and other writings, *without the consent of the authors or proprietors of such books* and writings, to their very great detriment, and too often to the ruin of them and their families :" for preventing, therefore, such practices for the future, and for the *encouragement of learned men to compose and write useful books,* may it please your Majesty that it may be enacted, and be it enacted by the Queen's most excellent Majesty, by and with the advice and consent of the Lords spiritual and temporal, and Commons, in this present Parliament assembled, and by the authority of the same, that from and after the tenth day of April, one thousand seven hundred and ten, the author of any book or books already printed, who hath not transferred to any other the copy or copies of such book or books, share or shares thereof, or the bookseller or booksellers, printer or printers, or other person or persons, who hath or have purchased or acquired the copy or copies of any book or books, in order to print or reprint the same, shall have sole right and liberty of printing such book and books for the term of one and twenty years, to commence from the said tenth day of April, and no longer ;

And that the author of any book or books already composed, and not printed and published, or that shall hereafter be composed, and his assignee or assigns, shall have the sole liberty of printing and reprinting such book and books for the term of fourteen years, to commence from the day of the first publishing the same, and no longer ;

And that if any other bookseller, printer, or other person whatsoever, from and after the tenth day of April, one thousand seven hundred and ten, within the times granted and limited by this act as aforesaid, shall print, reprint, or import, or cause to be printed, reprinted, or imported, any such book or books, without the consent of the proprietor or proprietors thereof, first had and obtained in writing, signed in the presence of two or more credible witnesses ; or knowing the same to be so printed or reprinted without the consent of the proprietors, shall sell, publish, or expose to sale, or cause to be sold, published, or exposed to sale, any such book or books, without such consent first had and obtained, as aforesaid ; then such offender or offenders shall forfeit such book or books, and all and every sheet or sheets, being part of such book or books, to the proprietor or proprietors of the copy thereof, who shall forthwith damask and make waste-paper of them : and farther, that every such offender or offenders shall forfeit one penny for every sheet which shall be found in his, her, or their custody, either printed or printing, published or exposed to sale, contrary to the true intent and meaning of this act ; the one moiety

the public to restrain the duration of copyright. The imaginary evil of its perpetuity (which will be afterwards investigated) was not then suggested. It is, indeed, quite manifest on the face of the act, that it originated with the aggrieved authors and publishers, and the Journals of the House of Commons (vol. xvi. p. 240) place this point beyond all doubt.

thereof to the Queen's most excellent Majesty, her heirs and successors, and the other moiety thereof to any person or persons that shall sue for the same ; to be recovered in any of Her Majesty's Courts of Record at Westminster, by action of debt, bill, plaint, or information, in which no wager of law, essoin, privilege, or protection, or more than one imparlance, shall be allowed.

II.---" And whereas many persons may through ignorance offend against this act, unless some provision be made, whereby the property in every such book as is intended by this act to be secured to the proprietor or proprietors thereof, may be ascertained, as likewise the consent of such proprietor or proprietors for the printing or reprinting of such book or books may from time to time be known ;" be it therefore further enacted by the authority aforesaid, that nothing in this act contained shall be construed to extend to subject any bookseller, printer, or other person whatsoever, to the forfeitures or penalties therein mentioned, for or by reason of the printing or reprinting of any book or books without such consent as aforesaid, unless the title to the copy of such book or books hereafter published, *shall, before such publication, be entered in the register book of the Company of Stationers, in such manner as hath been usual(a)* ; which register book shall at all times be kept at the hall of the said Company ; and unless such consent of the proprietor or proprietors be in like manner entered as aforesaid ; for every of which several entries sixpence shall be paid, and no more ; which said register book may at all seasonable and convenient times be resorted to, and inspected by any bookseller, printer, or other person, for the purposes before mentioned, without any fee or reward ; and the clerk of the said Company of Stationers shall, when and as often as thereunto required, give a certificate under his hand of such entry or entries, and for every such certificate may take a fee, not exceeding sixpence.

III.---Provided nevertheless, that if the clerk of the said Company of Stationers for the time being shall refuse or neglect to register, or make such entry or entries, or to give such certificate, being thereunto required by the author or proprietor of such copy or copies, in the presence of two or more credible witnesses, that then such person and persons so refusing, notice being first duly given of such refusal, or by an advertisement in the Gazette, shall have the like benefit as if such entry or entries, certificate or certificates, had been duly made and given ; and that the clerks so refusing shall, for any such offence, forfeit to the proprietor of such copy or copies the sum of twenty pounds, to be recovered in any of Her Majesty's Courts of Record at Westminster, by action of debt, bill, plaint, or information, in which no wager of law, essoin, privilege or protection, or more than one imparlance, shall be allowed.

IV.---Provided nevertheless, and it is hereby further enacted by the authority aforesaid, that if any bookseller or booksellers, printer or printers, shall, after the said five and twentieth day of March, one thousand seven hundred and ten, set a price upon, or sell or expose to sale, any book or books at such a price or rate as shall be conceived by any person or persons to be too *high and unreasonable ;* it shall and may be lawful for any person or persons to make complaint thereof to the Lord Archbishop of Canterbury for the time being ; the Lord Chancellor, or Lord Keeper of the Great Seal of Great Britain, for the time being ; the Lord Bishop of London for the time being ; the Lord Chief Justice of the Court of Queen's Bench, the Lord Chief Justice of the Court of Common Pleas, the Lord Chief Baron of the Court of Exchequer, for the time being ; the Vice-Chancellors of the two Universities for the time being, in that part of Great Britain called England ; the Lord President of the Sessions for the time being ; the Lord Justice General for the time being ; the Rector of the College of Edinburgh for the time being, in that part of Great Britain called Scotland ; who, or any one of them,

(a) An action may be maintained for damages by piracy without any entry at Stationers' Hall. 7 Term Rep. 620.

The act recites, that printers, booksellers, and other persons had of late frequently *taken the liberty* of printing, *re-printing*, and publishing books and other writings, *without the consent of the authors or proprietors*, to their very great detriment, and too often to the ruin of them and their families. For *preventing*, therefore, such *practices* for the future, and for

shall and have hereby full power and authority from time to time to send for, summon, or call before him or them, such bookseller or booksellers, printer or printers, and to examine and enquire of the reason of the dearness and enhancement of the price or value of such book or books by him or them so sold or exposed to sale; and if, upon such enquiry and examination, it shall be found that the price of such book or books is enhanced or anywise too high or unreasonable, then, and in such case, the said Archbishop of Canterbury, Lord Chancellor or Lord Keeper, Bishop of London, two Chief Justices, Chief Baron, Vice-Chancellors of the Universities in that part of Great Britain called England; and the said Lord President of the Sessions, Lord Justice General, Lord Chief Baron, and Rector of the College of Edinburgh, in that part of Great Britain called Scotland, or any one or more of them, so enquiring and examining, have hereby full power and authority to reform and redress the same, and to limit and settle the price of every such printed book and books, from time to time, according to the best of their judgments, and as to them shall seem just and reasonable; and in case of alteration of the rate or price from what was set or demanded by such bookseller or booksellers, printer or printers, to award and order such bookseller and booksellers, printer and printers, to pay all the costs and charges that the person or persons so complaining shall be put unto by reason of such complaint, and of the causing such rate or price to be so limited or settled; all which shall be done by the said Archbishop of Canterbury, Lord Chancellor or Lord Keeper, Bishop of London, two Chief Justices, Chief Baron, Vice-Chancellors of the two Universities in that part of Great Britain called England, and the said Lord President of the Sessions, Lord Justice General, Lord Chief Baron, and Rector of the College of Edinburgh, in that part of Great Britain called Scotland, or any one of them, by writing under their hands and seals, and thereof public notice shall be forthwith given by the said bookseller or booksellers, printer or printers, by an advertisement in the Gazette; and if any bookseller or booksellers, printer or printers, shall, after such settlement made of the said rate and price, sell or expose to sale any book or books at a higher or greater price than what shall have been so limited and settled as aforesaid, then, and in every such case, such bookseller and booksellers, printer and printers, shall forfeit the sum of five pounds for every such book so by him, her, or them sold or exposed to sale; one moiety thereof to the Queen's most excellent Majesty, her heirs and successors, and the other moiety to any person or persons that shall sue for the same; to be recovered, with costs of suit, in any of Her Majesty's Courts of Record at Westminster, by action of debt, bill, plaint, or information, in which no wager of law, essoin, privilege or protection, or more than one imparlance, shall be allowed.

V.---The fifth section, which relates to the delivery of nine copies of each book to the public libraries, will be inserted in the second part of the Historical View.

VI.---Provided always, and be it further enacted, that if any person or persons incur the penalties contained in this act, in that part of Great Britain called Scotland, they shall be recoverable by any action before the Court of Session there.

VII.---Provided, that nothing in this act contained do extend, or shall be construed to extend, or to prohibit, the importation, vending, or selling of any books in Greek, Latin, or any other foreign language, printed beyond the seas; any thing in this act contained to the contrary notwithstanding.

VIII.---And be it further enacted by the authority aforesaid, that if any action or suit shall be commenced or brought against any person or persons whatsoever, for doing, or causing to be done, any thing in pursuance of this act, the defendants in such action may plead the general issue, and give the special matter in evidence; and if upon such action a verdict be given for the defendant, or the plaintiff become nonsuited, or discontinue his action, then the defendant shall have and recover his full costs, for which he shall have the same remedy as a defendant in any case by law hath.

the *encouragement of learned men* to compose and write useful books, it was enacted, that the authors of books *already printed,* who had not transferred their rights, and the book-sellers or other persons who had purchased or acquired the copy of any book, in order to print or reprint the same, should have the sole right and liberty of printing them for a term of *twenty-one years,* from the 10th of April, 1710, *and no longer.*

And the authors of books already composed, but not printed, or that should thereafter be composed, and their assigns, should have the sole liberty of printing and reprinting such books for *fourteen years,* to commence from the first publishing the same, *and no longer.*

It then enacted the forfeiture of all books printed, re-printed, imported, or sold, without consent in writing of the proprietor, signed in the presence of two witnesses, and inflicted the penalties of confiscation of the pirated books, and one penny for every sheet; half the penalty to the owner, and the other to the informer.

And that persons might not through ignorance offend against the act, the forfeitures and penalties do not attach unless the title to the copy of the book be entered in the register book of the Stationers' Company, in such manner as had been usual.

The act authorizes the Archbishop of Canterbury and other dignitaries to settle the prices of books, upon complaint made that they were unreasonable.

It was also provided, that the act should not extend either to *prejudice or confirm* any right that the Universities, *or any person,* had, or claimed to have, to the printing or reprinting any book or copy already printed, or thereafter to be printed.

And the last clause directed that the sole right of printing or disposing of copies after the expiration of the first term of fourteen years, should *return* to the authors thereof, if they were then living, for another term of fourteen years.

IX.---Provided, that nothing in this act contained shall extend, or be construed to extend, either to prejudice or confirm any right that the said Universities, or any of them, or any person or persons have, or claim to have, to the printing or reprinting any book or copy already printed, or hereafter to be printed.

X.---Provided nevertheless, that all actions, suits, bills, indictments, or informations for any offence that shall be committed against this act, shall be brought, sued, and commenced within three months next after such offence committed, or else the same shall be void and of none effect.

XI.---Provided always, that after the expiration of the said term of fourteen years, the sole right of printing or disposing of copies shall return to the authors thereof, if they are then living, for another term of fourteen years.

In addition to this brief summary of the purport of the act, it has been deemed necessary to quote it fully in the notes; and we now proceed to the *intention of the Legislature*, deduced from the preamble of the act, and the language of its several clauses.

It is observable that the preamble of the act adopts a language which condemns the *liberty* then of late frequently taken, of printing books and writings without the consent of the author or proprietor, and treats it as an *abuse of a right*, not as an act done in assertion of any common law right, to which the statute intended to put only a temporary restraint, for the act declares it to be done " to the detriment of the *proprietors*, and the ruin of their families."

When the Legislature speak of a " liberty taken," it is obvious they could not mean a claim founded on any right. If such had been the intention, they would have so expressed themselves; and probably the preamble would have run thus: " Whereas booksellers and divers other persons have of late *claimed the right* of printing and reprinting," &c.

The word " reprinting," is also observable. For if the first printing a publication was a gift of the work to the public, it could be no injury to *re*print a second edition without consent. But without consent of *whom?* The author *or* proprietor (in the *dis*junctive); thereby clearly pointing out the persons entitled to this property, namely, the original author or his assignee. And by the words, " to the ruin of them and their *families*," the Parliament probably alluded to the dispositions of their works made by authors at their decease for the benefit of their families.

Again, in the enacting clause, " for preventing, therefore, the like practices in future," the Legislature, by the word *practices*, did not mean to describe the exercise of a legal right; but to point out acts committed in *fraud* and violation of private rights, which this act was made to prevent. The word " practices " is properly applied to the doing of *illegal* acts ; but is improperly and incongruously made use of to describe the exercise of right, either strictly legal, or even doubtful.

It is also worthy of notice, that the enacting clause adopts precisely the identical expressions anciently used in the decrees, ordinances, and statutes, alike speaking of the rights of authors as a known, subsisting, and transferable property. " The copy of the book," " the title to the copy," in the words of the act, form a technical recognition of the right.

The bill on which the act was founded, went to the committee as a bill to *secure* the undoubted property of copies *for
ever*. It seems that objections arose in the committee to the
generality of the proposition ; and that the debate ended in
securing the property in copies for a term---without prejudice
to either side of the question upon the general claim as to
the *right*. By the law and usage of Parliament, a *new* bill
cannot be made in a committee ; a bill to *secure* the property
of authors, could not be turned into a bill to *take it away*.
What the act gives with a sanction of penalties, is for a *term:*
the words, " and no longer," add nothing to the sense, any
more than they would in a will, if a testator gave an estate
for years(¹).

The preamble of the statute, as it was originally brought in and
went to the committee, was the fullest assertion of the legal property
and undoubted right of authors at common law, that could be, and
there was no saving clause at all in the act. When that florid introduction was abridged, it is most probable, as the fact appears, that a
saving clause was guardedly inserted.

The Universities had considerable copyrights. Lord Clarendon's
History was but lately published by the University of Oxford. The
third volume did not come out until 1707. They came out at different
times. The proviso, however, is general :---" That nothing in this act
contained shall extend either to prejudice or confirm any right that
the said Universities, or any of them, *or any person or persons*, have,
or claim to have, to the printing or reprinting *any* book or copy
already printed, or hereafter to be printed.

If there were not a common law right previous to this statute,
what is this clause to save? Not a right of publishing, to throw it
into universal communion as soon as it comes out. That was no
more worth while than the purchasing of a copy seems to be, if it be
left unprotected by the law, and open to every piratical practice.

This proviso seems to be the effect of extraordinary caution that
the rights of authors at common law might not be affected ; for if
it had not been inserted, they would not have been taken away by
construction, but the right and the remedy would still remain unaf-
fected by the statute(²).

The common law right, indeed, is admitted and recognized by providing a *remedy* for the injury ; although at
common law it has been said, that there is *no injury* whatever.
The statute professed to "encourage learning," and to prevent
" the printing of books without the consent of the authors or
proprietors, to their detriment," &c. Its object was avowedly
not to limit the right, but to facilitate the remedy. In giving
an additional protection to literary property by inflicting a

---

(1) 4 Burr. 2333.   (2) Ibid. 2352.

penalty, there might be some reason for limiting that species of punishment to a definite period. The penalty is not reserved to the author, but given to any one who may sue for it; and it is obvious, therefore, that it was designed as an act of *public justice,* independently of the *private* right to compensation at common law.

It should be recollected also, that it was a remedial statute, and ought to have been construed liberally: the contrary principle would assume, that the object of the act, as well as justice and policy, required the *suppression* of literature, rather than its " encouragement."

SECTION II.

Of the construction of the Statute before the year 1775.

The great question which has been discussed in the courts of justice regarding the limits of literary property, depended on the construction of the 8 Anne. Before adverting to the interpretation which was subsequently put upon it, we deem it appropriate, in the order of time, to notice the decisions in the courts of law and equity which took place from the passing of the act in question, down to the year 1774, when, contrary to all the previous decisions, it was determined by the House of Lords that the common law right was merged in the statute.

1. *Of the decisions in Equity.*

The earliest decisions on the general question of literary property occurred in the *courts of equity,* which were resorted to as affording a more speedy remedy against invasions of copyright by an immediate injunction, than could be obtained by an action at law for damages. Numerous decisions took place, founded upon the principles of the common law, and on the supposition that a *perpetual* copyright belonged to authors and their assignees. It is remarkable, that if the statute of Anne was intended to abridge the common law right, none of the lawyers who were engaged in the various cases which occurred after that act, should have advanced the argument. From the passing of the act in the year 1710, until 1775, when the question came before the House of Lords, there were numerous cases argued, yet in none of them was the point even in the slightest degree adverted to.

The question upon the common law right to old copies of works, could not arise until twenty-one years from the

10th of April, 1710; consequently, the soonest it could arise was in 1731.

In 1735, an injunction was granted by Sir Joseph Jekyll to restrain the printing of the *Whole Duty of Man*, the first assignment of which had been made seventy-eight years before that time.

In the same year, Lord Talbot restrained the printing of *Pope's* and *Swift's* Miscellanies, though many of the pieces were originally published prior to the act, namely, in 1701-2-8.

In 1736, Sir J. Jekyll granted another injunction for printing *Nelson's Festivals and Fasts*, though printed in 1703, in the life time of the author, and he died in 1714.

In 1739, an injunction was ordered by Lord Hardwicke against printing *Milton's Paradise Lost*, the title to which was derived by an assignment from the author seventy-two years antecedently.

And in 1752, another injunction issued in favor of Milton's Paradise Lost, with his Life by Fenton, and the Notes of all the former editions. It was an injunction to the *whole*, so that printing the Poem, *or* the Life, *or* the Notes, would have been a breach of the order.

The Court of Chancery, from the passing of the act of Anne, have been in error in all these decisions, if the whole right of an author in his copy depends upon this positive act, as introductive of a new law. For it is clear, the property of no book was intended to be secured by this act, unless it should be entered. No one offended against the act, unless the book was entered. Consequently, the sole copyright was not given by the act, unless the book was entered. Yet it was held unnecessary to the relief in Chancery that the book should be entered.

There is also an express proviso in the act, that all actions and suits for any offence against the act, should be brought within three months, or be of no effect. Now if all copies were open and free before, pirating is merely an offence against the statute, and can only be questioned in any court of justice as an offence against it. Yet it is not necessary that the bill in Chancery should be filed within three months.

Again, if the right vested, and the offence prohibited, by the act, be new, no remedy or mode of prosecution could be pursued, besides those prescribed by the act. But a bill in Chancery was not given, and consequently could not be brought upon the act. There is no ground upon which this jurisdiction has been exercised, or can be supported, except the antecedent property, confirmed and secured for a limited term by this act. In this light the entry of the book is a condition in respect of the statutory penalty only; so likewise the three months is a limitation in respect of the statutory penalty only. But the remedy by an action upon the case, or a bill in Chancery, is a consequence of the common law right ; and is not affected by the statutory condition or limitation([1]).

It has been urged in objection, that these injunction cases were only *preliminary* decisions, and that none of the suits were brought to a final hearing.

Great caution, however, has been always exercised in granting injunctions at the commencement of a suit, because if on further investigation it should be found erroneous, the loss of a defendant does not admit of reparation. The judgment, therefore, has been invariably given with great deliberation.

Lord MANSFIELD said he looked at the injunction which had been granted, or continued, before hearing, as equal to any final decree, for such injunction never is granted upon motion, unless the legal property is made out ; nor continued after answer, unless it remains clear. The Court of Chancery never grants injunctions in cases of this kind where there is any doubt([2]).

Lord ELDON, referring to the view taken by Lord Mansfield, also said, that in these cases a court of equity takes upon itself to determine, as well as it can, the rights in this period, and with a conviction that if then the cause was hearing, they would act upon the same rule. The court takes upon itself that which may involve it in mistake to determine the legal question. It is the decision of a judge sitting in equity upon a legal question, and therefore not having all the authority of a decision of a court of law, but giving an opinion, and pledged to maintain it, unless there should be occasion to alter it([3]).

So in the case respecting the publication of Lord Melville's Trial, Lord ERSKINE observed, that he was so much convinced by the arguments for the defendant as to the effect of an injunction, that unless he had a strong impression that at the hearing he should continue of the same opinion, and should grant a perpetual injunction, he would

(1) The statute of Anne is a *penal* statute, which prescribes the remedy for the party aggrieved, and the mode of prosecution to be commenced within three months. Upon such an act, if the offence, and consequently the right which arises from the prohibition, be *new*, no remedy or mode of prosecution can be pursued, except what is directed by the act.

If a conditional right is created by an Act of Parliament, the condition cannot be dispensed with. If the same act which creates the right, limits the time within which prosecutions for violation of it shall be commenced, that limitation cannot be dispensed with.

Therefore the whole jurisdiction by the Court of Chancery since 1710 against pirates of copies, is an authority that authors had a *property antecedent*, to which the act gives a *temporary additional security;* it can stand upon no other foundation(*a*).

(2) 4 Burr. 2303.   (3) 8 Vesey, 224.

(*a*) 4 Burr. 2323.

not grant the injunction then, which he only did as there was no probability that new facts would appear by the answer([1]).

Injunctions to stay printing, or the sale of books printed, it may be further observed, are in the nature of injunctions to stay *waste*---they never are granted but upon a *clear right*. If moved for upon filing the bill, the right must appear clearly by affidavit; if continued after the answer has been put in, the right must be clearly admitted by the answer, or at all events not denied.

Where the plaintiff's right is questioned and *doubtful*, an injunction is improper, because no reparation can be made to the defendant for the damage he sustains from the injunction.

There are several cases reported upon questions regarding infringements of copyright *within* the period protected by statutes : to these, of course, it is unnecessary in this place to advert, as the general principle was not in any way included in the determination ; and we refer them to the chapter on *pirating copyright*.

2.   *Of the Decisions at Law.*

The general question was first argued in a *court of law* in the case of Tonson v. Collins, in the year 1760, relative to the copyright in the *Spectator*. It appears from the best authority, that so far as the Court had formed an opinion, they all inclined to the plaintiff, and they were prepared to give judgment accordingly. But having received information that although the argument was conducted *bona fide* by the counsel, it was a collusive proceeding between the parties for the purpose of obtaining a judgment which might be set up as a precedent, they refused to pronounce any decision([2]).

In the year 1769, the subject was discussed at great length with respect to *Thomson's Seasons*, in the celebrated case of Millar v. Taylor([3]).

The counsel for the plaintiff insisted " that there was a real *property* remaining in authors *after publication* of their works ; and that *they only*, or those who claim under them, have a right to *multiply* the copies of such, their literary property, at their pleasure for sale." And they likewise insisted, " that this right is a *common law right*, which *always* has existed, and does still exist, independent of, and not taken away by, the statute of Anne."

On the other side, the counsel for the defendant denied that any such property remained in the author after the publication of his

(1) 13 Vesey, 505.   (2) 1 Blac Rep. 301, 321 ; 4 Burr. 2327.
(3) 4 Burr. 2303.

work, and they treated the pretensions of a common law right to it as mere fancy and imagination, void of any ground or foundation.

They insisted that if an original author publishes his work, he sells it to the public; and the purchaser of every book or copy has a right to make what use of it he pleases, and may multiply each book or copy to what quantity he pleases.

They also contended that the act of Anne vests the copies of printed books in the authors or purchasers of such copies during the times therein limited, but only during that *limited time,* and under the *terms* prescribed by the act.

There was a difference of opinion in the Court. Lord MANSFIELD and Judges ASTON and WILLES were in favor of the plaintiff's copyright, and Judge YATES was alone against it. Judgment was of course given according to the opinion of the majority.

Some years after this decision the question came before the HOUSE OF LORDS, upon an appeal from a decree of the Court of Chancery, founded on the judgment given in the Court of King's Bench in Millar v. Taylor, and it was ordered by the House, on the 9th of February, 1774, that the judges be directed to deliver their opinions upon the following questions :

1. Whether at common law, an author of any book or literary composition had the sole right of first printing and publishing the same for sale; and might bring an action against any person who printed, published, and sold the same without his consent?

Of eleven judges, there were eight to three in favor of the right at common law.

2. If the author had such right originally, did the law take it away upon his printing and publishing such book or literary composition; and might any person afterwards reprint and sell for his own benefit such book or literary composition, against the will of the author?

There were seven to four of the judges who held that the printing and publishing did not deprive the author of the right.

3. If such action would have lain at common law, is it taken away by the statute of 8th Anne? And is an author by the said statute precluded from every remedy, except on the foundation of the said statute, and on the terms and conditions prescribed thereby?

On this question there were only five judges who were of opinion that the action at common law was not taken away by the statute, and there were six of the opposite opinion.

It was well known that Lord MANSFIELD adhered to his opinion, and therefore concurred with the eight upon the first question ; with the seven upon the second, and with the five upon the third (which in the latter case would have made the votes equal).   But it being very unusual, from reasons of delicacy, for a Peer to support his own judgment upon an appeal to the House of Lords, he did not speak.

It was finally decided, that an action could not be maintained for pirating a copyright after the expiration of the time mentioned in the statute(¹).

SECTION III.

Of the Statutes 12 *Geo. II. and* 15 *and* 41 *Geo. III.*

The first of these statutes(²) was, " an act for prohibiting the importation of books reprinted abroad, and first composed

(1) Donaldson v. Becket, 4 Burr. 2408.
(2) By the 12 Geo. II. cap. 36, it was enacted, That from and after the 29th of September, 1739, it shall not be lawful for any person or persons whatsoever to import or bring into this kingdom for sale any book or books first composed or written and printed and published in this kingdom, and reprinted in any other place or country whatsoever ; and if any person or persons shall import or bring into this kingdom for sale any printed book or books so first composed or written and printed in this kingdom, and reprinted in any other place or country as aforesaid; or knowing the same to be so reprinted or imported, contrary to the true intent and meaning of this act, shall sell, publish, or expose to sale any such book or books; then every such person or persons so doing or so offending shall forfeit the said book or books, and all and every sheet or sheets thereof, and the same shall be forthwith damasked and made waste paper : and further, that every such offender or offenders shall forfeit the sum of five pounds, and double the value of every book which he or they shall so import or bring into this kingdom, or shall knowingly sell, publish, or expose to sale, or cause to be sold, published, or exposed to sale, contrary to the true intent and meaning of this act ; the one moiety thereof to the King's most excellent Majesty, his heirs and successors, and the other moiety to any person or persons that shall sue for the same ; to be recovered, with costs of suit, in any of His Majesty's courts of record at Westminster, by action of debt, bill, plaint, or information, in which no wager of law, essoine, or protection, or more than one imparlance, shall be allowed : and if the offence be committed in Scotland, to be recovered before the Court of Session there by summary action :
Provided that this act shall not extend to any book that has not been printed or reprinted in this kingdom within twenty-one years before the same shall be imported.
II.---Provided always, that nothing in this act contained shall extend to prevent or hinder the importation of any book first composed or written and printed in this kingdom, which shall or may be reprinted abroad, and inserted among other books or tracts, to be sold therewith in any collection, where the greater part of such collection shall have been first composed or written and printed abroad ; any thing in this act contained to the contrary notwithstanding.
III.---The third section recites the 4th clause in 8 Anne, c. 19, by which the price of books is subject to regulation, and repeals every part of that clause.   And then proceeds :
IV.---And be it further enacted, That this act (except so much thereof as repeals the before-mentioned clause in the said act of the eighth year of the reign of the late Queen Anne relating to the price of books) shall continue and be in force from the said 29th day of September, 1739, and from thence to the end of the then next Session of Parliament, and no longer.
This act was further continued by 27 Geo. II. cap. 18, and 33 Geo. II. cap. 16.

or written and printed in *Great Britain ;* and for repealing so much of an act made in the 8th year of the reign of her late Majesty, Queen Anne, as empowers the limiting the prices of books.

It recites in the preamble, that the duties on paper imported into this kingdom to be made use of in printing, greatly exceed those payable on the importation of printed books, whereby foreigners and others are encouraged to bring in great numbers of books originally printed and published in this kingdom, and reprinted abroad, to the diminution of His Majesty's revenue, and the discouragement of the trade and manufactures of the kingdom ; and, therefore, it prohibits the importation of books written and printed in *this*, and reprinted in another country, on pain of forfeiture of the books, and double their value, and five pounds for every offence.

But the act does not extend to books that have not been printed in this kingdom within twenty years, nor to their insertion among other books or tracts, where the greatest part have been composed and printed abroad.

The act then repeals the 4th section of the statute of Anne, relating to the limitation of the price of books.

15 *Geo. III. cap.* 53.

It is evident that the several Universities were as little prepared as any individual author or publisher, for the decision of the House of Lords, which overthrew the exercise of unlimited copyright, although it had prevailed, not only in all the time antecedent to the 8th Anne, but for sixty-five years subsequently. The Universities hastened immediately to Parliament, and in the same year, 1775, obtained an act " for enabling the two Universities in England, the four Universities in Scotland, and the several Colleges of Eton, Westminster, and Winchester, to hold in *perpetuity* their copyright in books given or bequeathed to the said Universities and Colleges, for the advancement of useful learning, and other purposes of education([1])."

(1) 15 Geo. III. c. 53. Whereas authors have heretofore bequeathed or given, and may hereafter bequeath or give, the copies of books composed by them, to or in trust for one of the two Universities in that part of Great Britain called England, or to or in trust for some of the colleges or houses of learning within the same, or to or in trust for the four Universities in Scotland, or to or in trust for the several colleges of Eton, Westminster, and Winchester, and in and by their several wills or other instruments of donation, have directed, or may direct, that the profits arising from the printing and reprinting such books shall be applied or appropriated as a fund for the advancement of learning, and other beneficial purposes of education within the said Universities and colleges aforesaid : And whereas such *useful purposes will frequently be frustrated*, unless the *sole printing* and reprinting of such books, the copies of which have been or shall be so bequeathed or given as aforesaid, be preserved and secured to the said Universities, colleges, and houses

It was enacted, that these Universities and Colleges should have *for ever* the sole liberty of printing and reprinting such books as had been, or should be, bequeathed to them, or in trust for them, unless the same had been, or should be, given for a limited time.

But it was provided, that the act should not extend to

of learning respectively *in perpetuity;* may it therefore please your Majesty that it may be enacted, and be it enacted by the King's most excellent Majesty, by and with the advice and consent of the Lords spiritual and temporal, and Commons, in this present Parliament assembled, and by the authority of the same, that the said Universities and colleges respectively shall, at their respective presses, have, *for ever,* the sole liberty of printing and reprinting all such books as shall at any time heretofore have been, or (having not been heretofore published or assigned) shall at any time hereafter be, bequeathed or otherwise given by the author or authors of the same respectively, or the representatives of such author or authors, to or in trust for the said Universities, or to or in trust for any college or house of learning within the same, or to or in trust for the said four Universities in Scotland, or to or in trust for the said colleges of Eton, Westminster, and Winchester, or any of them, for the purposes aforesaid, unless the same shall have been bequeathed or given, or shall hereafter be bequeathed or given, for any term of years, or other limited term; any law or usage to the contrary hereof in anywise notwithstanding.

II.----And it is hereby further enacted, that if any bookseller, printer, or other person whatsoever, from and after the 24th day of June, one thousand seven hundred and seventy-five, shall print, reprint, or import, or cause to be printed, reprinted, or imported, any such book or books; or knowing the same to be so printed or reprinted, shall sell, publish, or expose to sale, or cause to be sold, published, or exposed to sale, any such book or books; then such offender or offenders shall forfeit such book or books, and all and every sheet or sheets, being part of such book or books, to the University, college, or house of learning respectively, to whom the copy of such book or books shall have been bequeathed or given as aforesaid, who shall forthwith damask and make waste paper of them; and further, that every such offender or offenders shall forfeit one penny for every sheet which shall be found in his, her, or their custody, either printed or printing, published or exposed to sale, contrary to the true intent and meaning of this act; the one moiety thereof to the King's most excellent Majesty, his heirs and successors, and the other moiety thereof to any person or persons who shall sue for the same, to be recovered in any of His Majesty's Courts of Record at Westminster, or in the Court of Session in Scotland, by action of debt, bill, plaint, or information, in which no wager of law, essoine, privilege, or protection, or more than one imparlance, shall be allowed.

III.----Provided nevertheless, that nothing in this act shall extend to grant any exclusive right otherwise than so long as the books or copies belong to the said Universities or colleges are printed only at their own printing presses within the said Universities or colleges respectively, and for their sole benefit and advantage; and that if any University or college shall delegate, grant, lease, or sell their copyrights, or exclusive rights of printing the books hereby granted, or any part thereof, or shall allow, permit or authorize any person or persons, or bodies corporate, to print or reprint the same, that then the privileges hereby granted are to become void, and of no effect, in the same manner as if this act had not been made; but the said Universities and colleges, as aforesaid, shall nevertheless have a right to sell such copies so bequeathed or given as aforesaid, in like manner as any author or authors now may do under the provisions of the statute of the eighth year of Her Majesty Queen Anne.

IV.----And whereas many persons may through ignorance offend against this act, unless some provision be made whereby the property of every such book as is intended by this act to be secured to the said Universities, colleges, and houses of learning within the same, and to the said Universities in Scotland, and to the respective colleges of Eton, Westminster, and Winchester, may be ascertained and known, be it therefore enacted by the authority aforesaid, that nothing in this act contained shall be construed to extend to subject any bookseller, printer, or other person whatsoever, to the forfeitures or penalties herein mentioned, for or by reason of the printing or reprinting, importing or exposing to sale, any book or books, unless the title to the copy of such book or books

grant any exclusive right in such books longer than they were printed at the presses of the Universities or Colleges respectively. Yet they might sell their copyrights in the same manner as any individual author.

The provisions of the act are enforced by penalties and forfeitures ; but no person is subject to them on account of books *then already bequeathed,* unless they be entered in the register book of the Stationers' Company before the 24th of June, 1775; and all books which should be *thereafter* bequeathed, must be entered within two months after such bequest shall be known.

After making provision for enforcing the due entry in the register book, the act recites the statute of Anne, relating to the delivery of the copies to the public libraries, and enacts, that no person shall be subject to the penalties in

which has or have been already bequeathed or given to any of the said Universities or colleges aforesaid, be entered in the register book of the Company of Stationers kept for that purpose, in such manner as hath been usual, on or before the 24th day of June, one thousand seven hundred and seventy-five; and of all and every such book or books as may or shall hereafter be bequeathed or given as aforesaid, be entered in such register within the space of two months after any such bequest or gift shall have come to the knowledge of the Vice-Chancellors of the said Universities, or heads of houses and colleges of learning, or of the principal of any of the said four Universities respectively ; for every of which entries so to be made as aforesaid, the sum of sixpence shall be paid, and no more ; which said register book shall and may, at all seasonable and convenient times, be referred to and inspected by any bookseller, printer, or other person, without any fee or reward; and the clerk of the said Company of Stationers shall, when and as often as thereunto required, give a certificate under his hand of such entry or entries, and for every such certificate may take a fee not exceeding sixpence.

V.---And be it further enacted, that if the clerk of the said Company of Stationers for the time being shall refuse or neglect to register or make such entry or entries, or to give such certificate, being thereunto required by the agent of either of the said Universities or colleges aforesaid, lawfully authorized for that purpose, then either of the said Universities or colleges aforesaid, being the proprietor of such copyright or copyrights as aforesaid (notice being first given of such refusal by an advertisement in the Gazette), shall have the like benefit as if such entry or entries, certificate or certificates, had been duly made and given ; and the clerk so refusing shall, for every such offence, forfeit twenty pounds to the proprietor or proprietors of every such copyright, to be recovered in any of His Majesty's Courts of Record at Westminster, or in the Court of Session in Scotland, by action of debt, bill, plaint, or information, in which no wager of law, essoine, privilege, protection, or more than one imparlance, shall be allowed.

VI.---The next section, which relates to the delivery of the copies of books to the public libraries, will be found in the *second part.*

VII.---And be it further enacted by the authority aforesaid, that if any action or suit shall be commenced or brought against any person or persons whatsoever, for doing, or causing to be done, any thing in pursuance of this act, the defendants in such action may plead the general issue, and give the special matter in evidence ; and if upon such action a verdict, or if the same shall be brought in the Court of Session in Scotland, a judgment be given for the defendant, or the plaintiff become nonsuited, and discontinue his action, then the defendant shall have and recover his full costs, for which he shall have the same remedy as a defendant in any case by law hath.

VIII.---And be it further enacted by the authority aforesaid, that this act shall be adjudged, deemed, and taken to be a public act; and shall be judicially taken notice of as such, by all judges, justices, and other persons whatsoever, without specially pleading the same.

that act for printing any book, unless the title to the copy of *the whole* of such book be entered, and the copies of the whole delivered for the use of the several libraries.

41 *Geo. III. cap.* 107.

Immediately after the *Union* with *Ireland,* an act was introduced([1]) " for the further encouragement of learning in

(1) After the recital which is stated in the text, the statute 41 Geo. III. cap. 107, proceeds as follows :

That it be enacted by the King's most excellent Majesty, by and with the advice and consent of the Lords spiritual and temporal, and Commons, in this present Parliament assembled, and by the authority of the same, that the author of any book or books already composed, and not printed or published, and the author of any book or books which shall hereafter be composed, and the assignee or assigns of such authors respectively, shall have the sole liberty of printing and reprinting such book and books, for the term of fourteen years, to commence from the day of first publishing the same, and no longer ; and that if any other bookseller, printer, or other person whosoever, in any part of the said United Kingdom, or in any part of the British dominions in Europe, shall, from and after the passing of this act, print, reprint, or import, or shall cause to be printed, reprinted, or imported, any such book or books, without the consent of the proprietor or proprietors of the copyright of and in such book or books first had and obtained in writing, signed in the presence of two or more credible witnesses, or knowing the same to be so printed, reprinted, or imported, without such consent of such proprietor or proprietors, shall sell, publish, or expose to sale, or cause to be sold, published, or exposed to sale, or shall have in his or their possession for sale, any such book or books, without such consent first had and obtained as aforesaid, then such offender or offenders shall be liable to a special action on the case, at the suit of the proprietor or proprietors of the copyright of such book or books so unlawfully printed, reprinted, or imported, or published or exposed to sale, or being in the possession of such offender or offenders for sale as aforesaid, contrary to the true intent and meaning of this act ; and every such proprietor and proprietors shall and may, by and in such special action upon the case to be so brought against such offender or offenders in any Court of Record in that part of the said United Kingdom, or of the British dominions in Europe, in which the offence shall be committed, recover such damages as the jury on the trial of such action, or on the execution of a Writ of Enquiry thereon, shall give or assess, together with double costs of suit ; in which action no wager of law, essoine, privilege or protection, nor more than one imparlance, shall be allowed ; and all and every such offender or offenders shall also forfeit such book or books, and all and every sheet and sheets being part of such book or books, and shall deliver the same to the proprietor or proprietors of the copyright of such book or books, upon order of any Court of Record in which any action or suit in law or equity shall be commenced or prosecuted by such proprietor or proprietors, to be made on motion or petition to the said court ; and the said proprietor or proprietors shall forthwith damask or make waste paper of the said book or books, and sheet or sheets respectively ; and all and every such offender or offenders shall also forfeit the sum of *three pence* for every sheet which shall be found in his or their custody, either printed or printing, or published or exposed to sale, contrary to the true intent and meaning of this act, the one moiety thereof to the King's most excellent Majesty, his heirs and successors, and the other moiety thereof to any person or persons who shall sue for the same in any such Court of Record, by action of debt, bill, plaint, or information, in which no wager of law, essoine, privilege, or protection, nor more than one imparlance, shall be allowed : provided always, that after the expiration of the said term of fourteen years, the right of printing or disposing of copies shall return to the authors thereof, if they are then living, for another term of fourteen years.

II.---Provided also, and be it further enacted, that nothing in this act contained shall extend, or be construed to extend, to any book or books heretofore composed, and printed or published in any part of the said United Kingdom, nor to exempt or indemnify any person or persons whomsoever, from or against any penalties or actions, to which he, she,

the United Kingdom of Great Britain and *Ireland,* by securing
the copies and copyright of printed books to the authors of
such books, or their assigns, for the time therein mentioned."
It was passed on the 2nd of July, 1801, and recites in
the preamble, that it is expedient that further protection
should be afforded to the authors of books, and the purchasers

or they shall or may have become, or shall or may hereafter be liable, for or on account
of the unlawfully printing, reprinting, or importing such book or books, or the selling,
publishing, or exposing the same to sale, or the having the same in his or their possession
for sale, contrary to the laws and statutes in force respecting the same, at the time of the
passing an act in the Session of Parliament of the thirty-ninth and fortieth years of the
reign of his present Majesty, intitled, *An act for the union of Great Britain and
Ireland.*

III.--- And whereas authors have heretofore bequeathed, given, or assigned, and may
hereafter bequeath, give, or assign, the copies or copyrights of and in books composed by
them, to or in trust for the college of the Holy Trinity of Dublin; and in and by their
several wills or other instruments have directed or may direct, that the profits arising
from the printing and reprinting such books, shall be applied or appropriated as a fund
for the advancement of learning, and other beneficial purposes of education, within the
college aforesaid: and whereas such useful purposes will frequently be frustrated,
unless the sole right of printing and reprinting of such books shall be applied or appropriated
as a fund for the advancement of learning, and other beneficial purposes of education,
within the college aforesaid: and whereas such useful purposes will frequently be
frustrated, unless the sole right of printing and reprinting of such books, the copies of
which shall have been or shall be so bequeathed, given, or assigned as aforesaid, be
preserved and secured to the said college in perpetuity; be it therefore further enacted,
that the said college shall, at their own printing press, within the said college, have for
ever the sole liberty of printing and reprinting all such books as shall at any time
heretofore have been, or (not having been heretofore published or assigned) shall at any
time hereafter be bequeathed, or otherwise given or assigned by the author or authors of
the same respectively, or the representatives of such author or authors, to or in trust for
the said college for the purposes aforesaid, unless the same shall have been bequeathed,
given, or assigned, or shall hereafter be bequeathed, given or assigned, for any term of
years, or any other limited term; any law or usage to the contrary thereof in anywise
notwithstanding; and that if any printer, bookseller, or other person whosoever, shall
from and after the passing of this act unlawfully print, reprint, or import, or cause to be
printed, reprinted, or imported, or knowing the same to be so unlawfully printed,
reprinted, or imported, shall sell, publish, or expose to sale, or cause to be sold, published,
or exposed to sale, or have in his or their possession for sale, any such last mentioned
book or books, such offender and offenders shall be subject and liable to the like actions,
penalties, and forfeitures as are herein before mentioned and contained with respect to
offenders against the copyrights of authors and their assigns: provided, nevertheless, that
nothing in this act shall extend to grant any exclusive right to the said college of the Holy
Trinity of Dublin, otherwise than so long as the books or copies belonging to the said college
are and shall be printed only at the printing press of the said college, within the said college,
and for the sole benefit and advantage of the said college; and that if the said college
shall delegate, grant, lease, or sell the copyrights or exclusive rights of printing the books
hereby granted, or any part thereof, or shall allow, permit, or authorize any person or
persons, or bodies corporate, to print or reprint the same, then the privilege hereby
granted shall become void and of no effect, in the same manner as if this act had not
been made; but the said college shall nevertheless have a right to sell such copies so
bequeathed or given as aforesaid, in like manner as any author or authors can or may
lawfully do under the provisions of this act, or any other act now in force.

IV.---Provided also, and be it further enacted, that no bookseller, printer, or other
person whosoever, shall be liable to the said penalty of three pence per sheet, for or by
reason of the printing, reprinting, importing, or selling of any such book or books, or
the having the same in his or their custody for sale, without the consent of the proprietor
or proprietors of the copyright thereof as aforesaid, unless before the time of the publication

of the copies and copyright of the same, in the United
Kingdom of Great Britain and Ireland.

It enacts, that authors of books then already composed,
and not printed or published, and of books to be thereafter
composed, and the assigns of such authors, shall have the
sole right of printing such books for fourteen years, from
the day of first publishing the same, and no longer.

of such book or books by the proprietor or proprietors thereof (other than the said
college), the right and title of such proprietor or proprietors shall be duly entered in the
register book of the Company of Stationers in London, in such manner as hath been
usually heretofore done by the proprietors of copies and copyrights in Great Britain; nor
if the consent of such proprietor or proprietors for the printing, reprinting, importing, or
selling such book or books, shall be in like manner entered; nor unless the right and
title of the said college to the copyright of such book or books as has or have been
already bequeathed, given, or assigned to the said college, be entered in the said register
book before the 29th day of September, one thousand eight hundred and one, and of
all and every such book or books as may or shall hereafter be bequeathed, given, or
assigned as aforesaid, be entered in the said register book within the space of two
months after any such bequest, gift, or assignment shall have come to the knowledge of
the provost of the said college; for every of which several entries sixpence shall be paid,
and no more; which said register book shall at all times be kept at the hall of the
said Company, and shall and may at all seasonable and convenient times be resorted to
and inspected by any bookseller, printer, or other person, for the purposes before mentioned,
without any fee or reward; and the clerk of the said Company of Stationers shall, when
and as often as thereunto required, give a certificate under his hand of such entry or
entries, and for every such certificate may take a fee not exceeding sixpence; and the
said clerk shall also, without fee or reward, within fifteen days next after the 31st day of
December, and the 30th day of June, in each and every year, make or cause to be made,
for the use of the said college, a list of the titles of all such books, the copyright to
which shall have been so entered in the course of the half year immediately preceding
the said 31st day of December, and the 30th day of June respectively, and shall upon
demand deliver the said lists, or cause the same to be delivered, to any person or persons
duly authorized to receive the same for and on behalf of the said college.

V.---Provided also, and be it further enacted, that if the clerk of the said Company
of Stationers for the time being shall refuse or neglect to register or make such entry or
entries, or to give such certificate or certificates, being thereunto respectively required by
the author or authors, proprietor or proprietors, of such copies or copyrights, or by the
person or persons to whom such consent shall be given, or by some person on his or their
behalf, in the presence of two or more credible witnesses, then such party or parties so
refused, notice being first duly given by advertisement in the London Gazette, shall have
the like benefit as if such entry or entries, certificate or certificates, had been duly made
and given; and the clerk so refusing shall, for any such offence, forfeit to the author or
proprietor of such copy or copies, or to the person or persons to whom such consent shall
be given, the sum of twenty pounds; or if the said clerk shall refuse or neglect to make
the list aforesaid, or to deliver the same to any person duly authorized to demand the
same on behalf of the said college, the said clerk shall also forfeit to the said college the
like sum of twenty pounds; which said respective penalties shall and may be recovered
in any of His Majesty's Courts of Record in the said United Kingdom, by action of debt,
bill, plaint, or information, in which no wager of law, essoine, privilege, or protection, nor
more than one imparlance, shall be allowed.

VI.---The sixth section relates to the additional copies for the Irish libraries, and
will be stated in the next part.

VII.---And be it further enacted, that from and after the passing of this act, it shall
not be lawful for any person or persons whomsoever to import or bring into any part of
the said United Kingdom of Great Britain and Ireland for sale, any printed book or
books, first composed, written, or printed, and published in any part of the said United
Kingdom, and reprinted in any other country or place whatsoever; and if any person or

And that any bookseller or other person, in any part of the United Kingdom, or British Dominions in Europe, who shall print, reprint, or import any such book, without the consent of the proprietor of the copyright, shall be liable to an action for damages, and double costs, and shall also forfeit the books to the proprietor, and *three pence* per sheet, one moiety to the king, and the other to the informer.

The act also provides, that after the expiration of the fourteen years, the right of printing or disposing of copies shall return to the authors thereof, if they are then living, for another term of fourteen years.

It also enacts, that Trinity College, Dublin, shall *for ever* have the sole right of printing books given or bequeathed to them, unless they were given for a limited time only. And that if any printer, bookseller, or other person should unlawfully print such books, such offender should be subject to the like penalties as before mentioned.

The act, however, extends only to books printed at the

persons shall import or bring, or cause to be imported or brought for sale, any such printed book or books into any part of the said United Kingdom, contrary to the true intent and meaning of this act, or shall knowingly sell, publish, or expose to sale, or have in his or their possession for sale, any such book or books, then every such book or books shall be forfeited, and shall and may be seized by any officer or officers of Customs or Excise, and the same shall be forthwith made waste paper ; and all and every person and persons so offending, being duly convicted thereof, shall also, for every such offence, forfeit the sum of ten pounds, and double the value of each and every copy of such book or books which he, she, or they shall so import or bring, or cause to be so imported or brought, into any part of the said United Kingdom, or shall knowingly sell, publish, or expose to sale, or shall cause to be sold, published, or exposed to sale, or shall have in his or their possession for sale, contrary to the true intent and meaning of this act ; and the commissioners of Customs in England, Scotland, and Ireland respectively (in case the same shall be seized by any officer or officers of Customs), and the commissioners of Excise in England, Scotland, and Ireland respectively (in case the same shall be seized by any officer or officers of Excise), shall also reward the officer or officers who shall seize any books which shall be so made waste paper of, with such sum or sums of money as they the said respective commissioners shall think fit, not exceeding the value of such books; such reward respectively to be paid by the said respective commissioners out of any money in their hands respectively arising from the duties of customs and excise : provided that no person or persons shall be liable to any of the last mentioned penalties or forfeitures, for or by reason or means of the importation of any book or books which has not been printed or reprinted in some part of the said United Kingdom, within twenty years next before the same shall be imported, or of any book or books reprinted abroad, and inserted among other books or tracts to be sold therewith in any collection, where the greatest part of such collection shall have been first composed or written abroad.

VIII.---And be it further enacted, that if any action or suit shall be commenced or brought against any person or persons whomsoever, for doing or causing to be done any thing in pursuance of this act, the defendants in such action may plead the general issue, and give the special matter in evidence; and if upon such action a verdict shall be given for the defendant, or the plaintiff become nonsuited, or discontinue his action, then the defendant shall have and recover his full costs, for which he shall have the same remedy as a defendant in any case by law hath ; and that all actions, suits, bills, indictments, or informations, for any offence that shall be committed against this act, shall be brought, sued, and commenced within six months next after such offence committed, or else the same shall be void and of none effect.

college-press; but allows the college to sell their copy-rights.

Provision is then made for the entry at Stationers' Hall of the title to the copyright, without which the penalties are not incurred.

It is also enacted, that no person shall import into any part of the United Kingdom for sale, any book first composed within the United Kingdom, and reprinted elsewhere ; and the penalty for each offence is ten pounds, and double the value of each book.

But the act does not extend to books which have not been printed in the United Kingdom for twenty years.

We confine the statement of the statutory provisions in this place to those which relate to the *duration* of the copy-right, and refer to the next part the enactments relating to the delivery of copies to the libraries.

SECOND PART.

OF THE LIBRARY TAX.

CHAP. I.—FROM THE INVENTION OF PRINTING, TO THE
STATUTE OF ANNE.

SECTION I.—*Of the origin of the Tax.*

Having thus reviewed the laws, in relation to the limited period during which they protected the copyright of authors, we proceed to the history of the practice of delivering copies of books to the public libraries, which it has been assumed is calculated to encourage literature.

We purpose in the present chapter to consider the *origin* of the tax,

1st.   On public grounds,

Namely, for the purposes of state regulation. This division will include the *British Museum* and *Sion College.*

2nd.   On private grounds,

Or those which apply to the respective libraries in favor of which the tax was imposed.

The latter division will comprise the several claims made by the *Universities of Cambridge and Oxford,* and those of *Scotland and Ireland.*

Looking at the law in other countries of the civilized world, the evident interests of society, and considering the general principles of justice, it would not be easy to discover the origin of this extraordinary tax, or the pretensions on which it was instituted. We should be driven to ascribe it solely to the exercise of that arbitrary power which formerly prevailed in England, and for which it were vain to conjecture any just foundation.

We are not, however, left to surmise the circumstances under which the law originated. We have no trace of its existence from the commencement of printing in this country in the year 1471 (or 1468 as some insist), until the reign of Charles II., during which this notable plan was commenced for the encouragement of literature, and to induce learned men to write and compose useful books. During the lapse of nearly two hundred years, amidst the most unsettled state

of public affairs, and although there had been many severe
restraints upon printing, it had not occurred to the wisdom
or justice of Parliament to require the delivery of any number
of copies of books to the public libraries previous to publication.

Soon after the " Restoration," the press was put under
increased and most severe restraints, and the immediate control
of Government.   No printing press could exist unless by the
licence of the constituted authorities.   Hence the act was
called the " Licencing Act."

By this act (13th and 14th Car. II. c. 33), after prohibiting heretical or seditious publications, it was ordered that
no person should print any book unless it was first licenced and
authorized—law books by the Lord Chancellor, or Chief
Justices, or Chief Baron; books on history or state affairs
by the Secretary of State; books on heraldry by the Earl
Marshal; books on divinity, physic, philosophy, science, or
art, by the Archbishop of Canterbury or the Bishop of London.

It then declares, that in future no man should be a master
printer until the then master printers were reduced to twenty,
and the master letter founders were to be four.   The master
printers and letter founders were to be nominated and allowed
by the Archbishop of Canterbury and Bishop of London;
and no man, unless he had been master of the Stationers'
Company, was to keep more than two presses.

For the purpose of enforcing the act, very extensive
powers were given to messengers, authorized, by warrants
from the King, Secretary of State, or Master and Wardens
of the Stationers' Company, to enter at what time they should
think fit, and to search all houses where they should know,
or upon some probable cause suspect, any books to be printed,
bound, or stitched, and to examine whether the same be
licenced or not.

The statute, after imposing penalties sufficiently severe,
enacts, that every printer should send *three copies of every book*
new printed, or reprinted with additions, to the Stationers'
Company, to be sent to the *King's Library*, and the *Vice-Chancellors* of the two Universities of *Oxford and Cambridge*, for
the use of their public libraries.

The object of the act in requiring the delivery of the
three copies, was evidently to furnish the Ministers of State
and the Vice-Chancellors of the Universities with the ready
means of enforcing the intentions of the Legislature.   Thus
the first copy was to be transmitted to the King's Library,
where it would undergo the inspection of those whose busi-

ness it was to ascertain that nothing should be published which contained matter offensive to the *state*. And it is remarkable that the copies for the Universities were not ordered for the libraries of any of the colleges, but for the Vice-Chancellors in their official character:—thus evidently having relation to the interests of the *church*.

Severe as the statute was, its duration was at first limited to two years. It was afterwards continued from session to session for four years, and then was permitted to expire.

During a period of not less than twenty years, down to the reign of James II., no attempt was made to renew this odious restriction on the press, and the delivery of the three copies ceased to be required.

By the 1st of James II. it was revived for the term of seven years; the three copies to the same libraries were re-imposed, and continued to be exacted until a few years subsequently to the Revolution, when the licencing of printing presses finally ceased, and the copies of publications were no longer required.

It is observable that the *entries* of copies at Stationers' Hall prior to the Licencing Act, were unaccompanied by the delivery of any books ; and, as we have already seen, were designed by the booksellers of the Company to ascertain to each other their respective copyrights, and in some degree to advertise the works, as there were no newspapers.

It is also important to notice, that the first books recorded to have been *delivered* to the Company were in October, 1663, which was after the passing of the act of 13th and 14th Car. II., and the entries were only made during the several periods when the Licencing Acts were in force([1]).

To show more clearly the object of the act, we may present the following extract from Mr. BROUGHAM's argument (in the accuracy of which the court appears to have concurred) in the case of the University of Cambridge v. Bryer([2]).

He says, on this expired statute of Charles II. " I should take the liberty of concluding, first, from its being originally meant to be temporary, and next from its having been allowed to expire, and not being renewed, that those objects which the Legislature originally had in view, must be held to have been no longer in the view of the Legislature.

Mr. Justice BAYLEY---What do you say was the object of them?

Mr. BROUGHAM---That the object of them was to prevent unlicenced publications; and that in furtherance of that object, there is

(1) Reasons for a Modification of the Act of Anne, by *Sharon Turner*, Esq. 1813.
(2) Ib.

an order that copies of all books published shall be sent to the Universities, in order that it might appear, first, when a book had been published anonymously, if such a thing was attempted; and next, if published with the name of the author, that it might be immediately known whether any person had contravened the general prohibitions of the act by publishing an unlicenced book.

Mr. Justice BAYLEY---For that reason you contend that one was also to be sent to the King's Library.

Mr. BROUGHAM---Certainly, my lord, for the purpose of giving greater publicity to them, under the cognizance of the persons appointed to watch over the execution of the other sections of the act, and see that the provisions of the act were carried into force---the persons most sure to prevent all evasion of the act. It was taking the most public and the surest possible means of effecting the object of the act."

Such was the origin of this impost, which, it has been contended, is designed for the " encouragement of literature." It was by this act (says Sir Edgerton Brydges) that a delivery of copies was first enacted—not for the encouragement of learning; not as a consideration for the privileges given by that act, which, though it recognized the titles to copies against intruders (a property which the law of Parliament had previously enforced with equal strength, unalloyed by any such condition), was so far from an act of bounty, that it has ever since been branded with infamy for its usurpation of the free rights of the press---but unquestionably for the purpose of furnishing the Ministers of State, and the Vice-Chancellors of the Universities, with better means to put in force the despotic provisions of that act(1).

SECTION II.

Of the grounds of the Library Claim by the Universities of Cambridge and Oxford.

1st.   By the University of Cambridge.

It is urged on behalf of the Universities, that Henry VI. introduced printing into England at his own expence, that the crown had in consequence the sole privilege of printing; that Henry VIII. granted to *Cambridge*, and Charles II. to *Oxford*, the privilege of printing all books; and that the compulsory delivery of the copies is a proper commutation to the Universities for the loss of their exclusive privilege of printing.

(1) Reasons for a farther Amendment. 1817.

The pretensions of Oxford are also attempted to be maintained by the decrees of the Star Chamber, and an agreement between the Stationers' Company and Sir Thomas Bodley, the founder of the library at Oxford which bears his name. We will, in the first place, consider the historical evidence on the claim of the crown to the first importation of printing, under which the Cambridge University can alone establish its pretensions to a share of the Library Tax.

The claim of Henry VI. rests entirely upon a strange story told by one Atkyns, in a pamphlet published in the year 1664. He relates, that as soon as the art of printing made some noise in Europe, the Archbishop of Canterbury moved the King to procure a printing mould to be brought into England; and that Mr. Robert Turnour, the Master of the Robes, disguised himself by shaving his beard and hair, and taking to his assistance Mr. CAXTON, a citizen of good abilities, who traded to Holland,---that they went to Leyden, not daring to enter Haarlem, and succeeded in bringing away in the night one Corsells, or Corsellis. That Corsellis was carried, under guard, to Oxford, where the first printing press was thus set up at the King's expence. That afterwards the King set up a press at St. Albans, and another in Westminster. That the King permitted no law books to be printed, nor did any printer exercise the art but only such as were the King's sworn servants, the King himself having the price and emolument for printing.

Now, upon this singular narrative, and the inference attempted to be deduced from it, it may be observed, that the claim of Caxton to the honor of the first introduction of printing presses in England was never contested, until it became the *interest* of one of the parties, in a dispute with the Stationer's Company regarding a patent for printing, to set up the right of the Crown. We cannot, therefore, place much dependence upon a controversy introduced under such suspicious and interested motives, especially after nearly two centuries had elapsed, during which all the authorities had conceded the merit of Caxton; and it is reasonable to suppose, that the claim to the first acquisition of such an important art would not be allowed, during so long a period of time, to remain undisturbed without just cause.

" All our writers (says Dr. Middleton) before the Restoration [in 1660], who mention the introduction of the art amongst us, give Caxton the credit of it, without any contradiction or variation." Amongst these are *Stowe, Trussel, Sir Richard Baker, Leland,* and *Howell,* and the more modern authorities of *Henry*, *Wharton* and *Du Pin*---all of whom are strongly in favor of Caxton's claim([1]).

Mr. Bowyer, however, contends, that the *Oxford* press was prior to Caxton's, and thinks that those who have called Mr. Caxton "the first printer in England," (and Leland in particular) meant that he was the first who "practised the art in *fusile* types, and consequently first brought it to *perfection ;*" which is not inconsistent with Corsellis's having printed earlier at Oxford with *separate cut types in wood*, which was the only method he had learnt at Haarlem([2]).

Even upon this shewing it does not appear that the King's claim is established beyond the mere use of wooden types, and that the introduction of the metal types undoubtedly belongs to Caxton. The King's claim to the exclusive monopoly of the art, must therefore be confined at most to the use of wooden types.

But according to the authority of Lord Mansfield([3]), the King has no property in printing. The ridiculous conceit of Atkyns was exploded at the time.

Besides, it has been long decided at law, that if such patents were legal, they are merely permissions to the Universities to print books for their *own use*, and not to sell them exclusively to the public at large([4]).

In addition to the pamphlet of Atkyns, the claim set up

---

(1) 4 Burr. 2414. The Rev. Mr. Dibdin, in the first volume of his edition of " Ames's Typographical Antiquities," thus expresses himself on this very pretence : " The whole narrative is an absurd fabrication, and has been treated with proper ridicule and severity by Dr. Middleton, Oxonides, and subsequent bibliographical writers." Dibdin's Life of Caxton, 1 Ames, p. xcvii.

Mr. Nichols also, in his Essay on the Origin of Printing, says, " It is strange that a piece so fabulous, and carrying such evident marks of forgery, could impose upon men so knowing and inquisitive." See p. 7—18.

(2) 4 Burr. 2417.   (3) Ib. 2401.

(4) We subjoin the following extract on the question of the first inventor of printing from the Life of Caxton, published August, 1828, in the Library of Useful Knowledge : " It has been contended strenuously by several antiquarians, that Lewis Coster, of Haarlem, invented and used *wooden* types ; that he, therefore, was the original inventor of the art of printing, and that Haarlem was the place where the invention was first put into practice. But it is now proved, that this opinion is without foundation ; that wooden types were never used ; that the claims of Coster of Haarlem cannot stand the test of accurate investigation ; and that the art of printing, as at present practised with moveable *metal* types, was discovered by John Guthenberg, of Mayence, about the year 1438."

In a note in the Harleian Miscellany, single types of wood are said to have been used before the year 1440, by *Coster* at Haarlem, whence these characters were transferred to Mentz, either directly or by degrees ; probably by the elder *Genfleisch ;* who, with his brother, John *Guttemberg*, cut metallic types under the patronage of *Faust*, whose son in law, Schoeffer, cast his own types(*a*).

(*a*) Vol. I. p. 528, note on Essay from the Anthology, 1696.

by the University to a priority in the use of printing is founded on the date of a book in the Cambridge Library bearing the date 1468, but it is liable to the following objections :

1. The date MCCCCLXVIII. is probably a mistake, owing to the omission of a second numerical letter X.

2. It is printed with separate fusile metal types, which, it appears, were not in use so early as 1468.

3. No other book than the one in dispute was issued from the Oxford press until 1479; and it is highly improbable that during eleven years this press, the first, as it was alleged, would remain so long unused, whilst Caxton's press at Westminster, and subsequently others, were in full operation.

2nd. As to the Oxford University.

It appears by the records at Stationers' Hall, that on November 15, 1609, an agreement was entered into with the University of Oxford for delivering " one book of every new copy" to the Public Library; and on November 14, 1610, Sir Thomas Bodley, who had then recently founded the Library, was appointed by the University the receiver of these books([1]).

This agreement, although made between two public institutions, was evidently of a private character, and could be binding only on the contracting parties. It continued for several years unsupported by any authority of the state. In 1637, however, it became the policy of the Government to extend and enforce this agreement; and accordingly, on the 11th of July in that year, a decree was made by the Star Chamber, which contained nearly all the provisions which the Licencing Act of Charles II. afterwards established, but it did not comprise the proviso for delivering three copies to the King's Library and the Universities of Oxford and Cambridge. Instead, however, of that clause, it recited the agreement between Sir Thomas Bodley and the Company of Stationers, and ordered the copy to be delivered which had been bargained for between them.

The following are the words of the clause. " XXXIII. Item. That whereas there is an agreement betwixt Sir Thomas Bodley,

---

(1) The Public Library at Oxford was first founded by Humphrey Duke of Gloucester in 1439. Anthony Wood says it remained desolate from Edward VI. to the end of the reign of Queen Elizabeth, when Sir Thomas Bodley applied his fortune to restore it. Wood's account of the above contract is—" So great was his zeal for obtaining new books, that he did not only search all places in the nation for antiquated copies, and persuade the Society of Stationers in London to give a copy of every book that was printed, but also searched for authors in the remotest places beyond the sea."

Knight, founder of the University Library at Oxford, and the Master, Wardens, and Assistants of the Company of Stationers, viz. that one book of every sort that is new printed, or reprinted with additions, be sent to the University of Oxford, for the use of the Public Library there, the Court do hereby order and declare, that *every printer* shall reserve one book new printed, or reprinted by him with additions, and shall, before any public venting of the said book, bring it to the common hall of the Company of Stationers, and deliver it to the officer thereof, *to be sent to the library at Oxford* accordingly, upon pain of imprisonment, and such further order and direction therein as to this Court, or the High Commission Court, respectively, as the several causes shall require, shall be thought fit."

This decree, it will be observed, is confined to Oxford, and neither the King's Library nor that of Cambridge is mentioned.

This delivery of copies of books to Oxford is not expressed to be founded on any public right, but on a specific agreement between Sir Thomas Bodley on behalf of the University, and the Stationers' Company. It appears from the recital, that it was merely a private agreement between the two bodies. It would bind the Stationers' Company in its capacity as far as the usual operation of law on such instruments allows; but it could impose no obligation on authors then unborn, nor on publishers not members of that Company, nor could it be extended to any object to which its actual tenor did not apply(¹).

That the arbitrary Court of Star Chamber enacting expressly, as it declares, " to prevent libellous, seditious, and mutinous books," should condescend to notice a specific contract between two public bodies, can only be accounted for (says Mr. Sharon Turner) on the supposition that the thing enacted had some particular reference to the main object of the act. Both Oxford and the Stationers' Company had each, no doubt, a great number of contracts with various persons which the Court of Star Chamber never troubled itself to enforce. To have stooped to order the performance of this particular agreement, must be referred to its connection with the avowed purpose of this decree; and what connection could this be but that it was perceived that the delivery of a copy of every book to a public body, very friendly to the royal cause, would be an useful auxiliary in enforcing the vindictive and inquisitorial government and superintendence of the press, which the Star Chamber had resolved to exercise ?

(1) Mr. Sharon Turner's " Reasons for a Modification," 1813. The books printed by the Stationers' Company in their corporate capacity, are chiefly school books, psalms, and almanacs.

But in 1640 the Star Chamber was abolished; and, to use the words of Judge Willes, " all regulations of the press, and restraints of unlicenced printing by proclamation, decrees of the Star Chamber, and charter powers given to the Stationers' Company, were deemed to be, and certainly were, illegal([1]).

Therefore, *after* 1640, Oxford had no other claim to any copy of any book than what could be made from this specific agreement with Sir Thomas Bodley in 1609, which, of course, could have no public operation.

3rd.   As to the Universities of Scotland and Ireland.

The English libraries having no legal right to the delivery of the copies, except under the recent statutes, it remains only to consider the situation of Scotland and Ireland.

Is it supposed that the delivery of five copies to the Scottish libraries, can be a compensation to the printers and publishers of Scotland for being deprived of the right of pirating English books? There can be no compensation for the forbearance to do an illegal thing. Scotland at the Union incurred the full legal obligation to respect the rights of property in England. Who would insult (says Mr. Sharon Turner) this high-spirited and noble nation by offering it a compensation *not to steal?* If English authors and book-sellers had a property in copyright, Scotland was as much bound to respect that right, as every honest Englishman was bound to respect the Scottish copyrights. The just compensation to Scotland for any such right of publication, if she had possessed it, was, that by the act her copyrights became also protected and secured to her authors. This was fair reciprocity, and this is the true view of the question. The act with equal impartiality prohibited Englishmen from pirating her books, as it prohibited her publishers from pirating the books of Englishmen. The delivery of the copies is an extraneous circumstance.

The same remarks apply to *Ireland,* on the subsequent statute as to her copies([2]).

---

(1) 4 Burrow's Rep. 2313.   (2) Sharon Turner's Reasons for a Modification.

E

CHAP. II.

FROM THE ACT OF ANNE, TO THE YEAR 1814.

SECT. I.——*Of the Statutes.*

The 5th section of the 8th Anne, chap. 9, enacted, that *nine* copies of each book, upon the best paper, that after the 10th of April, 1710, should be printed and published " as aforesaid," or reprinted and published with additions, should be delivered to the warehouse-keeper of the Stationers' Company, before publication, for the use of the Royal Library, the libraries of the Universities of Oxford and Cambridge, the libraries of the four Universities in Scotland, the library of Sion College in London, and the library of the Faculty of Advocates in Edinburgh. The warehouse-keeper to deliver the same to the libraries in ten days.

And in case of default, a forfeiture of the books was inflicted, and of five pounds for every copy not delivered([1]).

The 15th Geo. III. chap. 53, besides securing the copyright of the several Universities therein named([2]) *in perpetuity,* " for the advancement of useful learning, and other purposes of education," had also for one of its objects the " amending so much of an act of the eighth year of the reign of Queen Anne, as relates to the delivery of books to the warehouse-keeper of the Stationers' Company, for the use of the several libraries therein mentioned."

---

(1) V.---Provided always, and it is hereby enacted, that nine copies of each book or books, upon the best paper, that from and after the said tenth day of April, one thousand seven hundred and ten, shall be printed and published, as aforesaid, or reprinted and published with additions, shall, by the printer and printers thereof, be delivered to the warehouse keeper of the said Company of Stationers for the time being, at the hall of the said Company, before such publication made, for the use of the Royal Library, the libraries of the Universities of Oxford and Cambridge, the libraries of the four Universities in Scotland, the library of Sion College in London, and the library commonly called the library belonging to the Faculty of Advocates at Edinburgh, respectively; which said warehouse-keeper is hereby required, within ten days after demand by the keepers of the respective libraries, or any person or persons by them or any of them authorized to demand the said copy, to deliver the same, for the use of the aforesaid libraries; and if any proprietor, bookseller, or printer, or the said warehouse-keeper of the said Company of Stationers, shall not observe the direction of this act therein, that then he and they so making default in not delivering the said printed copies, as aforesaid, shall forfeit, besides the value of the said printed copies, the sum of five pounds for every copy not so delivered, as also the value of the said printed copy not so delivered; the same to be recovered by the Queen's Majesty, her heirs and successors, and by the Chancellor, Masters, and Scholars of any of the said Universities, and by the President and Fellows of Sion College, and the said Faculty of Advocates at Edinburgh, with their full costs respectively.

(2) Page 33 *Ante.*

In the 6th section of this statute is recited the enactment of the statute of Anne, regarding the library copies ; and it is then alleged, that the provision in that act had not proved effectual, but had been eluded by the entry only of the title to a single volume, or of some part of the book.

It was therefore enacted, that no person should be subject to the penalties in the act, unless the title to the copies of the whole of such book, and every volume, be entered in the register book of the Stationers' Company, and nine such copies of the whole book, and every volume, should be actually delivered to the warehouse-keeper of the company, for the several uses of the libraries in the act mentioned([1]).

The 41st Geo. III. chap. 107, section 6, enacted, that in addition to the nine copies then required by law, one other copy should be delivered in like manner as the former, for the use of the library of Trinity College, Dublin, and also one for the library of the society of the King's Inns, Dublin, by the printer or printers of *all such books* as should thereafter be printed and published, and *the title to the copyright whereof should be entered* in the register book of the Stationers' Company.

(1) VI.---And whereas in and by an Act of Parliament, made in the eighth year of the reign of her late Majesty Queen Anne, intituled, *An act for the encouragement of learning, by vesting the copies of printed books in the authors or purchasers of such copies during the times therein mentioned,* it is enacted, that nine copies of each book or books, upon the best paper, that, from and after the tenth day of April, one thousand seven hundred and ten, should be printed and published, as therein mentioned, or reprinted and published with additions, shall, by the printer and printers thereof, be delivered to the warehouse-keeper of the said Company of Stationers for the time being, at the hall of the said Company, before such publication made, for the use of the Royal Library, the libraries of the Universities of Oxford and Cambridge, the libraries of the four Universities in Scotland, the library of Sion College in London, and the library commonly called the library belonging to the Faculty of Advocates in Edinburgh, respectively; which such warehouse-keeper was thereby required, within ten days after demand by the keepers of the respective libraries, or any person or persons by them, or any of them, authorized to demand the said copy, to deliver the same for the use of the aforesaid libraries; and if any proprietor, bookseller, or printer, or the said warehouse-keeper of the said Company of Stationers, should not observe the direction of the said act therein, that then he and they so making default in not delivering the said printed copies as aforesaid, should forfeit as therein mentioned: and whereas the said provision has not proved effectual, but the same hath been eluded by the entry only of the title to a single volume, or of some part of such book or books so printed and published, or reprinted and republished, as aforesaid, be it enacted by the authority aforesaid, that no person or persons whatsoever shall be subject to the penalties in the said act mentioned, for or by reason of the printing or reprinting, importing or exposing to sale, any book or books, without the consent mentioned in the said act, unless the title to the copy of the whole of such book, and every volume thereof, be entered in manner directed by the said act, in the register book of the Company of Stationers, and unless nine such copies of the whole of such book or books, and every volume thereof printed and published, or reprinted or republished, as therein mentioned, shall be actually delivered to the warehouse-keeper of the said Company, as therein directed, for the several uses of the several libraries in the said act mentioned.

E 2

And penalties were inflicted for default, similar to those which were enacted regarding the previous nine copies([1]).

Of the interpretation of the Statutes regarding Books not registered at Stationers' Hall.

It was for a long series of years considered as the sound and unquestionable interpretation of the statute of 8th Anne, that the Universities were entitled to copies of *such books as were registered at Stationers' Hall, and no others.*

It is by the 2nd section of the 8th Anne that the entry at Stationers' Hall is directed to be made. The *object* of the provision is recited to be, *that persons may not through ignorance offend against the act;* but, that the property in the book may be ascertained. And the penalties do not attach for printing without the consent of the proprietor, *unless* the title to the book shall be entered before publication in the registry of the company.

It has been contended, that this provision as to the registry is confined to the penalties mentioned in the first section of the act; and that in the 5th section, by which the nine copies are given, there is no reference to the prevention of persons being unwarily led into the penalties given by the first section. For the intention of the legislature, we ought, however, to look at the *preamble* of the act, which, after reciting the invasions upon the rights of authors and proprietors, " to their very great detriment and ruin," proceeds to enact the remedies contained in the statute: and the whole of the act is, to prevent the injuries in future, and to encourage learned men to compose and write useful books.

----

(1) The following is a copy of the clause:—

VI.---Provided also, and be it further enacted, that from and after the passing of this act, in addition to the nine copies now required by law to be delivered to the warehouse-keeper of the said Company of Stationers, of each and every book and books which shall be entered into the register book of the said company, one other copy shall be in like manner delivered for the use of the library of the said college of the Holy Trinity of Dublin, and also one other copy for the use of the library of the society of the King's Inns, Dublin, by the printer or printers of all and every such book and books as shall hereafter be printed and published, and the title to the copyright whereof shall be entered in the said register book of the said company ; and that the said college and the said society shall have the like remedies for enforcing the delivery of the said copies, and that all proprietors, booksellers, and printers, and the warehouse-keeper of the said company, shall be liable to the like penalties for making default in delivering the said copies for the use of the said college and the said society, as are now in force with respect to the delivering, or making default in delivering, the nine copies now required by law to be delivered in manner aforesaid.

The tax of the copies surely could not be construed as a protection to literary property, or to prevent the ruin of authors. It was evidently a payment, exacted for the supposed benefits conferred by the statute, and a condition precedent to any claim on the remedies it provides. The first section (after stating the general object of the act) secures the copyright for a term of years, by certain penalties.—The 2nd provides that the works shall be registered. —The 3rd imposes a penalty on the Stationers' clerk for breach of his duty.—The 4th regulates the price of books (afterwards repealed).—The 5th contains the proviso, that nine copies shall be delivered to the warehouse-keeper for the use of the University Libraries, &c.

Now it is true, that the words "provided always," which commence the sections of many of the Acts of Parliament, are not invariably to be taken as referring to all the previous enactments; and sometimes these words very absurdly introduce an enactment perfectly distinct from any thing that precedes it; yet, here the common sense of the whole statute stands thus:—"Authors have sustained very great detriment, ---to prevent which in future, and to encourage the composition of useful books, the legislature inflicts certain penalties on the invasion of copyrights, *provided* the books be registered, and provided *also*, that nine copies be presented to the public libraries."

Although there are two intervening sections on other subjects, the 1st, 2nd, and 5th are, in all fair construction, one enactment. It is impossible that the 5th section can be connected with either the 3d or 4th, which relate to the Stationers' clerk, and the price of books.

If the conditions of registry and delivery are not complied with, the party cannot avail himself of the remedies afforded by the act.—They are conditions *precedent*, and he has no claim under the act unless he performs them; but if he is satisfied with the remedy at common law, and chooses to abandon the protection of the statute, there seems no ground for imposing on him the tax inflicted by the statute, when he seeks no benefit under its provisions. It was, indeed, understood by every one, for nearly a century, that the entry was necessary for no other purpose than to enforce the penalties against pirating the copyright. In the majority of cases no entry was made; because it is only in relation to some peculiar works that the remedy under the statutes for the penalties is preferable to the ordinary action for damages.

It appears that the books entered in the registry of

the Stationers' Company during a period of fifty years, sub-sequently to the statute of Anne, were not altogether at the rate of fifty annually; and it was the invariable custom to deliver to the libraries those works only which were so entered.

Such was not only the understanding of the publishers and the Stationers' Company, but of those who, acting for the libraries, were the most interested in a contrary construction. Until the case of the Cambridge University v. Bryer, which was decided in November, 1812, it was never pretended that the statute entitled the Universities to copies of *un*registered books. Nay, further, it appears by the journals of the House of Commons in 1775(¹) that the House ordered " that the Committee make provision in the Bill (then pending in Parliament) for enforcing the execution of a clause in the act of Anne, which provides that the several copies of each book, printed *and registered* under the direction of the act, be delivered to the warehouse-keeper of the Stationers' Company, for the use of the several libraries therein described.

Then the act 15th Geo. III. chap. 53, section 6, *recites,* that the provision relative to the delivery of the copies had not proved effectual, but had been eluded by the entry only of the title to a single volume, or of some part of the book; and *enacts,* that no person should be subject to the penalties, unless the title to the copy of the whole book, and every volume, should be entered—*and unless* nine copies of the whole should be actually delivered for the use of the several libraries, &c.

Here it is evident that the delivery of the presentation copies was a mere condition, attached to the remedy by way of penalties given by the statute against pirating.

So also the 41st Geo. III. chap. 107, directs, that in addition to the nine copies required by law to be delivered of each book *which should be entered in the register book of the Stationers' Company,* one other copy should be delivered for Trinity College, and one for the King's Inns, Dublin, of all books which should thereafter be printed and published; *and the title to the copyright whereof should be entered in the register book of the Company.*

It is clear, therefore, that before the right of the Univer-sities could attach, the entry must be made. There is nothing in the act to compel the entry. It was necessary only that those who sought protection under the statute, should conform to its conditions: the one was, to enter the book,—the

(1) Page 351.

other, to deliver certain copies. If the protection was not needed, the entry was not made, and consequently the copies ought not to have been required.

SECTION III.

Of the Legal Decisions relating to Unregistered Books.

The only case on this subject was that of the University of Cambridge v. Bryer('), in which the Court of King's Bench

(1) 16 East, 317.

The following is an extract of the judgment, taken from the short-hand writer's notes, for which we are indebted to Messrs. Longman, Rees, and Co., the eminent publishers.

The University of Cambridge against Henry Bryer.—Judgment, 20th November, 1812. L RD ELLENBOROUGH.—The grand rule of construing any statute, as indeed it is the grand rule of construing any instrument, be it statute, be it will, be it deed, is to look into the body of the thing to be construed, and to collect, as far as you can, what is the intrinsic meaning of that thing to be construed, and if that thing be clearly intelligible in reference to its own contents, I should not be inclined to raise a doubt upon the construction drawn *aliunde*, if I can help it. I may certainly by subsequent statutes be obliged to put a perverse, and what I should consider an unnatural interpretation, on the statute as originally passed. I may be under such compulsion, but I should certainly endeavour, as far as I can, without violating the fair rules of construction, to maintain the integrity of the original text unvitiated by subsequent misconstruction, if I may so say.

Now the statute of 8th Anne, cap. 19, I think is susceptible of one doubt, and that one doubt has been pointed out, which is in the section respecting the delivery, where it is enjoined to be by the printer, after a demand made by the warehouse-keeper; and it then goes on, "and if any proprietor, bookseller, or printer, or the said warehouse-keeper of the said Company of Stationers, shall not observe the directions of this act therein, then he and they so making default in not delivering the said printed copies as aforesaid, shall forfeit, besides the value of the said printed copies, the sum of five pounds for every copy not so delivered." Now there is certainly something doubtful there, because a duty is enjoined to be performed by the printer and the warehouse-keeper only, and there appears to be a penalty imposed upon the proprietor and bookseller, in respect to whom no particular duty has been previously enjoined; that is therefore susceptible of some doubt ; probably it might receive a construction that these persons, booksellers and proprietors, were to procure the thing to be done by the printer or bookseller, and that they would not be exempt from the penalty if it was not done by the manual hand of the bookseller or printer.

It has been said the act has three objects; I cannot subdivide the first into two---I think it has only two. Mr. Littledale contended that there was no right at common law ; perhaps there might not be ; but with that we have not particularly any thing to do. He considered the first, the protection of authors, by vesting the right in them ; then the fortifying their right by penalties; and, thirdly, the encouragement of literature. I think it has simply but two, the object of protecting the copyright, and the object of the advancement of learning ; and there is a section in this statute which has that in view, which it is singular enough has not been adverted to by either of the gentlemen who have argued this case. The first, second, and third sections relate to the protection of the right of the author, and to the protection of the right of the person having the property in the copy, or the purchaser ; the fourth and fifth have for their objects the advancement of literature, and they are pregnant with this purpose, that literature should be made accessible, at easy rates and prices, to persons desirous of purchasing books, and therefore they subject to the Archbishops and the Chiefs of the Courts of Law the power of settling the prices of books. I am aware that that provision is repealed by the 2nd

decided, that it was necessary to deliver a copy to the warehouse-keeper of the Stationers' Company, although the book was not entered in the registry :

This determination was founded on the construction put by the court on the 8th Anne, chap. 19, and is admitted to be a construction opposed to the provisions of the subsequent sta-

Geo. II. cap. 36, but though repealed, it makes a part of the one entire act, and shews the purpose of the legislature. The purpose of the legislature by the 4th section was to make learning easy of access. The purpose of the fifth was to secure the delivery of the books printed to the King's Library, the libraries of the Universities of Oxford and Cambridge, the libraries of the four Universities of Scotland, the library of Sion College in London, and the library belonging to the Faculty of Advocates---I think five copies out of the nine being to be transmitted to Scotland---in order to secure a deposit accessible by literary persons, for the books might have been of such considerable price, that they might not be easily attainable by scholars of ordinary means. These are the two objects, and in furtherance of these objects are the provisions contained in this statute to be construed.

The first branch of the first section provides, " That the author of any book or books already composed, and not printed and published, or that shall hereafter be composed, and his assignee or assigns, shall have the sole liberty of printing and reprinting such book and books for the term of fourteen years, to commence from the day of the first publishing the same." That may be considered as a substantive provision vesting the copyright, and for any violation of that right, it is considered in Beckford v. Hood that an action is maintainable, independently of the penalties which are accollary to the protection of the right. There is not only given to the proprietors, but to the common informer, a right to bring that action ; and therefore in Beckford v. Hood it was properly observed, that unless the proprietor of a book had an action at law, his remedy might be anticipated, or rather precluded by a common informer, who might by some species of collusion, difficult to detect, have stopped the course of his remedy entirely, and therefore in Beckford v. Hood that was maintained, and I think it has not been impeached ; it was brought before the court, but I think it was generally recognized as law, that an action was maintainable on this branch of the section independently of the penalties. It was decided in the same case, that the penalties accrue on the entering at Stationers' Hall, as the act itself says in the latter part of the first section. It is provided, " that if any bookseller, printer, or other person, shall, within the times granted and limited by this act," that is fourteen years, "print, reprint, or import any such book, without the consent of the proprietor, or knowing the same to be so printed or reprinted, without the consent of the proprietor, shall sell, publish, or expose to sale any such book, he shall forfeit the same ; and he shall forfeit a penny for every sheet found in his custody, published or exposed to sale, contrary to the true intent and meaning of this act, the one moiety thereof to the Queen, and the other moiety to any person who shall sue for the same."

The second section provides, " Whereas many persons may through ignorance offend against this act, unless some provision be made whereby the property of a book, as is intended to be secured to the proprietor thereof, may be ascertained, it is enacted, that no person shall be subjected to the forfeitures or penalties therein mentioned, for or by reason of the printing or reprinting of any book without consent, unless the title to the copy of such book shall, before such publication, be entered in the register book of the Company of Stationers ;" therefore it is quite clear, that by the express provisions of the statute there must be a previous entry at Stationers' Hall to found an action for penalties.

Then the third provides, " That if the clerk of the Company of Stationers shall refuse or neglect to make such entry, or to give such certificate, the proprietor shall supply the place of that entry in a way there pointed out."

Then the fourth section is directed to the settling the prices of books, with reference to which is a very prominent object of this act, the cheapness of books ; and then comes the fifth section, and that provides, "that nine copies of each book or books, upon the best paper that shall be printed and published as aforesaid, or reprinted and published with additions, shall, by the printer, be delivered to the warehouse-keeper of the said

tutes of 15th Geo. III. and 41st Geo. III. Besides this conflict of legislative enactment, it also appears, that Lord Ellenborough, before whom the cause was tried, observed, that he would reserve his opinion, as it might very fitly be made the subject of discussion elsewhere, and perhaps in some ulterior *Court of Appeal, to which it might not unfitly be carried.*

Company of Stationers for the time being, at the hall of the said Company, before such publication made." Now the question arises upon this section, what is the meaning of the words, "shall be printed and published as aforesaid?" And printed and published as aforesaid relates not merely to any mode of printing and publishing, if mode of printing and publishing had been previously mentioned, but it relates likewise to the persons entitled to print and publish; it relates to the persons whose property is protected for the period for which it is protected; that is the thing referred to; that shall be printed by the owner or author entitled to protection during the respective periods, that is twenty-one years for works printed before the act, and fourteen years for works printed after the act, that is during the period stated by the act, in reference to these particular works. When it directs that nine copies shall be delivered, it relates therefore to every person standing in that situation; the act directs that the copy shall be delivered to the warehouse-keeper, and it has not in this case been delivered to the warehouse-keeper.

It is said, that the entry at Stationers' Hall is necessary to recover the copies; but the entry in the terms of the act is required only to enable them to recover the forfeitures and penalties, and not the value of the book, distinct from the forfeiture. I do not advert particularly to the prior statutes, the object of which was to give the Universities copies, nor the policy of them, only as shewing that this was a matter not perfectly new, but that under former statutes the Universities had derived similar benefits. But there come two further statutes; and it is contended, that by the 15th Geo. III. cap. 53, and the 41st Geo. III. cap. 107, a sense is put upon the statute of Anne, which sense we are bound to adopt in the construction of it here. The statute of 15th Geo. III. says, "Whereas the said provision has not proved effectual, but the same hath been eluded by the entry of the title to a single volume, or of some part of such book or books so printed and published, or reprinted and republished." What is the meaning of the word eluded? It means, that the person entitled to the right has by some deception or other lost the benefit of it. Eluded means, that he was tricked or deceived as to the thing he was otherwise entitled to have. It does not mean that he was defeated, that he was effectually defeated; and unless it means effectually defeated, it is not pregnant of the construction endeavoured to be put upon it. At the same time, my difficulty has arisen here, and here only. The framers of this statute did certainly, in framing this law, advert to that as the supposed construction of the act of Anne; but have they thrown upon the court, by any enactment, the necessity of adopting that which I must assume to be their error, if the words of the act are intelligible in themselves? If the entry is not a condition precedent to the recovering of the value of the copy, which by looking at the act *per se* I may say is very clear, I cannot say that the person drawing this act, and the legislature in passing it, can over-run the intelligible sense of an Act of Parliament, such as it is.

There is a further provision in this act, and a further condition precedent to the right, "that no one shall be subject to the penalties in the statute of Anne, for printing or reprinting, importing or exposing to sale, any book or books, without the consent mentioned in the said act, unless the title to the copy of the whole of such book, and every volume thereof, be entered in the register of the Company of Stationers, and unless nine such copies of the whole of such book or books, and every volume thereof, shall be actually delivered to the warehouse-keeper of the said Company, as therein directed, for the several uses of the several libraries in the said act mentioned." Therefore, the delivery of the nine copies, in furtherance of the object of the act, is made a condition precedent to the right of maintaining an action for the penalties.

This statute of the 41st Geo. III. clearly was meant to put the Universities of Dublin in the same situation in point of benefit with the Universities of Great Britain, and the other bodies entitled to copies under the statute of Queen Anne. It says, "that

On the argument of the case in the Court of King's
Bench, the court held, that though there arose some difficulty in the construction arising out of the two statutes of
15th and 41st Geo. III. the construction which was to be collected from those statutes as being intended by the legislature
at subsequent periods, was not sufficiently strong and cogent

in addition to the nine copies now required by law to be delivered to the warehousekeeper of the said Company of Stationers, of each book which shall be entered in the
register book of the said Company, one other copy shall be in like manner delivered for
the use of the library of the said College of the Holy Trinity of Dublin, and also one
other copy for the use of the library of the Society of the King's Inns, Dublin." It has
been argued, that it was presumed, that inasmuch as both these things were required to
be done, the copies to be delivered and the entry made, the legislature supposed both
should be done, in obedience to the law; but when they appear to make the title of the
University of Dublin depend upon the copy of the title being entered, it certainly
appears to me at present to make the entry of the copy of the title at Stationers' Hall
a condition precedent to the vesting of that right in the Universities. Certainly, therefore, there does arise some difficulty in the construction arising out of these two statutes;
but I think the construction which is to be collected from these statutes, as being intended by the legislature at subsequent periods, is not sufficiently strong and cogent to
overturn what I understand to be the clear distinct sense of the statute of 8th Anne,
cap. 14, in which there is nothing ambiguous. But what I have adverted to as to the
printer, bookseller, and author, where the duty is required only of the printer and warehouse-keeper, and the words "as aforesaid" are only intelligible in the way I have
stated. Upon these grounds, it appears to me, from the clear understanding of the 8th
Anne, cap. 14, not so impeached by a reference to the other statutes, as to take away its
clear and intelligible sense, that the plaintiff is entitled to recover.

Mr. Justice LE BLANC.—This question arises upon the construction to be put upon
the statute of Anne. That construction may certainly be materially aided and explained by the language of other statutes, but it is upon the construction of that statute
that the court must act, and if the court are clear in their construction of this Act of
Parliament, although they should be of opinion that an erroneous construction may have
been put by others upon that act, they will be bound to give effect to it.

The previous acts of Charles II. seem to me to be so far only material to be called
in aid, as shewing the attention of the legislature to have been at former periods directed
to the Universities, when they were making any provisions respecting the publication of
books, and that when those publications were under the consideration of the legislature,
they imposed a restriction upon the authors, that copies should be sent to the Universities; thereby shewing that they considered learning to be advanced by these libraries
being kept constantly supplied with books.

Then came the statute of 8th Anne, which gives this copyright to authors for a
certain time; the title of it is, "An act for the encouragement of learning, by vesting
the copies of printed books in the authors or purchasers of such copies, during the times
therein mentioned." The legislature thought that learning would be encouraged by
vesting the right, for a certain time, in the copies of printed books, in the authors or
the purchasers of those books; and then they enacted that the authors, or purchasers from
the authors, should have a right vested in them, in one case for twenty-one years, and in
the other case for fourteen years; and then the legislature went on to guard that by the
penalties which are imposed by the first section [of the act, that is, to guard this right
which they have given for twenty-one years in the one case, and fourteen years in the
other; and then comes the second clause of the act, which contains the direction that a
copy shall be entered with the Stationers' Company, and the object of it is this, as contained in the recital to that clause: "Whereas many persons may through ignorance
offend against the act, unless provision is made whereby the property in every such book
as intended by this act to be secured to the proprietor thereof may be ascertained, as
likewise the consent of such proprietor for the printing or reprinting of such book or
books may from time to time be known, it is enacted, that nothing shall extend to sub

to overturn what the court understood to be the clear, distinct
sense of the statute of 8th Anne, in which, the court was of
opinion there was nothing ambiguous.

The court having decided in favor of the University,
some discussion took place as to the defendant's right to
take the case into the Court of Exchequer Chamber; and

ject any bookseller, printer, or other person, to the forfeitures or penalties mentioned
therein, for or by reason of printing or reprinting of any book or books without such
consent as aforesaid, unless the title to the copy of such book or books;" the forfeitures
and penalties are those mentioned in the first section, and the first section only.—" That
nothing therein contained shall be construed to extend to subject any bookseller, printer,
or other person whatsoever, to the forfeitures or penalties therein mentioned, for or by
reason of the printing or reprinting of any book or books without such consent as
aforesaid, unless the title to the copy of such book or books hereafter published shall,
before such publication, be entered in the register book of the Company of Stationers."
Therefore it shews clearly that the object of this provision is to prevent persons being
misled by publishing works, the sole copyright of which was given to the author, or the
purchaser under the author, for a certain limited time, which they might be unless they
had notice of such right or title, and therefore that which was required to be entered
in the book of the Stationers' Company, was with reference only to the penalties contained in the first section of the act.

I will pass over those clauses which have been referred to by my lord, the object of
which appears to be the rendering books easy of access; and then comes the fifth
section, in which there is no reference to the preventing their being unwarily led into
the penalties given by the first section.—That provides, " that nine copies of each book
that shall be printed and published, or reprinted and published as aforesaid, or reprinted
and published with additions, shall be delivered to the warehouse-keeper of the Company of Stationers, at the hall of the Company, before such publication made, for the
use of the libraries therein mentioned." The doubt arises upon the words, printed and
published as aforesaid. Suppose the clause had been only that nine copies of each book
that shall be printed or published, or reprinted and published, shall be delivered to the
warehouse-keeper; that could not have been the intention of the legislature, because they
never meant, I apprehend, to say that nine copies of any book which at any time should
be printed or reprinted should be delivered, but it was, that nine copies of every book
which should be printed or reprinted by any persons to whom the exclusive right of
printing or reprinting is given by the first clause, shall be delivered to the register or
clerk of the Company, for the use of the Universities; and as aforesaid means, that shall
be printed and published, not under the restrictions of the registry, but that shall be
printed and published by the persons to whom this right or privilege is given by the first
section of the act, and that appears to me the meaning of the term "as aforesaid," instead of confining it, as contended on the part of the defendant, to printed and published,
and entered as aforesaid; if that had been the object of the legislature, it would have
said, that nine copies of each book which shall be printed and published, and entered as
aforesaid, shall be delivered to the clerk for the use of the Universities, instead of which
it is printed and published as aforesaid, which means printed and published by those to
whom the exclusive right of printing and publishing is given by the preceding section of
the act; and that appears to me perfectly clear.

It then goes on to direct that if any proprietor, bookseller, or printer, or the warehouse-keeper of the Company of Stationers, shall not observe the direction of the act, the
person making default shall forfeit, above the value of the printed copies, the sum of
five pounds. It directs the printer to deliver the copy, the warehouse-keeper to transmit
it to the public libraries, and then it says, that if any proprietor, bookseller, or printer
shall not observe the direction of the act, he shall incur a penalty; perhaps if the proprietor had insisted on the printer not doing it, he might have been subject to the penalty.
It seems to me, therefore, that if it stood simply upon the construction of this Act of
Parliament, and if we had been called upon to put a construction upon it the day after
it passed, this is the clear obvious meaning of the Act of Parliament; and that connecting

Lord Ellenborough observed, that the question affected a great quantity of interest, and that no person could blame the defendant in having it further considered. It appears, however, that the defendant did not avail himself of the opportunity afforded him, but relied on the justice of Parliament, to which an application was ineffectually made, and it was then too late to appeal to the Court of Error.

that fifth section with the second section requiring the copy to be delivered to the clerk of the Company, would be fettering the act by a provision made *diverso intentu.*

But it has been stated, that a construction has since been put by the legislature as to this Act of Parliament, and of those persons under whose consideration this act may have been supposed to have been brought, and great reliance is placed on the provisions of the 15th Geo. III. and the 41st Geo. III. The 15th of the King was brought in for the purpose of securing to the Universities their copyright, and an argument arises upon the particular recital rather more than the provision; but coupling the recital with the provision in the sixth section of the act, that section recites the provision made by the statute of Anne, for securing to the Universities the nine copies which are to be delivered to the Stationers' Company for their benefit; it recites only that the nine copies shall be delivered, it does not recite that they are to be delivered only of the books so printed and entered, but it recites that provision in the language of the fifth section; and then it recites, "And whereas the said provision has not proved effectual, but the same has been eluded by the entry only of the title to a single volume, or of some part of such book or books so printed and published, or reprinted and republished;" and then it goes on to say, that no person shall be subject to the penalties inflicted by the statute of 8th Anne, which are the penalties of the first section of that act, "that no person shall be liable to the penalties in the said act mentioned, for printing or reprinting, importing or exposing to sale, any book or books, without the consent mentioned in the act, unless the title of the whole of such book and every volume be entered in the manner directed in the act, and also the nine copies shall be delivered to the University;" and therefore, in order to prevent that elusion or evasion by entering only the title of a single volume, where perhaps the work might consist of a great number of volumes, and to make it necessary that the titles of all the volumes should be entered with the clerk of the Company, the legislature make that which was not a condition precedent before, namely, the delivery of the nine copies to the Universities, a condition precedent to the party suing for penalties under the first section. Now, how can it be said that this right of the University can be rendered not so effectual, or eluded by the entry of the title of a single volume in the books of the Stationers' Company? That entry is originally directed by the statute of Anne, to be made for the purpose of giving notice, that there may be a place where every person may go and see every thing which is published. The clause giving the nine copies to the different libraries is only guarded by a penalty to be recovered and sued for within three months after the offence is committed, and therefore that would be ineffectual if the Universities or the owners of the libraries could be kept in the dark three months as to the books published; and if this register, which is the public notice, contains only the title of a single volume, and that is the place they are to have resort to, the three months may be elapsed before they have notice of any more than a single volume being published, and then their whole remedy would be at an end, as it respected the right vested in them by the 8th Anne; but it appears to me that the act makes the use of entering in that register that which is described, namely, that it is for the purpose of notice, to prevent ignorant people being led into penalties; therefore it provides, that the whole title shall be entered there, and the copies delivered; it seems to me, therefore, that the words of the recital of that sixth clause in the 15th of the present King is perfectly consistent with the construction of this act, though it may appear at first sight to have a different effect, for as the right to protect the privileges of the libraries could be exercised only within three months after the publication of the book, it was an elusion and a rendering ineffectual that provision in their favor, if a false account were given of the number of volumes.

The next act is the 41st of the king; and it appears upon that act, that the construc-

On a question which seems to depend rather on the
technical constructions of lawyers, than on the rational grounds
of the subject, it may not be unimportant, on the authority
of Mr. Sharon Turner([1]), to state, that when the action was
brought by the University of Cambridge, the opinion of the
then Attorney General([2]) was taken on behalf of the printer;

tion of the statute of Anne was misunderstood, for at that time it is recited as if the
entry of the book at the Company's hall was a condition precedent; it is provided at
least, that in future copies shall be delivered to the Universities of Ireland in the same
manner as before they had been delivered to the Universities in England and Scotland;
and in future it makes it a condition precedent to the delivery of the copies, that they
shall have been entered. This act certainly acts upon a misunderstanding, and a misconstruction, in my opinion, of the statute of Anne; for it must certainly have been the
intention of the legislature to put these learned bodies of Ireland upon the same footing
as those of England and Scotland were before placed by the statute of Anne; but as the
construction of the statute of Anne appears to me clear, when I do not give it that misconstruction which in later times appears to have been applied to it, I am of opinion that
cannot control us in the construction to be put upon that act. I admit the force of the
observations; but here it is not a positive interpretation imposed by the legislature, but
only by the provisions of the legislature they seem to have apprehended such was the
construction of the statute of Anne. If the court is clear that the construction is otherwise, that cannot bind us in the construction we put upon it; and it appears to me, that
notwithstanding the title of the book has not been entered with the clerk of the Stationers'
Company, yet inasmuch as the author of this book is, according to the decision of this
court in Beckford v. Hood, entitled to all the privileges granted by the statute of Anne,
and all the privileges granted by a much more effectual remedy than the penalties which
are given by the first section of the act, namely, by action to recover damages against
any person who shall infringe his right, this privilege to the different libraries is given by
the fifth section of this act, notwithstanding he may not have complied with that which is
required by the second section, but which is totally for a different purpose than that of
securing the right to the Universities; therefore it appears to me, upon these grounds,
the *postea* ought to be delivered to the plaintiffs.

Mr. Justice BAYLEY---I am entirely of the same opinion; but as my lord and my
brother Le Blanc have gone so fully into it, I shall not enter into it.

Mr. BROUGHAM---My lord, on the reservation to turn this into a special verdict, if
the court shall so please, I request to know whether it is your lordship's pleasure.

Mr. Justice BAYLEY---It is upon the record, is it not, that it was not entered at
Stationers' Hall?

Mr. MARRYAT---It is not found that it was not entered at Stationers' Hall.

Lord ELLENBOROUGH---It was a point reserved at the trial.

Mr. MARRYAT---Yes, my lord.

Lord ELLENBOROUGH---There is no objection in the court to its being done; but the
terms of the reservation are, " If the court shall so please." The University oppose no
objection, I suppose, if the court do not.

Mr. Serjeant LENS---Unless the court entertain some doubt about it, we do not feel
ourselves called upon to consent; we conceive that was left to the judgment of the court.
If the court think there is a doubt, and it ought to be put into a course of further investigation, we do not wish to interpose any objection.

Lord ELLENBOROUGH---The court do not wish to enter into it. The words, " if the
court shall so please," are general words, introduced for the purpose of enabling the
court, if they shall have a doubt upon the subject, to let it go to the Court of Appeal;
that is the way in which it is framed. It is very often put, that it shall be turned into a
special verdict upon the application of either of the parties.

Mr. BROUGHAM---Your lordship at the trial was pleased to observe, that you would
reserve your opinion, as it might very fitly be made the subject of discussion elsewhere,
and perhaps in some ulterior Court of Appeal, to which it might not unfitly be carried.

(1) See his Address to the Chairman of the Committee on the Copyright Laws, 1818.
(2) Sir Vicary Gibbs.

and he thought that the 15th Geo. III. and 41st Geo. III. were legislative expositions of the statute of Anne, and shewed that the nine copies directed to be delivered, were nine copies of *such books as should be entered at Stationers' Hall*. And that, on a view of all the statutes taken together, and on the *reason of the thing*, he was of opinion that the Universities and other public libraries mentioned in the statutes were not entitled to have copies of such books as were *not entered* in the register book of the Stationers' Company.

Lord ELLENBOROUGH---Very well; there can be no objection on the part of the court, certainly.

Mr. Serjeant LENS---I understand that the court have given leave to my learned friend to turn it into a special verdict. The *postea* then is to be stayed ; and it is to be put into that shape.

Mr. Justice LE BLANC---Upon the application of the party, it must be done without delay.

Mr. Serjeant LENS---I only wish to know whether they have the option at any future time, or whether it is to be done now ?

Mr. Justice LE BLANC---On application of the counsel for the defendant, on leave given at *Nisi Prius* that they may turn it into a special verdict, that must be done within a reasonable time.

Lord ELLENBOROUGH---It must be done with our judgment upon it ; we must not have it argued again.

Mr. MARRYAT---Certainly not, my lord ; we have no desire for that.

Mr. Serjeant LENS---I dare say they will proceed as fast as they can to have the judgment upon it ; that they will not take it into the Exchequer Chamber for delay.

Lord ELLENBOROUGH---You may get them on as fast as you can.

Mr. BROUGHAM---We merely want a fair time to consider whether it is fit to carry it elsewhere.

Lord ELLENBOROUGH---Certainly these things have been agitated, and they affect a great quantity of interest. No person can say you are to blame in having it further considered ; certainly not ; only it should be done soon.

BOOK II.

THE

PRESENT STATE

OF

THE LAW.

BOOK II.

Œhe Present State of the Law.

FIRST PART.

OF THE DURATION AND EXTENT OF COPYRIGHT.

CHAP. I.——OF THE DURATION OF COPYRIGHT *IN BOOKS*, GENERALLY.

SECT. I.——*Analysis of the Statute* 54 *Geo. III. cap.* 156.

1st. Its general scope.

The principal statute by which Literary Property is at present regulated, was passed the 29th of July, 1814. It is entitled, " An act to amend the several acts for the *encouragement of learning*, by securing the copies and *copyright* of printed books to the *authors* of such books, and their assigns."

The statute not only repealed several of the former enactments, and amended others, but in effect consolidated within it the whole of the provisions relating to Literary Property(¹).

It is remarkable that the act does not commence, like the statute of Anne, by providing for the protection of copyright, and prescribing the period during which the protection was to be afforded. Although expressly entitled for " securing the copies and copyright of printed books," it begins with repealing the former enactments by the 8th Anne and 41st Geo. III. regarding the delivery of copies to the public libraries, and substitutes other provisions on the same subject, which will be hereafter stated(²). In effect, it imposes the tax before it bestows the protection. In support of the exaction it has been urged, that it is a reasonable compensation for the additional and superior security afforded by the statute. The legislative boon, therefore, ought to have preceded the duty, in consideration of which it was imposed. But as the act is differently constructed, its title should have been varied accordingly, and called *An act for securing* (not the copyright of authors, but) *eleven copies of the whole of every book, with all maps and prints belonging thereto, to be delivered on demand to*

(1) Godson on Patents and Copyright, 208.
(2) Vide Part II. of the Second Book.

F

certain corporate bodies, and [subordinately] to protect copyright for a *limited* term: such is the true description of this last act for " the encouragement of learning."

Reserving the statement of the provisions of the act relating to the library copies to the next division of our subject, we proceed in this place to set forth the several clauses which apply to the duration of copyright in books.

2nd.   *Of the Term during which Copyright in Books is protected.*

By the 4th section of the act, after reciting the statute of 8th Anne, and 41st Geo. III., by which the author of any book and his assigns had the sole liberty of printing such book for fourteen years, and no longer; and reciting, that *it will afford further encouragement to literature if the duration of copyright were further extended* ; it is enacted, that after the passing of the act, the author of any book, and his assigns, shall have the sole liberty of printing and reprinting such book for *the full term of twenty-eight years,* to commence from the day of first publishing the same.

And if the author shall be living at the end of that period, for the residue of his natural life.

The following is the language, fully detailed, of this part of the statute :—

IV.   And whereas by the said recited acts of the eighth year of Queen Anne, and the forty-first year of his present majesty's reign, it is enacted, that the author of any book or books, and the assignee or assigns of such author respectively, should have the sole liberty of printing and reprinting such book or books for the term of fourteen years, to commence from the day of first publishing the same, and no longer ; and it was provided, that after the expiration of the said term of fourteen years, the right of printing or disposing of copies should return to the authors thereof, if they were then living, for another term of fourteen years.   And whereas it will afford further encouragement to literature if the duration of such copyright were extended in manner hereinafter mentioned, be it further enacted, that from and after the passing of this act, the author of any book or books composed and not printed and published, or which shall hereafter be composed, and be printed and published, and his assignee or assigns, shall have the sole liberty of printing and reprinting such book or books for the full term of twenty-eight years, to commence from the day of first publishing the same ; and also, if the author shall be living at the end of that period, for the residue of his natural life.

The 5th section relates to the entry of the title of all books at Stationers' Hall, within one month after publication([1]).   But provides, that no failure in making any such

---

entry shall in any manner affect any copyright, but shall only subject the person making default to the penalty under the act.

3rd.   Of the Penalties for Pirating Copyright.

It is then enacted, that if any bookseller, printer, or other person, in any part of the United Kingdom, or British Dominions, shall print, reprint, or import any such book, without the consent in writing of the author or other proprietor; or knowing the same to be so printed, shall sell, publish, or expose to sale such book, without the like consent; such offender shall be liable to an action, to be brought in any Court of Record, for damages, and to double the costs of suit.

The forfeiture of the book, to be damasked or made waste, is also enacted; and to this is added a penalty of three pence for every sheet printed, published, or exposed to sale, contrary to the act; one moiety to the King, and the other to the informer.

In Scotland, the action may be brought in the Court of Sessions; and where damages are awarded, double costs or expences are also to be allowed.

We insert the remainder of the fourth section, to shew the precise language of the act, and the places to which it extends.

And that if any bookseller or printer, or other person whatsoever, in any part of the United Kingdom of *Great Britain* and *Ireland,* in the Isles of *Man, Jersey,* or *Guernsey,* or in any other part of the *British dominions,* shall, from and after the passing of this act, within the terms and times granted and limited by this act as aforesaid, print, reprint, or import, or shall cause to be printed, reprinted, or imported, any such book or books, without the consent of the author or authors, or other proprietor or proprietors of the copyright of and in such book and books, first had and obtained in writing; or, knowing the same to be so printed, reprinted, or imported, without such consent of such author or authors, or other proprietor or proprietors, shall sell, publish, or expose to sale, or cause to be sold, published, or exposed to sale, or shall have in his or their possession for sale, any such book or books, without such consent first had and obtained as aforesaid, then such offender or offenders shall be liable to a special action on the case, at the suit of the author or authors, or other proprietor or proprietors of the copyright of such book or books so unlawfully printed, reprinted, or imported, or published or exposed to sale, or being in the possession of such offender or offenders for sale as aforesaid, contrary to the true intent and meaning of this act: and every such author or authors, or other proprietor or proprietors, shall and may, by and in such special action upon the case, to be so brought against such offender or offenders, in any Court of Record in that part of the United Kingdom, or of the British Dominions, in which the offence shall be committed, recover such damages as the jury on the trial of such action, or on the execution of a writ of enquiry thereon, shall give or assess, together with double costs of suit; in which action no wager of law, essoine, privilege, or protection, nor more than one imparlance, shall be allowed; and all and every such offender and offenders shall also forfeit such book or books, and all and every sheet being part of such book or books, and shall deliver the same to the author or authors, or other proprietor or proprietors of the copyright of such book or books, upon order of any Court of Record in which any action or suit in law or equity shall be commenced or prosecuted by such author or authors, or other proprietor or proprietors, to be made on motion or petition to the said court; and the said author or authors, or other proprietor or proprietors, shall forthwith damask or make waste paper of the said book or books and sheet or sheets; and all and every such offender and offenders shall also forfeit the sum of three pence for every sheet thereof, either printed or printing, or published or exposed to sale, contrary to the true intent and meaning of this act; the one moiety thereof to the King's most excellent Majesty, his heirs and successors, and the other moiety thereof to any person or persons who shall sue for the same, in any such Court of Record, by action of debt, bill, plaint, or information, in which no wager of law, essoine, privilege, or protection, nor more than one imparlance, shall be allowed : provided always, that in Scotland such offender or offenders shall be liable to an action of damages in the Court of Session in Scotland, which shall and may be brought and prosecuted in the same manner in which any other action of damages to the like amount may be brought and prosecuted there; and in any such action where damages shall be awarded, double costs of suit or expences of process shall be allowed.

4th.   Of the Copyright of Authors living at the passing of the Act, but dying before the expiration of the first fourteen years.

The eighth section enacts, that the *representatives of authors* of books published before the passing of the act, shall have the *benefit of the extension of the term,* if such authors be living at the passing of the act, and die before the expiration of the first fourteen years.   But such provision is not to affect the right of the assigns of authors, or any contracts between them.
The following is the section in full :—

VIII.   And whereas it is reasonable that authors of books already published, and who are now living, should also have the benefit of the extension of copyright, be it further enacted, that if the author of any book or books which shall not have been published fourteen years at the time of passing this act shall be living at the said time, and if such author shall afterwards die before the expiration of the said fourteen years, then the personal representative of the said author, and the assignee or assigns of such personal representative, shall have the sole right of printing and publishing the said book or books for the further term of fourteen years after the expiration of the first fourteen years : provided that nothing in this act contained shall affect the right of the assignee or assigns of such author to sell any copies of the said book or books which shall have been printed by such assignee or assigns within the first fourteen years, or the terms of any contract between such author and such assignee or assigns.

5th. Of the Copyright of Authors living at the end of twenty-eight years, in Books published before the Act.

By the ninth section, if the *authors* of books then already published, be *living at the end of twenty-eight years* after the first publication, they shall have the sole right of printing and publishing the same for the *remainder of their lives.* But without prejudice to the right of the assigns of authors, or any contract between them.

The wording of the act is as follows :—

IX. And be it also further enacted, that if the author of any book or books which have been already published shall be living at the end of twenty-eight years after the first publication of the said book or books, he or she shall for the remainder of his or her life have the sole right of printing and publishing the same : provided that this shall not affect the right of the assignee or assigns of such author to sell any copies of the said book or books which shall have been printed by such assignee or assigns within the said twenty-eight years, or the terms of any contract between such author and such assignee or assigns.

6th.   Limitation of Proceedings under the Act.

The last clause limits the commencement of legal proceedings under the act to twelve months after the offence committed, and is as follows :

X. Provided nevertheless, and be it further enacted, that all actions, suits, bills, indictments, or informations for any offence that shall be committed against this act, shall be brought, sued, and commenced within twelve months next after such offence committed, or else the same shall be void and of no effect.

SECTION II.

Digest of Cases relating to the Duration of Copyright.

A question has arisen on the construction of the statute 54th Geo. III. cap. 156,

Whether an author whose work had been published *more* than twenty-eight years before the passing of the act, was entitled to the copyright for the remainder of his life.

This question was decided against the author in the case of Brooke v. Clarke([1]). In that case, (which was determined

---

(1) 1 Barn. and Ald, 396. We subjoin a full report of the argument in this important case.
Mr. DENMAN, for the plaintiff.—The question depends on the statute 54th Geo. III.

in 1818) *Mr. Hargrave*, the author of Notes or Annotations on Lord COKE's First Institute or Commentary upon Littleton, had assigned in the year 1784, to the *defendants*, his copyright therein, and such *further property* as he might thereafter become entitled to by virtue of the Act of 8th Anne, or any other law or usage. In 1817, he executed another assignment

cap. 156, which, as appears from the preamble, was passed for the express purpose of extending the rights of authors. It recites the 8th Anne, cap. 19, (which first gave to authors a copyright for fourteen years) and the 41st Geo. III. cap. 107, which gave the authors living at the end of the first fourteen years, a further right for a like term; and then it proceeds to state, "that it will afford further encouragement to literature, if the duration of such copyright were extended." The object of the legislature, therefore, was to extend the duration of the copyright; and, if in the subsequent clauses any words of doubtful import occur, they should be construed with reference to the general purpose, thus expressly avowed by the legislature. The ninth section of the act (which is applicable to this case) is free from any such ambiguity. It provides, "that if the author, who might under the former act have acquired a right for twenty-eight years, shall be living at the end of such twenty-eight years, after such first publication, he shall then have the copyright for his life." The author in this case *is living*, and the twenty-eight years have expired: he is, therefore, within the very words of the act, and thereby becomes entitled to the copyright for his life, and the assignment to the plaintiffs is consequently valid. It may be argued, however, that the legislature contemplated the term then to expire, and not already expired; and the author's term having actually been exhausted when this act passed, that this case is not within its meaning. But it must then be made out that the words, "at the end of twenty-eight years," are expressive of the very moment of time at which they should expire. That would, however, be a very narrow construction of these words, and not warranted by the meaning generally given to them in common usage. The words, "at the end of any term," mean after that term is expired. In stating, that at the end of a King's reign such things were done, it would not signify that they were done at the moment he ceased to reign, but only after he had ceased to reign. So if a right of way were granted for a number of years, over certain closes, and at the end of those years the right is to cease, it would mean, that after these years are expired the right was to cease. It, therefore, appears that these words are used in the common intercourse of mankind, and not to express a precise point of time, but the expiration of a period as a thing passed. Then if the words are capable of this sense (although they may admit also of the other construction), they should be construed in this case so as to effect the general purpose of the legislature, viz., the extension of the duration of the copyright of authors. By this construction, the right of the author living at the end of twenty-eight years (expired at the time of passing this act) will be extended: by the other construction, his right will not be extended or enlarged, and the object of the legislature will therefore be defeated. By construing these words so as to give the author the copyright for his life, the court will give full effect to the words of the ninth section, and will further the general intention of the legislature, viz., the encouragement of literature, by extending the rights of authors.

Mr. RICHARDSON, contra. This Act of Parliament does not re-vest in an author a copyright, which, under the then existing laws, was spent and terminated; it only *extends*, but does not *create* a right. The language and meaning of the statute is wholly prospective. The fourth section provides, that from and after the passing of the act, the author of any book, composed and not printed and published, or which shall hereafter be composed and be printed and published, shall have the copyright for twenty-eight years; and if he be living *at* the end of that period, for the term of his life. This section, therefore, makes an alteration in the then law, by extending the author's copyright, first for twenty-eight years, and if he be living at the end of twenty-eight years, for his life. It, however, provides only as to future publications, for the work may be written either before or after the act, but unless it be *published after* the act, this clause does not attach, and it goes on to inflict very severe penalties upon persons printing the works of any authors without their consent. So far the statute had provided for the cases of authors who published after the printing of the act. It occurred, however, to the legislature, that some provisions should be made for existing authors, whose rights under former acts had not

to the *plaintiff* of all his copyright (as far as he lawfully could) in the Notes or Annotations in question, *for the remainder of his* (Mr. Hargrave's) *life.*

This case depended upon the eighth and ninth sections; the former of which recites, that it is reasonable that authors of books already published, and who where then living, should have the benefit of the *extension* of copyright.

then expired, but were concurrent; and the eighth and ninth sections provide for these cases: the eighth section recites, " that whereas it is reasonable that authors of books already published, and who are now living, should have the benefit of the *extension* of copyright." This word extension is a term properly used for the purpose of enlarging or giving further duration to any existing right, but does not import the re-vesting of any expired right; that would not be an *extension*, but a *re-creation.* The object, therefore, of the eighth section is to extend to living writers the benefit of their unexpired rights, and therefore it only applies to cases where the first fourteen years had not expired. The object of this act is to give authors an absolute right for twenty-eight years; and in pursuance of that intention, it gives a continuing interest for fourteen years to those who should be living, and whose copyright under former acts had not expired; the words following the recital in that section are, " be it further enacted, that if the author of any book, which shall not have been published fourteen years at the time of passing this act, shall be then living, and if such author shall afterwards die before the expiration of the fourteen years, then the personal representative shall have the copyright for the further term of fourteen years, provided that nothing in the act shall affect any right of the assignee to any of the books of the author, printed within the first fourteen years ;" the eighth and ninth sections both contemplate the case of living authors; the eighth, where the first fourteen years have not yet expired, and the ninth where they have; the ninth section applies to the case where the author is living at the end of the first fourteen years, but before the expiration of the second fourteen years; these are the only two cases in which, before the passing of this act, an author could have any right capable of extension, and this statute does not create a new right not already existing, but only extends an existing right; the ninth section goes on, " and be it *also* further (i. e. upon the same recital as that which precedes the eighth section) enacted, that if the author of any book already published, shall be living at the end of twenty-eight years after such publication, he shall have the copyright for his life ;" the words "*shall* be living," are prospective. The legislature does not suppose the time to have been already expired, but it contemplates a further extension of time then unexpired ; the language is prospective in its terms, and the sense requires that it should be so. For taking the two sections together, it appears clearly that the legislature intended only to extend the already existing right of authors, and not to create a right then expired. This is perfectly consistent with the meaning of the word *shall*, and also with the meaning of the words, *at the end of twenty-eight years.* The words, at the expiration of a term, mean immediately after. Thus, if speaking of a reversioner who is to come into possession at the expiration of the term, that could not be said to mean after the expiration of the term, and at any future period, for the reversion attaches at the expiration of the term. But admitting that the words are capable of either sense, they must be construed so as to give effect to the other words used in these two sections, and particularly with reference to the word " shall," which is prospective in its meaning, and the word " extension," which imports the enlargement of an existing thing, and not a creation. The contrary construction would, indeed, produce an inconvenience and an injustice which could not be intended by the legislature; for at the time of passing this Act of Parliament, the author's right having become extinguished, it was competent to any person to publish the work in question, and such publications may have actually taken place at a great expence to the individual; yet according to the construction contended for, if the author's right were re-vested, the innocent publisher might have his work taken from him, and would be subject to the penalties imposed by this act: so that an individual would be guilty of an offence, and subject to a penalty for exercising his legal right. The legislature could not have intended to produce so much public inconvenience, to benefit a small, though highly

Lord ELLENBOROUGH, C. J., said the word *extension* imports the continuance of an existing thing, and must have its full effect given to it where it occurs. It is expressly used in the recital of the eighth section, which is connected with the ninth, by the subject matter, as well as by the words " be it also further enacted;" and it seems to me, that predicating the purpose to be to benefit the author by the *extension* of his rights, is adopting a very different idea from re-creating an expired right. The word extension, is too strong for me to grapple with; and, if the court were to get rid of its operation, a great public injury would be effected, by calling back a right, that by lapse of time had become extinct.

ABBOTT, J., further observed, it is admitted, that if the public had exercised their rights, by publishing the work before the act passed, that the author could not interfere with the parties who had so exercised the right: and there are no words in the Act of Parliament which admit of one construction where the public have exercised the privileges which have devolved upon them by the lapse of twenty-eight years, and another construction where they have not exercised that

meritorious, class of individuals; and that cannot be the true construction of the Act of Parliament from which such a consequence would follow. Looking, therefore, to the language of the section itself, and the general intention to be collected from the several clauses, as well as the great inconvenience that would follow if the opposite construction were to prevail, it does clearly seem that the intention of the act will be best effected by confining its operation to those authors who at the time of passing the Act of Parliament had existing rights; or in other words, to those whose twenty-eight years had not then elapsed.

Mr. DENMAN, in reply.---The word " extension" does occur in the eighth section, but *not* in the ninth: it is there studiously left out; and the benefit conferred by that section need not, therefore, come within the meaning of the term extension, and there is no expression that connects the two clauses so as to make that word applicable to the ninth.

ABBOTT, Justice.---Will you mention any words in the *English* language more appropriate or apposite to connect one section with another than the words " Be it also further enacted ?"

Mr. DENMAN. They are separate clauses, and are not necessarily connected; and the ninth section does not say that the author's right shall be extended, but generally, that, if living, he shall have the copyright for his life : an extension of a right is given by one clause, and a right generally conferred by the other. With respect to the inconvenience which, it is said, will result from this construction of the act, it is not true that an innocent publisher would be subjected to the penalties inflicted by the fourth section, for those penalties only attach on offences comprised in that section.

BAYLEY, J.---Is not a man penally affected who has legally vested his money in a printed book, and is afterwards prevented from selling it ?

Mr. DENMAN. The act could not be meant to operate as an ex post facto law in a case where a party had exercised rights vested in the public. Certainly no right actually vested in and exercised by the public, was intended to be divested. If such rights had indeed been exercised, the case might have been very different as to the parties so exercising them ; but the fact is otherwise, and therefore that question is immaterial. And that being so, then the case comes within the very words of the ninth section, and is embraced within the general object the legislature had in view in passing the Act of Parliament, viz., the extension of the copyright of authors.

privilege. The act makes no distinction between these two cases.

The COURT afterwards certified their opinion, that the plaintiff, by virtue of the last mentioned assignment, took no interest in the Notes or Annotations.

In the case of Carnan v. Bowles([1]) it was also decided, that an author who sells his work in general terms, without making any limitations, has no resulting right against his own assignee after the first term has expired, formerly of fourteen, but now of twenty-eight years([2]).

Although a general assignment of a copyright in writing endures only for fourteen years, yet where an author by parole gave a compilation to a publisher unconditionally, it was holden that such gift was not impliedly limited to the term of fourteen years([3]).

The distinction between the point decided in the case of Carnan v. Bowles, and the eighth section of the 54th Geo. III. cap. 156, appears to be this :

If an author who has assigned his right, *outlive the first fourteen years*, (or twenty-eight years now allowed) his *assignee*, by the general assignment, will have the benefit of the resulting term, fourteen years, or the remainder of the author's life.

But if an author die after the enactment, but *within* that

---

(1) Carnan v. Bowles, 2 Brown's Chancery Rep. 80.

(2) The eleventh section of 8 Anne provides, that after the expiration of the term of fourteen years, the sole right of printing or disposing of copies of books shall *return* to the authors thereof, if they are then living, for a further term of fourteen years. In the case cited in the text, the author, Captain Paterson, having sold " all his right" in a Book of Roads to the plaintiff, which was printed in letter-press, after the expiration of the first fourteen years, sold it to the defendant, who published the high roads upon copper-plates, and the cross roads in letter-press.

Mr. MANSFIELD, on the part of the plaintiff, contended, that the expression in the act meant to secure something to authors even against their own acts. It gives the right to authors and their assigns during the first fourteen years, and no longer ; and then, by the proviso, the right shall *return to the authors* (not their assigns), if living. So that it is a personal bounty to the authors only. In selling the right, the author sells all that is in him, not the contingent right that may return to him.

The SOLICITOR-GENERAL, on the other side, argued, that the author has an absolute and a contingent right ; they are both capable of being disposed of. There is nothing in the act to make a difference between them. The *return* is only between the public and the author, not between him and his assignee. There are no negative words in the act to prevent his assigning that, as well as his other rights. In many cases, if he could not assign it, the disability would be productive of great inconvenience.

LORD CHANCELLOR.---The *contingent* interest must pass by the word " interest" in the grant. The author conveys all his interest in the copyright. The assignment must have been made upon the idea of a perpetuity. It is probable not a syllable was said or thought of respecting the contingent right. They merely followed the old precedents of such conveyances. It must, I think, be considered as conveying his whole right. If he had meant to convey his first term only, he should have said so. An injunction was therefore granted as to the letter-press.

(3) Rudell v. Murray, 1 Jacob, 311. 6 Petersdorff's Abr. 564.

term, then his assignee will enjoy the copyright for the first
fourteen years only, and the *personal representatives* of the
deceased will have the benefit of a further term of fourteen
years, without prejudice to the sale of the books printed by
the assignee within the first term([1]).

SECTION III.

*Digest of Cases relating to the extent of Copyright—works comprised
in the Statute, or protected by the Common Law.*

1st.   *Of Manuscripts.*

Although the common law, on the subject of copyright
in *printed* books, has been superseded by the statutes, the
ancient protection afforded to all kinds of property still remains in full force in favor of literary *manuscripts*.

With the single exception of Mr. Baron Eyre, all the
judges decided in the case of Donaldson v. Becket([2]), that an
author has complete control over his works, so long as they
remain in manuscript.

Of these there are several kinds, consisting of

1. Unpublished works in general.

2. Dramatic works, whether they have been represented
or not.

3. Epistolary writings.

These several descriptions of literary works are protected
from invasion, and the Courts of Equity, at the instance of
the author or proprietor, will stay the publication of them:
and an action at law can be maintained in trover, detinue,
or trespass([3]).

2nd.   *Of Printed Books.*

The statute, according to its construction by the courts, is
not limited to publications usually termed " books," but includes every original work, however insignificant it may be
in extent.   There is a property even in a single page.

There is nothing (said Mr. Erskine) in the word *book* to require
that it should consist of several sheets, bound in leather, or stitched in
a marble cover. *Book* is evidently the Saxon 𝔅𝔬𝔠, and the latter
term is from *beech tree*, the rind of which supplied the place of paper
to our German ancestors.   The latin word *liber* is of a similar etymo-
logy, meaning originally only the bark of a tree.   *Book* may therefore

---

(1) Godson on Patents and Copyright, 211.
(2) 4 Burr. 2408.
(3) For the details on *pirating the copyright* of these works, vide Part III.

be applied to any writing, and it has often been so used in the English language([1]).

If a different construction were put upon the act, many productions of the greatest genius, both in prose and verse, would be excluded from its benefits. But might the papers of the *Spectator,* or *Gray's Elegy* in a Country Church-yard, have been pirated as soon as they were published, because they were given to the world on single sheets? The voluminous extent of a production cannot in an enlightened country be the sole title to the guardianship the author receives from the law. Every man knows that the mathematical and astronomical calculations which will inclose the student during a long life in his cabinet, are frequently reduced to the compass of a few lines; and is all this profundity of mental abstraction, on which the security and happiness of the species in every part of the globe depend, to be excluded from the protection of British jurisprudence?

The point was not further argued. The rule was made absolute([2]).

In a subsequent case this decision was referred to, and Lord ELLENBOROUGH said([3]),

I do not at present see why a composition, printed on a single sheet, should not be entitled to the privileges of the statute. We say, "sit liber index," without referring to a volume either printed or written. I was at first startled at a single sheet of paper being called a *book;* but I was afterwards disposed to think that it might be so considered, within the meaning of this Act of Parliament; and when the matter came before the court, the other judges inclined to the same opinion([4]).

This point was afterwards settled and confirmed by the whole court([5])

The statute comprises not only original works, but *Translations,* both from the ancient and modern languages([6]).

(1) Sometimes the most humble and familiar illustration is the most fortunate. The *Horn Book,* so formidable to infant years, consists of one small page, protected by an animal preparation, and in this state it has universally received the appellation of a *book.* So in legal proceedings, the copy of the pleadings after issue joined, whether it be long or short, is called the Paper *Book,* or the Demurrer *Book.* In the Court of Exchequer, a roll was anciently denominated a book, and continues in some instances to the present day. An oath as old as the time of Edward I. runs in this form : " And you shall deliver into the Court of Exchequer a *book* fairly written." But the book delivered into court in fulfilment of this oath, has always been a roll of parchment. 2 *Camp.* 29.

(2) Hine v. Dale, 2 Camp. 28, *note.*   (3) Clementi v. Golding, 2 Camp. 30.

(4) Mr. SCARLETT, in his argument for the plaintiffs, ably contended, that the legislature by the word *book,* could not be considered as meaning only a number of printed sheets bound up together, since they talked in section 2 of a literary composition, as a book before it was printed at all. According to its original meaning, it signifies any writing, without reference to size or form, and it is so used by the most celebrated authors. Thus in Shakespeare, Henry IV., *book* stands for the indenture or instrument by which Mortimer, Glendower, and Hotspur, agreed to divide England between them(*a*), and the commentators upon that passage point out various other instances in which the word is employed in the same sense.

(*a*) *Mort.* By that time will our *book* I think be drawn. Hen. IV. Part I. Act 3. Scene 1. The instrument is a little before called *an indenture tripartite.*

(5) 11 East, 244.   (6) 3 Ves. and B. 77.

It also includes *Abridgments* and *Compilations,* provided
they are *bona fide,* and not fraudulently or colourably,
made(¹).

And after the time limited by the statute has expired, if
the author, or any other writer, should reprint the book with
original

Notes or *additions,*

the latter are entitled to the same degree of protection as any
other original composition, for the whole time allowed by the
statute(²).

3rd.   Of Musical Compositions.

The statute has further received a liberal interpretation
in favor of musical compositions, which have also been held,
as a branch of science, to be comprehended within the meaning of the act.   The work thus printed and published contains a representation (so to speak) of original musical ideas,
and therefore receives the same protection, both in extent and
duration, as publications which convey ideas more purely
intellectual.

Lord MANSFIELD said, the words of the Act of Parliament are very
large---*books and other writings.* It is not confined to language or letters.
Music is a science : it may be *written ;* and the mode of conveying
ideas is by signs and marks.   If the narrow interpretation contended
for in the argument were to hold, it would equally apply to algebra,
mathematics, arithmetic, hieroglyphics.   All these are conveyed by
signs and figures.   There is no colour for saying that music is not
within the act(³).

CHAP. II.

OF COPYRIGHT IN ENGRAVINGS, ETCHINGS, PRINTS, MAPS, AND CHARTS.

In the historical view of the law of copyright in general,
we have not adverted to the statutes regarding engravings,
etchings, and prints, inasmuch as they have not been recently
consolidated, like those which relate to printed books.   In
treating of the present state of the law on this branch of the
fine arts, which is so intimately connected with literature,
we may properly consider, under one view, the *three* Acts of
Parliament which have been passed for " the encouragement
of the arts of designing, engraving, and etching."

---

(1) Amb. 403, Lofft. Rep. 775.   Vide Part III. for the details regarding piracy in
these compositions.

(2) 1 East, 358.   (3) Bach v. Longman, Cowp. 623.

SECTION I.

Analysis of the Statutes.

The 8th Geo. II. cap. 13, is entitled, An act for the encouragement of the arts of designing, engraving, and etching historical and other prints, by vesting the properties thereof in the inventors and engravers during the time therein mentioned.

It recites, that divers persons have, by their own genius, industry, pains and expence, invented and engraved, or worked in *mezzotinto* or *chiaro oscuro*, sets of historical and other prints, in hopes to have reaped the sole benefit of their labors; and that printsellers and other persons have of late, without the consent of the inventors, designers, and proprietors of such prints, frequently taken the liberty of copying, engraving, and publishing, or causing to be copied, engraved, and published, base copies of such works, designs, and prints, to the very great prejudice and detriment of the inventors, designers, and proprietors thereof.

For remedy thereof, and for preventing such practices for the future, the act vests the sole right and liberty of printing and reprinting the same for fourteen years, to commence from the day of first publishing thereof.

The date to be engraved, with the name of the proprietor, on each plate, and printed on every print.

The penalties for pirating, or selling, or exposing to sale, either the whole or a part of any print, without the consent of the proprietor in writing, signed in the presence of two witnesses, are a *forfeiture* of the prints, and a *fine* of five shillings each.

The act does not extend to purchasers of plates from the original proprietors. And there is a clause in favor of certain engravings then designed, relating to the Spanish invasion.

Actions under the statute must be brought within three months. The general issue may be pleaded.

We consider it essential, as a part of the present law, to set forth the remainder of the act in full. The following is the enacting part, together with the subsequent clauses.

That from and after the 24th of June, which will be in the year of our Lord, 1735, every person who shall invent and design, engrave, etch, or work in *mezzotinto*, or *chiaro oscuro*, or from his own works and inventions, shall cause to be designed and engraved, etched, or worked in mezzotinto or chiaro oscuro, any historical or other print or prints, shall have the sole right and liberty of printing and reprinting the same for the term of fourteen years, to commence from the day of the first publishing thereof, which shall be truly engraved with the name of the proprietor on each plate, and printed on every such print or prints ; and that if any printseller or other person whatsoever, from and after the said 24th day of June, 1735, within the time limited by this act, shall engrave, etch, or work as aforesaid, or in any other manner copy and sell, or cause to be engraved, etched, or copied and sold, in the whole, or in part, by varying, adding to, or diminishing from the main design, or shall print, reprint, or import for sale, or cause to be printed, reprinted, or imported for sale, any such print or prints, or any part thereof, without the consent of the proprietor or proprietors thereof first had and obtained in writing, signed by him or them respectively, in the presence of two or more credible witnesses, or knowing the same to be so printed or reprinted without the consent of the proprietor or proprietors, shall publish, sell, or expose to sale, or otherwise or in any other manner dispose of, or cause to be published, sold, or exposed to sale, or otherwise or in any other manner disposed of, any such print or prints, without such consent first had and obtained as aforesaid, then such offender or offenders shall forfeit the plate or plates on which such print or prints are or shall be copied, and all and every sheet or sheets (being part of or whereon such print or prints are or shall be so copied and printed), to the proprietor or proprietors of such original print or prints, who shall forthwith destroy and damask the same; and further, that every such offender or offenders shall forfeit five shillings for every print which shall be found in his, her, or their custody, either printed or published and exposed to sale, or otherwise disposed of, contrary to the true intent and meaning of this act: the one moiety thereof to the King's most excellent Majesty, his heirs and successors, and the other moiety thereof to any person or persons that shall sue for the same ; to be recovered in any of His Majesty's Courts of Record at Westminster, by action of debt, bill, plaint, or information, in which no wager of law, essoine, privilege, or protection, nor more than one imparlance, shall be allowed.

II.   Provided nevertheless, that it shall and may be lawful for any person or persons who shall hereafter purchase any plate or plates for printing from the original proprietors thereof, to print and reprint from the said plates, without incurring any of the penalties in this act mentioned.

III.   And be it further enacted by the authority aforesaid, that if any action or suit shall be commenced or brought against any person or persons whatsoever for doing, or causing to be done, any thing in pursuance of this act, the same shall be brought within the space of three months after so doing, and the defendant and defendants in such action or suit shall or may plead the general issue, and give the special matter in evidence ; and if upon such action or suit a verdict shall be given for the defendant or defendants, or if the plaintiff or plaintiffs become nonsuited, or discontinue his or their action or actions, then the defendant or defendants shall have and recover full costs, for the recovery whereof he shall have the same remedy as any other defendant or defendants in any other case hath or have by law.

IV.   Provided always, and be it further enacted by the authority aforesaid, that if any action or suit shall be commenced or brought against any person or persons for any offence committed against this act, the same shall be brought within the space of three months after the discovery of every such offence, and not afterwards; any thing in this act contained to the contrary notwithstanding.

V.   And whereas John Pine, of London, Engraver, doth propose to engrave and publish a set of prints copied from several pieces of tapestry in the House of Lords and His Majesty's wardrobe, and other drawings relating to the Spanish invasion in the year of our Lord 1588, be it further enacted by the authority aforesaid, that the said John Pine shall be entitled to the benefit of this act to all intents and purposes whatsoever, in the same manner as if the said John Pine had been the inventor and designer of the said prints.

VI.   And be it further enacted by the authority aforesaid, that this act shall be deemed, adjudged, and taken to be a public act, and be judicially taken notice of as such by all judges, justices, and other persons whatsoever, without specially pleading the same.

The next act is the 7th Geo. III. c. 38, and is entitled, An act to amend and render more effectual an act made in the eighth year of the reign of King George II. for encouragement of the arts of designing, engraving, and etching historical and other prints, and for vesting in and securing to Jane Hogarth, widow, the property in certain prints.

By this act, the term of copyright is extended to twenty-eight years.

And it includes " the prints of any portrait, conversation, landscape, or architecture, *map, chart, or plan*, or any other print."

By the 2nd section, engravings, etchings, or works taken from " any picture, drawing, model, or sculpture, either ancient or modern," are entitled to the protection of the act.

The remedies provided by this statute must be sued for within *six months* after the offence committed.

It is observable that this act does not expressly require the name of the proprietor and the date of publication to be engraved on the print; but it seems probable that the provision of the previous statute, 8 Geo. II. in that respect should be considered as included([1]); and the insertion is necessary for the recovery of the penalties, though not for the purpose of maintaining an action for damages([2]).

The following is an accurate statement of the act :

It recites---

That an Act of Parliament passed in the eighth year of the reign of His late Majesty King George II. intituled, An act for encouragement of the arts of designing, engraving, and etching historical

(1) 2 Evans's Stat. 637, *note.*   (2) 1 Camp. 98; but see the next section.

and other prints, by vesting the properties thereof in the inventors and engravers during the time therein mentioned, had been found ineffectual for the purposes thereby intended.

And it is then enacted,

That from and after the first day of January, 1767, all and every person and persons who shall invent or design, engrave, etch, or work in mezzotinto or chiaro oscuro, or from his own work, design, or invention, shall cause or procure to be designed, engraved, etched, or worked in mezzotinto or chiaro oscuro, any historical print or prints, or any print or prints of any portrait, conversation, landscape, or architecture, map, chart, or plan, or any other print or prints whatsoever, shall have, and are hereby declared to have, the benefit and protection of the said act, and this act, under the restrictions and limitations hereinafter mentioned.

II. And be it further enacted by the authority aforesaid, that from and after the said first day of January, one thousand seven hundred and sixty seven, all and every person and persons who shall engrave, etch, or work in mezzotinto or chiaro oscuro, or cause to be engraved, etched, or worked, any print taken from any picture, drawing, model, sculpture, either ancient or modern, shall have, and are hereby declared to have, the benefit and protection of the said act, and this act, for the term hereinafter mentioned, in like manner as if such print had been graved or drawn from the original design of such graver, etcher, or draughtsman ; and if any person shall engrave, print, and publish, or import for sale, any copy of any such print, contrary to the true intent and meaning of this and the said former act, every such person shall be liable to the penalties contained in the said act, to be recovered as therein and hereinafter is mentioned.

III. The sole right of printing and reprinting the late W. Hogarth's prints, vested in his widow and executrix for twenty years.

IV. Penalty of copying, &c. any of them before expiration of the term ; such copies excepted as were made and exposed to sale after the term of fourteen years, for which the said works were first licenced, &c.

V. And be it further enacted by the authority aforesaid, that all and every the penalties and penalty inflicted by the said act, and extended and meant to be extended to the several cases comprised in this act, shall and may be sued for and recovered in like manner, and under the like restrictions and limitations, as in and by the said act is declared and appointed ; and the plaintiff or common informer in every such action (in case such plaintiff or common informer shall recover any of the penalties incurred by this or the said former act) shall recover the same, together with his full costs of suit.

VI. Provided also, that the party prosecuting shall commence his prosecution within the space of six calendar months after the offence committed.

VII. And be it further enacted by the authority aforesaid, that the sole right and liberty of printing and reprinting intended to be secured and protected by the said former act, and this act, shall be extended, continued, and be vested in the respective proprietors for the space of twenty-eight years, to commence from the day of the first publishing of any of the works respectively herein before, and in the said former act, mentioned.

VIII. And be it further enacted by the authority aforesaid, that if any action or suit shall be commenced or brought against any person or persons whatsoever for doing, or causing to be done, any thing in pursuance of this act, the same shall be brought within the space of six calendar months after the fact committed ; and the defendant or defendants in any such action or suit shall or may plead the general issue, and give the special matter in evidence ; and if upon such action or suit a verdict shall be given for the defendant or defendants, or if the plaintiff or plaintiffs become nonsuited, or discontinue his, her, or their action or actions, then the defendant or defendants shall have and recover full costs ; for the remedy whereof, he shall have the same remedy as any other defendant or defendants in any other case hath or have by law.

The last act on this subject is the 17th Geo. III. c. 57, and is entitled, An act for more effectually securing the property of prints to inventors and engravers, by enabling them to sue for and recover penalties in certain cases.

By this statute an *action for damages* and *double costs* is given for engraving, etching, or printing any historical print, or any portrait, &c. without the consent of the proprietor, within the time limited by the former acts. The remedies provided by the former statutes were by fine and forfeiture.

The act recites---

That an act of Parliament passed in the eighth year of his late Majesty, King Geo. II. intituled, An act for the encouragement of the arts of designing, engraving, and etching historical and other prints, by vesting the properties thereof in the inventors and engravers during the time therein mentioned ; and that by an Act of Parliament passed in the seventh year of the reign of his present Majesty, for amending and rendering more effectual the aforesaid act, and for purposes therein mentioned, it was (among other things) enacted, that from and after the first day of January, 1767, all and every person or persons who should engrave, etch, or work in mezzotinto or chiaro oscuro, or cause to be engraved, etched, or worked, any print taken from any picture, drawing, model, or sculpture, either ancient or modern, should have, and were thereby declared to have, the benefit and protection of the said former act, and that act, for the term thereinafter mentioned, in like manner as if such print had been graved or drawn from the original design of such graver, etcher, or draughtsman : and that the said acts have not effectually answered the purposes for which they were intended ; and it is necessary, for the encouragement of artists, and for securing to them the property of and in their works, and for the advancement and improvement of the aforesaid arts, that such further provisions should be made as are hereinafter mentioned and contained.

G

It is therefore enacted,

That from and after the 24th day of June, 1777, if any engraver, etcher, print-seller, or any other person, shall within the time limited by the aforesaid acts, or either of them, engrave, etch, or work, or cause or procure to be engraved, etched, or worked, in mezzotinto or chiaro oscuro, or otherwise, or in any manner copy in the whole or in part by varying, adding to, or diminishing from the main design, or shall print, reprint, or import for sale, or cause or procure to be printed, reprinted, or imprinted or imported for sale, or shall publish, sell, or otherwise dispose of, or cause or procure to be published, sold, or otherwise disposed of, any copy or copies of any historical print or prints, or any print or prints of any portrait, conversation, landscape, or architecture, map, chart, or plan, or any other print or prints whatsoever which hath or have been, or shall be, engraved, etched, drawn, or designed in any part of Great Britain, without the express consent of the proprietor or proprietors thereof first had and obtained in writing, signed by him, her, or them respectively, with his, her, or their own hand or hands, in the presence of, and attested by, two or more credible witnesses, then every such proprietor or proprietors shall and may, by and in a special action upon the case to be brought against the person or persons so offending, recover such damages as a jury on the trial of such action, or on the execution of a Writ of Enquiry thereon, shall give or assess, together with double costs of suit.

SECTION II.
Digest of Cases.

The acts are not confined in their protection to *inventions*, strictly speaking, but comprise the designing or engraving any thing that is already in nature(¹).

The *degree of originality* which entitles the inventor to the protection of the statute, has been well defined by Lord ELLENBOROUGH, who states the question thus: Whether the defendant has copied the main design? Whether there be such a similitude and conformity between the prints, that the person who executed the one set, must have used the others as a model? In that case, he is a copyist of the main design. But if the similitude can be supposed to have arisen from accident, or necessarily from the nature of the subject, or from the artist having sketched his design merely from reading the letter-press of the plaintiff, the defendant is not answerable(²).

A question has arisen, whether it be absolutely necessary to support an action at law, or a bill in equity, that the *date of publication*, and the *name of the proprietor*, be engraved on each plate and print.

(1) 2 Atkins, 293.   (2) 1 Camp. 94, Roworth v. Wilkes.

It is said(¹) that there is a contrariety of opinion in the authorities as to the true construction of the act. *Lord Hardwicke* and *Lord Ellenborough* being on one side, and *Lord Alvanley, Lord Kenyon,* and *Judge Buller,* on the other. The case referred to, however, was not decided on the point in question, and *Lord Kenyon* himself does not appear very decided in his opinion. He says, had the question turned entirely on the point on which it has been argued, I should have thought it involved in considerable difficulty : upon that head *my opinion has floated during the course of the argument.* It should seem, that the reason for requiring the name and the date to appear on the print, was, that they might convey some useful intelligence to the public. The *date* is of importance, that the public may know the period of the monopoly. The *name* of the proprietor should appear, in order that those who wish to copy it, might know to whom to apply for consent. It seems, therefore, necessary, that the date should remain, but that the name of the proprietor should be altered as often as the property is changed(²).

This decision was in the year 1792. At a subsequent period, namely, in 1807, Lord ELLENBOROUGH said, although the plaintiff's name is not engraved upon the prints, if there has been a piracy, I think the plaintiff is entitled to a verdict. *The interest being vested, the common law gives the remedy.* I have always acted on the case of Beckford v. Hood(³), in which the Court of King's Bench held, that an author whose work is pirated, may maintain an action on the case for damages, although the work was not entered at Stationers' Hall, and although it was first published without the name of the author affixed(⁴).

We have-stated the preceding case, which arose more directly out of the *construction* of the Acts of Parliament; and for the decisions relating to the invasion of copyright in engravings and prints, we refer to the *third part of this book,* in which the whole subject of "piracy" will be considered.

CHAP. III.

OF THE RIGHT IN ORIGINAL SCULPTURE, MODELS, AND CASTS.

There are two statutes on the subject of original sculpture, models, and casts, which may not inappropriately be introduced in this place as a branch of the fine arts.

(1) Godson on Patents and Copyright, 290.
(2) 5 T. R. 45, Thompson v. Symonds.　　　(3) 7 T. R. 620.
(4) 1 Camp. 98. See also 2 Vesey, 327, and Law Journal, May, 1827. In Newton v. Cowie, the Common Pleas held both date and name to be essential.

The first of these acts was passed in the year 1798 ; and the last, a short time previously to the general Copyright Act in 1814.

SECTION I.

Analysis of the Statutes.

The 38th Geo. III. chap. 71, is entitled, " An act for encouraging the art of making new models and casts of busts, and other things therein mentioned."

It vests in the proprietor the sole right and property of making new models, or copies or casts from such models, of any bust, figure, or any statue, &c. during the term of fourteen years, provided the name of the maker and the date of publication be put thereon.

Persons making copies, without the written consent of the proprietor, may be sued for damages in a special action on the case.

The act recites---

That divers persons have by their own genius, industry, pains, and expence, improved and brought the art of making new models and casts of busts, and of statues of human figures and of animals, to great perfection, in hopes to have reaped the sole benefit of their labors ; but, that divers persons have (without the consent of the proprietors thereof) copied and made moulds from the said models and casts, to the great prejudice and detriment of the original proprietors, and to the discouragement of the art of making such new models and casts as aforesaid ; FOR REMEDY WHEREOF, AND FOR PREVENTING SUCH PRACTICES FOR THE FUTURE, IT IS ENACTED, that from and after the passing of this act, every person who shall make, or cause to be made, any new model or copy or cast made from such new model of any bust, or any part of the human figure, or any statue of the human figure, or the head of any animal, or any part of any animal, or the statue of any animal, or shall make or cause to be made any new model, copy, or cast from such new model, in alto or basso relievo, or any work in which the representation of any human figure or figures, or the representation of any animal or animals, shall be introduced, or shall make, or cause to be made, any new cast from nature of any part or parts of the human figure, or of any part or parts of any animal, shall have the sole right and property in every such new model, copy, or cast, and also in every such new model, copy, or cast in alto or basso relievo, or any work as aforesaid, and also in any such new cast from nature as aforesaid, for and during the term of fourteen years from the time of first publishing the same ; provided always that every person who shall make, or cause to be made, any such new model, copy, or cast, or any such new model, copy, or cast in alto or basso relievo, or any work as aforesaid, or any new cast from nature as aforesaid, shall cause his or her name to be put thereon, with the date of the publication, before the same shall be published and exposed to sale.

II. And be it further enacted, that if any person shall, within the said term of fourteen years, make, or cause to be made, any copy or cast of any such new model, copy, or cast, or any such model, copy, or cast in alto or basso relievo, or any such work as aforesaid, or any such new cast from nature as aforesaid, either by adding to, or diminishing from, any such new model, copy or cast, or adding to or diminishing from any such new model, copy or cast in alto or basso relievo, or any such work as aforesaid, or adding to or diminishing from any such new cast from nature, or shall cause or procure the same to be done, or shall import any copy or cast of such new model, copy, or cast in alto or basso relievo, or any such work as aforesaid, or any copy or cast of any such new cast from nature as aforesaid for sale, or shall sell or otherwise dispose of, or cause or procure to be sold or exposed to sale, or otherwise disposed of, any copy or cast of such new model, copy, or cast in alto or basso relievo, or any such work as aforesaid, or any copy or cast of any such new cast from nature as aforesaid, without the express consent of the proprietor or proprietors thereof first had and obtained in writing, signed by him, her, or them respectively, with his, her, or their hand or hands, in the presence of, and attested by, two or more credible witnesses, then, and in all or any of the cases aforesaid, every proprietor or proprietors of any such original model, copy, or cast, and every proprietor or proprietors of any such original model or copy or cast in alto or basso relievo, or any such work as aforesaid, or the proprietor or proprietors of any such new cast from nature as aforesaid, respectively, shall and may, by and in a special action upon the case, to be brought against the person or persons so offending, recover such damages as a jury on the trial of such action, or on the execution of a writ of enquiry thereon, shall give or assess, together with costs of suit.

III. Provided nevertheless that no person who shall hereafter purchase the right either in any such models, copy, or cast, or in any such model, copy, or cast in alto or basso relievo, or any such work as aforesaid, or any such new cast from nature of the original proprietor or proprietors thereof, shall be subject to any action for vending or selling any cast or copy from the same ; any thing contained in this act to the contrary thereof notwithitanding.

IV. Provided also, that all actions to be brought as aforesaid against any person or persons for any offence committed against this act, shall be commenced within six calendar months next after the discovery of every such offence, and not afterwards.

These provisions were rendered more effectual by the 54th Geo. III. c. 56, by which double costs were given, and an additional term of fourteen years in case the maker of *original sculpture, models, &c.* should be living, except he should have divested himself of the right previous to the passing of the act.

Before proceeding to the construction which has been put on these acts, we deem it necessary to insert the several clauses of the last act.

It is intituled,

An act to amend and render more effectual an act of his present majesty for encouraging the art of making new models and casts of busts, and other things therein mentioned, and for giving further encouragement to such arts.

It recites---

That by an act passed in the 38th year of the reign of his present majesty, intituled An act for encouraging the art of making new models and casts of busts, and other things therein mentioned, the sole right and property thereof were vested in the original proprietors for a time therein specified---that the provisions of the said act having been found ineffectual for the purposes thereby intended, it is expedient to amend the same, and make other provisions and regulations for the encouragement of artists, and to secure to them the profits of and in their works, and for the advancement of the said arts.

It is therefore enacted---

That from and after the passing of this act, every person or persons who shall make, or cause to be made, any new and original sculpture or model, or copy or cast of the human figure or human figures, or of any bust or busts, or of any part or parts of the human figure, clothed in drapery or otherwise, or of any animal or animals, or of any part or parts of any animal combined with the human figure or otherwise, or of any subject being matter of invention in sculpture, or of any alto or basso relievo, representing any of the matters or things herein before mentioned, or any cast from nature of the human figure, or of any part or parts of the human figure, or of any cast from nature of any animal, or of any part or parts of any animal, or of any such subject containing or representing any of the matters and things hereinbefore mentioned, whether separate or combined, shall have the sole right and property of all and in every such new and original sculpture, model, copy and cast of the human figure and human figures, and of all and in every such bust or busts, and of all and in every such part or parts of the human figure, clothed in drapery or otherwise, and of all and in every such new and original sculpture, model, copy and cast representing any animal or animals, and of all and in every such work representing any part or parts of any animal, combined with the human figure or otherwise, and of all and in every such new and original sculpture, model, copy and cast of any subject, being matter of invention in sculpture, and of all and in every such new and original sculpture, model, copy and cast in alto or basso relievo, representing any of the matters or things hereinbefore mentioned, and of every such cast from nature, for the term of fourteen years, from first putting forth or publishing the same, provided in all and every case the proprietor or proprietors do cause his, her, or their name or names, with the date, to be put on all and every such new and original sculpture, model, copy or cast, and on every such cast from nature, before the same shall be put forth or published.

II. And be it further enacted, that the sole right and property of all works which have been put forth or published under the protection of the said recited act, shall be extended, continued to, and vested into the respective proprietors thereof, for the term of fourteen years, to commence from the date when such last mentioned works respectively were put forth or published.

III. And be it further enacted, that if any person or persons shall, within such term of fourteen years, make or import, or cause to be made or imported, or exposed to sale, or otherwise disposed of, any pirated copy or pirated cast of any such new and original sculpture or model, or copy or cast of the human figure or human figures, or of any such bust or busts or of any such part or parts of the human figure, clothed in drapery or otherwise, or of any such work of any animal or animals, or of any such part or parts of any animal or animals, combined with the human figure or otherwise, or of any such subject being matter of invention in sculpture, or of any such alto or basso relievo, representing any of the matters or things hereinbefore mentioned, or of any such cast from nature as aforesaid, whether such pirated copy or pirated cast be produced by moulding or copying from, or imitating in any way, any of the matters or things put forth or published under the protection of this act, or of any works which have been put forth or published under the protection of the said recited act, the right and property whereof is and are secured, extended, and protected by this act in any of the cases aforesaid, to the detriment, damage, or loss of the original or respective proprietor or proprietors of any such works so pirated, then and in all such cases the said proprietor or proprietors, or their assignee or assignees, shall and may, by and in a special action upon the case to be brought against the person or persons so offending, receive such damages as a jury on a trial of such action shall give or assess, together with double costs of suit.

IV. Provided nevertheless, that no person or persons who shall or may hereafter purchase the right or property of any new and original sculpture or model, or copy or cast, or of any cast from nature, or of any of the matters and things published under or protected by virtue of this act, of the proprietor or proprietors, expressed in a deed in writing signed by him, her, or them respectively, with his, her, or their own hand or hands, in the presence of, and attested by, two or more credible witnesses, shall be subject to any action for copying, or casting, or vending the same, any thing contained in this act to the contrary notwithstanding.

V. Provided always, and be it further enacted, that all actions to be brought as aforesaid against any person or persons for any offence committed against this act, shall be commenced within six calendar months next after the discovery of every such offence, and not afterwards.

VI. Provided always, and be it further enacted, that from and immediately after the expiration of the said term of fourteen years, the sole right of making and disposing of such new and original sculpture, or model, or copy, or cast of any of the matters or things herein before mentioned, shall return to the person or persons who

originally made, or cause to be made, the same, if he or they shall be
then living, for the further term of fourteen years, excepting in the
case or cases where such person or persons shall, by sale or otherwise,
have divested himself, herself, or themselves, of such right of making
or disposing of any new and original sculpture, or model, or copy, or
cast of any of the matters or things herein before mentioned, previous
to the passing of this act.

<hr>

SECTION II.
Construction of the Acts.

The first act on this subject (38 Geo. III. c. 71) was
found to be so defective, that it was held to be no offence to
make a cast of a bust, provided it was a *perfect* fac-simile of
the original([1]).

It was also held, in the case of Gahagan v. Cooper, to
be no offence under that act to *sell* a pirated cast of a bust,
if the piracy had any addition to, or diminution from, the
original([2]).

The declaration, however, confined the case to the selling
exact copies.   But in West v. Francis (which has been
referred to by Mr. Godson on this subject), there was a count
for selling copies in part by small variations from the main
design, and therefore the point did not arise([3]).

The second act remedied these defects ; but no case has
been decided under that act as to the insertion of the name
and day of publication ; yet it seems clear that the construction of the statutes relating to engravings and prints
will equally apply to sculpture, models, &c.   It appears also
that the reasoning on the statutes regarding patterns for
linen, are applicable to the present subject([4]).

<hr>

CHAP. IV.
OF WORKS EXCLUDED FROM LEGAL PROTECTION.

The consideration of works excluded from legal protection, on the ground of their unlawful and immoral nature,
has been reserved for this part of the treatise ; inasmuch as
the same principle which excludes a *book*, will equally apply
to an *engraving* and to *sculpture*.   The cases, therefore, of
this kind, whether referring to books, prints, or sculpture,
will be arranged according to the nature of their injurious or
illegal character.

(1) Godson on Patents, &c. 305.   (2) 3 Camp. 111.
(3) 5 Barn. and Ald. 737.   (4) Godson on Patents, &c. 306.

SECTION I.

Of Works injurious to public morals.

The courts of justice endeavour to protect society from the publication of works which tend to degrade the morals of the people; and so strong is the objection to an immoral work, that Lord ELLENBOROUGH held an apprehension of a prosecution for the immorality or illegality of a work (if proved to be well founded by the production of the part printed), would justify a person for refusing to supply a bookseller with the remainder of the manuscript agreeable to a contract.

The author might say, I now feel convinced that this work cannot be committed to the press with safety, that it is not a proper one for me to publish, or for you (the bookseller) to print; here I will pause, and will proceed no further in that which will place both of us in peril(¹).

It has also been held, that a Court of Equity has a superintendency over all books, and may in a summary way restrain the printing or publishing every thing that contains reflections on religion or morality.

Protection has been denied to a *translation* of an immoral work. In the case of Burnett v. Chetwood, in the year 1720, the LORD CHANCELLOR said,

Though a translation might not be the same with the reprinting the original, on account that the translator had bestowed his care and pains upon it, yet this being a book which to his knowledge contained strange notions, intended by the author to be concealed from the vulgar in the Latin language, in which language it could not do much hurt, the learned being better able to judge of it, he thought it proper to grant an injunction to the printing and publishing it in English(²).

And an action cannot be maintained to recover the value of obscene or libellous prints or caricatures. Mr. Justice LAWRENCE observed, that

For prints whose objects are general satire, or ridicule of prevailing fashions or manners, he thought a plaintiff might recover; but he could not permit him to do so for such whose tendency was immoral or obscene(³).

SECTION II.

Of Publications injurious to Religion.

Works which deny the truth of, or vilify, the sacred scriptures, or which tend to bring them into disrepute, or

---

(1) Gale v. Leckie, 2 Stark. 109-10. (2) 2 Meriv. 441, n.
(3) Fores v. Jones, 4 Esp. N. P. C. 97.

which lead to a disbelief in revelation, are strictly excluded from legal protection in the Courts of Justice in this country, all of which acknowledge Christianity as part of the law of the land.

Thus in the case of *Murray v. Benbow*, in which an injunction was applied for to restrain a pirated edition of Lord BYRON's Cain, Lord ELDON said,

The jurisdiction of this court in protecting literary property is founded on this, that where an action will lie for pirating a work, then the court, attending to the imperfection of that remedy, grants its injunction, because there may be publication after publication which you may never be able to hunt down by proceeding in the other courts. But where such an action does not lie, I do not apprehend that it is according to the course of the court to grant an injunction to protect the copyright. Now this publication, if it is one intended to *vilify* and bring into discredit that portion of *scripture history* to which it relates, is a publication, with reference to which, if the principles on which that case at Warwick (Dr. Priestley's case) was decided by just principles of law, the party could not recover any damages in respect of a piracy of it. This court has no criminal jurisdiction, it cannot look on any thing as an offence ; but in those cases it only administers justice for the protection of the civil rights of those who possess them, in consequence of being able to maintain an action. You have alluded to MILTON's immortal work ; it did happen in the course of last long vacation, I read that work from beginning to end; it is therefore quite fresh in my memory, and it appears to me that the great object of its author was to promote the cause of Christianity ; there are, undoubtedly, a great *many passages* in it, of which, if that were not its object, it would be *very improper by law* to vindicate the publication ; but, *taking it altogether*, it is clear that the object and effect were not to bring into disrepute, but to promote, the reverence of our religion. Now the real question is, looking at the work before me, its preface, the poem, its manner of treating the subject, particularly with reference to the *fall* and the *atonement*---whether its intent be as innocent as that of the other with which you have compared it; whether it be to traduce and bring into discredit that portion of sacred history. This question I have no right to try, because it has been settled, after great difference of opinion among the learned, that it is for a jury to determine that point ; and where, therefore, a reasonable doubt is entertained as to the character of the work (and it is impossible for me to say I have not a doubt---I hope it is a reasonable one), another course must be taken for determining what is its true nature and character.

There is a great difficulty in these cases, because it appears a strange thing to permit the multiplication of copies, by way of preventing the circulation of a mischievous work (which I do not presume to determine that this is) ; but that I cannot help ; and the singularity of the case, in this instance, is more obvious, because here is a defendant who has multiplied his work by piracy, and does not think proper to appear. If the work be of that character which a Court of Common Law would consider criminal, it is pretty clear why he does not appear, because he would come *confitens reus*, and for the same reason the question may, perhaps, not be tried by an action at law ; and if it turns out to be the case, I shall be bound to give my own opinion. That opinion I express no further now than to say, that after having read the work, I cannot grant the injunction until you shew me that you can maintain an action for it. If you cannot maintain an action, there is no pretence for granting an injunction ; if you should not be able to try the question at law with the defendant, I cannot be charged with impropriety if I then give my opinion upon it.

It is true that this mode of dealing with the work, if it be calculated to produce mischievous effects, opens a door for its wide dissemination ; but *the duty of stopping the work does not belong to a Court of Equity*, which has no criminal jurisdiction, and cannot punish or check the offence. If the character of the work is such, that the publication of it amounts to a temporal offence, there is another way of proceeding, and the publication of it should be proceeded against directly as an offence ; but whether this or any other work should be so dealt with, it would be very improper for me to form or intimate an opinion([1]).

In the same year (1822) occurred another case, which may be classed in the same order, namely, that of *Lawrence v. Smith;* and considering the importance of the principle established by these decisions, we deem it proper to set forth the judgment of the court at large.

It appeared that Mr. Lawrence published his Lectures on Physiology, in which, mixed with a great collection of valuable and appropriate facts, were some episodical theories on the nature of the soul, and the origin of mankind, which were supposed to lead to a *disbelief in revelation*. The lectures were soon pirated. An application was made by the piratical publisher to dissolve the injunction.

It was moved on the ground that the " the evil tendency of the work was as clear as the sun at noon([2])." The defendant was heard by his counsel to maintain that " his publication denied Christianity and revelation, and was contrary to public policy and morality ; that it was more dangerous from the author's scholar-like command of the language, and his scientific mode of treating the subject, which, acting upon undisciplined minds, was calculated to bring them under its control, and thereby work the greater mischief : and that

(1) 6 Petersdorff Abr. 558-9.
(2) Was this " coming into court with *clean hands?*" Was it consistent with the principle which maintains that *a man shall not avail himself of his own wrong?*

therefore the restraint which the injunction imposed on its dissemination must be removed !"

The Lord Chancellor said, that this case had been argued at the bar with great ability. He would explain in a few words the principles on which his decision would be founded. On the observations which had been made on the College of Surgeons, as the place in which these lectures had been read, he would not touch ; he would only treat the plaintiff as the author of the work. This case had been introduced by a bill filed by Mr. Lawrence, in which he stated that he was the author of this book, which the defendant had also published; and that he was entitled to the protection of this court, in preservation of the *profits* resulting from its publication. Undoubtedly the jurisdiction of this court was founded on this principle, that where the law will not afford a complete remedy to literary property when invaded, this court will lend its assistance ; because, where every publication is a distinct cause of action, and where several parties might publish the book, if a man were obliged to bring an action on each occasion, the remedy would be worse than the disease. But then this court will only interfere where he can by law sustain an action for damages, equal to the injury he has sustained. He might then come here to make his legal remedy more effectual. But if the case be one which it is not clear will sustain an action at law, then this court will not give him the relief he seeks.

The present case had been opened as an ordinary case of piracy, and he took it that nothing was then said as to the general tenor of the work, or of particular passages in it. He, the Lord Chancellor, was bound to look, not only to the tenor, but also to *particular passages unconnected with its general tenor*([1]) ; for if there were any parts of it which denied the *truth of scripture*, or which furnished a doubt as to whether a court of law would not decide that they had denied the truth of scripture, he was bound to look at them and decide accordingly.

There was a peculiar circumstance attending this case, which was, that the defendant possessed no right to the work, but said to the plaintiff, " this book is so original in its nature, as to deprive you of all protection at law against others and myself, and I will therefore publish it."

Now his Lordship knew it to be said that in cases where the work contained criminal matter, the court, by refusing the injunction, allowed the greater latitude for its dissemination. But his answer to that was, that this court possessed no criminal jurisdiction. It could only look at the civil rights of the parties, and therefore whether a different proceeding were hereafter instituted against the defendant or the plaintiff, or both, was a circumstance with which he had nothing to do. The only question for him to determine was, whether it was so clear that the plaintiff possessed a civil right in this publication, as

---

(1) But see the preceding case, in which it is laid down that the true criterion is to ke the publication *altogether*, and thus to judge of the general intent.

to have no doubt upon his mind that it would support an action in a Court of Law.

He had read the whole of this book with attention, and it certainly did raise such a doubt in his mind. It might probably be expected, that after the able and learned. argument which had gone forth to the world upon a subject so materially affecting the happiness of mankind, he should state his answer to that argument; but if he left these parties to a Court of Law (and he should leave them to a Court of Law), his opinion might have the effect of prejudicing the question to be there determined; all he would say, therefore, was, that entertaining a rational doubt upon some parts of the work as to their being directed against the truth of scripture, he would not continue this injunction, but the plaintiff might apply for another after he had cleared away that doubt in a Court of Law. Further than this, his Lordship would not interfere([1]).

SECTION III.
Of Works injurious to Public Peace and Justice.

Publications which are calculated to disturb the public peace, or to be injurious to the good government of the state, or which tend to bring into contempt the administration of justice, are all shut out of the pale of the law. There can be no right of property in such compositions.

The first case in which this doctrine was judicially pronounced was that of Dr. *Priestley*, who brought an action against the hundred for damages for the injuries sustained by him in consequence of the riotous proceedings of the mob at Birmingham; and among other property alleged to have been destroyed, claimed compensation for the loss of certain unpublished MSS. offering to produce booksellers as witnesses to prove that they would have given considerable sums for them.

On behalf of the hundred it was alleged, that the plaintiff was in the habit of publishing works *injurious to the government of the state;* upon which, Lord Chief Justice EYRE said, if any such evidence had been produced, he should have held it fit to be received as against the claim made by the plaintiff([2]).

In another case, that of Hime v. Dale([3]), which was an

(1) Petersdorff's Abr. 559-60.   (2) 2 Meriv. 437.
(3) The mischievous tendency of the production would sufficiently appear (it was contended) from the following stanza:

> The world is inclined
> To think justice blind;
> Yet what of all that?
> She will blink like a bat
> At the sight of friend *Abraham Newland,*
> Oh! *Abraham Newland!* magical *Abraham Newland!*
> Tho' justice 'tis known
> Can see thro' a mill stone,
> She can't see thro' *Abraham Newland.*

action for pirating the words of a song called " Abraham Newland," Mr. *Garrow* contended that the song was of such a description that it could not receive the protection of the law.

It professed, he said, to be a panegyric on money, but was in reality a gross and nefarious *libel* on the solemn *administration* of British *justice*. The object of this composition was not to satirize folly, or to raise the smile of innocent mirth, but being sung in the streets of the capital to excite the indignation of the people against the sacred ministers of the law, and the awful duties they were appointed to perform([1]).

Lord ELLENBOROUGH. If the composition appeared on the face of it to be a libel, so gross as to affect the public morals, I should advise the jury to give no damages. I know the Court of Chancery on such an occasion would grant no injunction.

But I think the present case is not to be considered one of that kind.

LAWRENCE, J. The argument used by Mr. GARROW on this fugitive piece as being a libel, would as forcibly apply to the *Beggar's Opera*, where the language and allusions are sufficiently derogatory to the administration of justice.

The last case of this kind was that of *Southey v. Sherwood*, which was decided in the year 1822. The author had written a seditious poem, called " Wat Tyler," which, having come into the defendant's possession, he published it without Mr. Southey's consent, and the latter applied to the Court of Chancery for an injunction.

The work was composed in the year 1794, when the author was under twenty-one. In that year there was an intention to publish it. It was sent by the plaintiff to Mr. Ridgway. The latter gave no account how it passed out of his hands.

The LORD CHANCELLOR said, if a man leaves a book of this description in the hands of a publisher, without assigning any satisfactory reason for doing so, and has not enquired about it during twenty-three years, he can have no right to complain of its being published at the end of that period.

But his lordship, in another part of his judgment, said, there is a difference between the case of an actual publication by the author, which all the world may pirate, and that of a man, who having composed a work, of which he afterwards repents, and wishes to withhold it from the public. I will not say that a principle might not be found which would apply to such a case as that; but then it is necessary to take all the circumstances of the case into consideration([2]).

The LORD CHANCELLOR subsequently delivered the following judgment.

(1) 2 Camp. 29.   (2) Meriv. 438.

" I have looked into all the affidavits, and have read the book itself. The bill goes the length of stating, that the work was composed by Mr. Southey in 1794, that it is his own production, and that it has been published by the defendant, without his sanction or authority; and therefore seeking an account of the profits which have arisen from, and an injunction to restrain, the publication. I have examined the cases that I have been able to meet with, containing precedent for injunctions of this nature, and I find that they all proceed upon the ground of a title to the property in the plaintiff. On this head a distinction has been taken, to which a considerable weight of authority attaches, supported, as it is, by the opinion of Lord C. J. EYRE, who has expressly laid it down that a person cannot recover in damages for a work which is in its nature to do injury to the public. Upon the same principle this court refused an injunction in the case of *Walcot v. Walker*, inasmuch as he could not have recovered damages in an action. After the fullest consideration, I remain of the same opinion as that which I entertained in deciding the case referred to. It is very true, that in some cases it may operate so as to multiply copies of mischievous publications, by the refusal of the court to interfere by restraining them; but to this my answer is, that sitting here as a judge upon a mere question of property, I have nothing to do with the nature of the property, nor with the conduct of the parties, except it relates to their civil interests; and if the publication be mischievous, either on the part of the author or the publisher, it is not my business to interfere with it. In the case now before the court, the application made by the plaintiff is on the ground only of his civil interest, and this is the proper place for such an application. I shall say nothing as to the nature of the book itself, because the grounds upon which I am about to declare my opinion, render it unnecessary that I should do so."

His Lordship then recapitulated the circumstances of the original intention to publish, the subsequent abandonment of the intention, the length of time during which the plaintiff had suffered the work to remain out of his possession, without inquiry, and its recent publication by the defendant.

" Taking," said his Lordship, " all these circumstances into my consideration, and having consulted all the cases which I could find at all regarding the question, entertaining also the same opinion with C. J. EYRE as to the point above noticed, it appears to me that I cannot grant this injunction, until after Mr. Southey shall have established his right to the property by an action([1]).

(1) 2 Meriv. 438.

The question of the protection claimed for illegal works is one of general importance, and has been productive of much litigation. It has been ably discussed by Mr. PETERS-DORFF, in his comprehensive abridgment, and we subjoin the *substance* of his observations thereon.

From the decisions of Lord ELDON, it will appear that that learned judge was well aware of the ground he was treading on, in refusing those injunctions which he felt himself bound to do from acknowledged law and precedent; but he shows that the rule, with all its practical evils and absurdities, is now part of the law of the land; and that it is only by an alteration of the law that it can be got rid of.

Two arguments are urged in defence of this system.

There is this distinction in *Southey's* case from that of *Byron and Lawrence*, that the former required the suppression of a work which had been published without his consent, which he had never previously published himself, and desired to be suppressed. In the latter instances, the object of the suit was to preserve the profit of exclusively printing and publishing the work.

It would seem that Mr. Southey might have put his case on the footing of those of *Pope* and *Swift*, in which the exclusive right to the manuscript was decided. Mr. Southey did not complain that he was deprived of the profits which he might derive from publishing the work himself, but he objected to the publication altogether. During the lapse of a quarter of a century, his views had undergone a change. He came within the reasoning advanced by Lord Mansfield([1])

1st. Admitting the incidental advantage that would arise by the protection from piracy of a work, however libellous, such protection cannot be afforded without violating the established principle of law, that *there can be no property in what is injurious.*

Waiving the answer afforded by the equally established principle that *a man shall not profit by his own wrong ;* and that a defendant cannot plead that his own act is criminal, to support a maxim, established only because it is generally useful, in the cases in which it is hurtful, is a puerile preference of the means to the end.

2ndly. It is said, that by destroying the profit, it prevents the publication of injurious works.

Now, if it were true that it destroys the profit, it does not follow that it will prevent the publication. The desire of obtaining notoriety, and of producing an effect, are (often) much stronger motives to authors, than the mere contingency of profit.

Besides, the profit will not be destroyed; it will not necessarily be diminished when the piracy has been foreseen. The publisher must protect himself from being undersold, by reducing both the cost and the price of the work ; and trust to a small profit on a wide scale, instead of a profit greater in each individual instance, but not so often repeated.

If *Don Juan*, and such like publications, had been the subject of copyright, and had been confined by its price to a class of readers with whom its faults might have been somewhat compensated by its merits, with whom, in fact, the ridicule which it endeavours to throw upon virtue, might have been partially balanced by that with which it over-whelms vice, no evil, comparatively speaking, would have accrued to the public. The proprietor's price was intended to confine the circulation amongst those to whom each side of the question was familiar ; that of the pirate's, to diffuse it among readers with whom its impieties have all the face of novelty, and to whom the answers are unknown (*a*).

As a remedy for these evils, the Quarterly Review(*b*) suggests, that it would be sufficient if a short Act of Parliament were passed, declaring that the libellous character of the work shall never be resorted to in bar of any proceeding at law or in equity for the infringement of copyright. The effect of such an act would be to subject the piratical publisher, whatever may be the tendency of the work, to those restraints which the law has imposed upon piracy, namely, an injunction, with an account of the profits, and an action at law for damages. We at first thought (say the reviewers) of excluding the two latter remedies, and merely proposing an injunction. This would be a slighter alteration of the law, and spare the prejudices of those whom no advantage can reconcile to the enabling a plaintiff to demand damages, and an account of " the unhallowed profits of a libellous publication;" but it would leave these unhallowed profits where they ought *still less* to be—in the hands of a libellous pirate.

(*a*) 6. Petersdorff Abr. 560-1.   (*b*) April, 1822.

(1) Vide pages 8, 9, *ante*.---In *Macklin v. Richardson*, it was also decided, that the author has a property in an unpublished work, independent of the statute of Anne, which is capable of being protected by injunction. *Amb.* 694.

—he had repented, and become ashamed of his former sentiments; he wished to suppress their publication; and ought to
have been allowed the exclusive dominion over his own
manuscript.

SECTION IV.

Of Publications injurious to private Individuals.

The Courts of Equity will not assist an author, whose
work contains a libel on private character. The criterion
of exclusion may be stated to be the liability of the writer
to an action for damages, or a prosecution for the libel.

A case in illustration of this principle was that of *Dr.
Walcot*, who filed a bill against booksellers of the name of
Walker for an injunction to restrain them from publishing two
editions of his works, upon a dispute as to the construction
of the agreement between the parties.

The defendants by their answer admitted that they had
published in one of the editions some of the plaintiff's works,
which they were not authorized to publish. As to that
edition, therefore, they submitted.

The LORD CHANCELLOR, in his judgment, observed, " If the doctrine of Lord C. J. Eyre is right, (and I think it is) that publications
may be of such a nature that an author can maintain no action at law,
it is not the business of this court, even upon the submission in the
answer, to decree either an injunction, or an account of the profits of
works of such a nature that the author can maintain no action at law
for the invasion of that which he calls his property, but which the policy
of the law will not permit him to consider his property. It is no answer
that the defendants are as criminal. It is the duty of the court to
know whether an action at law would lie; for if not, the court ought
not to give an account of the unhallowed profits of *libellous* publications. At present, I am in total ignorance of the nature of the work,
and whether the plaintiff can have any property in it or not. But I
will see these publications, and determine upon the nature of them,
whether there is question enough to send to law, as to the property in
these copies; for if not, I will act upon that submission in the answer.
If upon inspection the work appears innocent, I will act upon
that submission; if criminal, I will not act at all; and if doubtful,
I will send that question to the law(¹).

It seems doubtful whether an action could be maintained
for destroying a picture containing a scandalous libel upon
individuals, and which had been publicly exhibited; but it

----

(1) 7 Vesey, 1.   6 Petersdorff Abr. 557.

has been decided that the owner of such a libellous picture so destroyed, is, at most, only entitled to recover the value of the materials.

Thus, in the case of *Du Bost v. Beresford*, it appeared, that the picture in question, entitled *La Belle et la Bête,* or "Beauty and the Beast," was a scandalous libel upon a gentleman of fashion and his lady, who was the sister of the defendant. It was exhibited in a house in Pall Mall, for money, and great crowds went daily to see it, till the defendant one morning cut it in pieces.

Lord ELLENBOROUGH. The only plea on the record being the general issue of not guilty, it is unnecessary to consider whether the destruction of this picture might or might not have been justified. The material question is, as to the value to be set upon the article destroyed. If it was a libel upon the persons introduced into it, the law cannot consider it valuable as a picture. Upon an application to the Lord Chancellor, he would have granted an injunction against its exhibition, and the plaintiff was both civilly and criminally liable for having exhibited it. The jury, therefore, in assessing the damages, must not consider this as a work of art, but must award the plaintiff the value of the canvas and paint which formed its component parts(¹).

SECTION V.

Of Piratical Works.

As the law will not protect works which are immoral and unlawful, because there can be no right of property in such productions, so also it refuses its aid in preserving the exclusive use of books which have been pirated from previous publications. The law will not assist the robber in multiplying his spoil.

We reserve to the third part of this book the full consideration of the subject of literary piracy. It will be sufficient, in this place, to state, generally, that the law not only withholds its protection from books which are *wholly pirated,* but from those which are, *in substance,* merely *copies* and *imitations ;* or which, although in some parts different, yet are in general the same.

Thus in a book of *chronology*(²), though the same facts must be related, yet if the new work transcribes literally page after page, although other parts of it are original, the former author will be entitled to recover damages, and consequently the pirate would be excluded from proceeding against any one who had subsequently copied the passages thus illegally taken.

So also in the publication of *original poems,* together with

(1) 2 Camp. 511.   (2) Trusler v. Murray, 1 East, 363, *note.*

others which had been *before published*, a Court of Equity will grant an injunction to restrain the publication([1]), and it follows that the pirated part of the work will receive no protection.

A similar decision was made with respect to an *abridgment* of Cook's Voyage round the World([2]). A *bona fide* abridgment or compilation is considered in the nature of an original work; but whole passages must not be transcribed to the injury of the original author, nor the work abridged in a merely colorable manner([3]). It seems clear, that where these rules are violated, the law will not interfere between the first and subsequent pirates, or lend itself to the protection of property thus fraudulently obtained.

CHAP. V.

OF THE SPECIAL COPYRIGHT OF THE CROWN AND THE UNIVERSITIES, AND OF PUBLISHING PARLIAMENTARY AND JUDICIAL PROCEEDINGS.

SECT. I.——*Of the former prerogative Copyright in Law Books, Almanacs, and the Latin Grammar.*

In the review which we have taken of the progressive stages of the law in relation to copyright in general, we passed over the peculiar and special nature of *prerogative* copyright. Before entering on the present state of the law in this respect, we may advert briefly to its past condition, and set forth the instances in which the Universities and the Stationers' Company, as well as the Crown, claimed an exclusive right of printing; but which claims have been exploded by the learning and independence of the distinguished judges in recent times.

We avail ourselves of the language of Mr. ERSKINE in describing the monopoly of printing, which formerly was exercised by the Crown.

" On the first introduction of printing (says this distinguished advocate), it was considered, as well in England as in other countries, to be a matter of state. The quick and extensive circulation of sentiments and opinions which that invaluable art introduced, could not but fall under the gripe of Governments, whose principal strength was built upon the ignorance of the people who were to submit to them. The *press* was therefore wholly under the coercion of the Crown; and

---

(1) Case of Mason's Poems, *per Lord Bathurst.*   (2) 1 East, 363, *note.*
(3) Vide p. 76 *ante*, and Part III. *post.*

H 2

all printing, not only of *public* books containing ordinances, religious or civil, but *every species of publication* whatsoever, was regulated by the King's proclamations, prohibitions, charters of privilege, and, finally, by the decrees of the Star Chamber.

"After the demolition of that odious jurisdiction, the Long Parliament, on its rupture with Charles the First, assumed the same power which had before been in the crown; and after the Restoration, the same restrictions were re-enacted, and re-annexed to the prerogative by the statute of the 13th and 14th Charles II., and continued down by subsequent acts till after the revolution."

" The expiration of these disgraceful statutes (in 1694), by the refusal of Parliament to continue them any longer, formed the *great æra of the liberty of the press in this country*, and stripped the crown of every prerogative over it, except that which, upon just and rational principles of Government, must ever belong to the executive magistrate, namely, the exclusive right to publish religious or civil constitutions; in a word, to promulgate every ordinance which contains the rules of action by which the subject is to live and to be governed(¹)."

Amongst the works formerly claimed as exclusively belonging to the crown, or its patentees, were law books, almanacs, and the Latin grammar.

From the time of 26th Henry VIII. down to the 12th Anne, various patents were granted to different persons, giving them full power to print and re-print prerogative copies, in exclusion of all other persons.

The King's printer in England enjoys the benefit to be derived from printing the Acts of Parliament, and other documents of the state; and the King's printers for Scotland and Ireland possess similar patents.

The Universities of Oxford and Cambridge, in common with the King's printer, claim a right to print all Bibles to be circulated in England; and the Company of Stationers *formerly* exercised, in conjunction with the Universities, an exclusive power of printing almanacs.

We shall proceed to consider in their order the several works which were thus anciently monopolized under the charters and patents granted by the crown.

1st.   Of Law Books.

The following were the reasons on which the monopoly

(1) Ridgway's Coll. 1st. vol.

in law books was attempted to be upheld, namely—that this privilege had been always allowed, which was a strong argument in its favor; although it could not be said to amount to a prescription, as printing was introduced within time of memory;—that it concerned the state, and was matter of public care;—that it was in nature of a proclamation, which none but the King could make;—that the King had the making of judges, serjeants, and officers of the law;—that though it could not be extended to a book containing a quotation of law, it applied to those in which the principal design was to treat on that subject([1]).

The King's prerogative in law publications is now, however, treated as perfectly ridiculous([2]). Nothing, indeed, could be more preposterous than the argument, that because the King appointed the judges, he had a monopoly in the publication of their decisions! It was urged, also, that as he paid for the composition of the year books, he was entitled to them on the ground of purchase. Mr. Justice YATES, however, in the cause of Millar v. Taylor([3]) observed, that the expence of printing prerogative books was, "in fact, no private disbursement of the King, but done at the public charge, and formed part of the expences of Government."

It could hardly, he said, be contended, that the produce of expences of a public sort, were the private property of the King, when purchased with the public money. He could not sell or dispose of one of those compositions. How, then, could they be his private property, like private property claimed by an author in his own compositions?

Besides, the purchase by the King could only comprise the right of an individual author. He did not compose the works personally, and could only acquire such right as a subject was able to dispose of. It has never been contended that the mere act of purchasing a work, conferred on the purchaser of the manuscript a copyright beyond the interest

(1) *Roper* and *Streater*, 4 Bac. Ab. Art. "Prerogative."—In this case, Roper bought of the executors of Justice *Croke*, the 3rd part of his Reports, which he printed. Colonel Streater had a grant for years from the crown for printing all law books, and printed upon Roper, on which Roper brought an action on the statute 13th and 14th Car. II. c. 33. Streater pleaded the King's grant.
On demurrer, it was adjudged in B. R. for the plaintiff, against the validity of the patent; on these reasons, that this patent tended to a monopoly—that it was of a large extent—that printing was a handicraft trade, and no more to be restrained than other trades—that it was difficult to ascertain what should be called a law book—that the words in the patent, *touching or concerning the common or statute law*, were loose and uncertain—that if this were to be considered as an office, the grant for years could not be good, as it would go to executors and administrators, and that there was no adequate remedy in the way of redress in case of abuses by unskilfulness, selling dear, printing ill, &c.
But this judgment was reversed on a writ of error in Parliament.
(2) 4 Burr. 2315. 3 Pere Williams, 255.　　　(3) 4 Burr. 2384.

possessed by the author. The duration or extent of the right can in no degree depend on the purchaser : if it did so, it would follow, that under the present Acts of Paliament the copyright in a book would continue for the life of the assignee, and not for the life time of the author ; and a copy-right might thus easily be perpetuated, by the author selling his interest to two or more persons, and on the death of one of them, the survivors might transfer the copy to others, and so on for ever.

2nd. Of Almanacs.

A patent was granted by James I. for the exclusive printing of almanacs, and the right continued to be insisted upon by the Universities and Stationers' Company as matter of prerogative, after the final decision of the general question of literary property in 1774.

The origin of the prerogative claim in these publications, is put upon the following curious reasons :—

1st. Because derelict.

2nd. Because almanacs regulate the feasts of the church(¹).

In the year 1778, Mr. Carnan having made several improvements in the nature of the work, and published it on his own account, the Universities and the Stationers' Company filed a bill in Chancery to restrain the publication.

The court having doubted the legality of the patent, directed a case to the Common Pleas ; the judges of which court, after two arguments, decided that the patent was void(²).

A bill was then brought in " to revest the monopoly in almanacs, which had fallen to the ground by the above-mentioned judgments in the King's Courts."

Mr. ERSKINE was heard against the bill at the bar of the House of Commons, and it was rejected by a majority of forty-five votes(³).

(1) Mod. 256.   (2) 2 Blac. Rep. 1004.
(3) Vol. 37, *Journals*, 388. It is from the splendid speech on this occasion that we have made the extract at the commencement of this section.

In contrast to the title of the bill given to it by its proposer, Mr. Erskine face-tiously adduced the following, as more truly characterizing its nature :—

" Whereas the Stationers' Company and the two Universities, for above a century last past, *contrary to law*, usurped the right of printing almanacs, in exclusion of the rest of His Majesty's faithful people, and have from time to time harassed and vexed divers good subjects of our Lord the King for printing the same, till checked by a late decision of the Courts of Law :

Be it therefore enacted, that this usurpation be made legal, and be confined to them in future."

" This would have been a curiosity indeed, and would have made some noise in the House, yet it is nothing but the plain and simple truth ; the bill could not pass without making a sort of bolus of the preamble to swallow it in."

3rd. *Of the Latin Grammar.*

The claim to a prerogative copyright in the old Latin grammar, was grounded on the allegation that the work had been originally written and composed at the King's expence([1]).

But this pretension, like that in favour of law books, is now considered as wholly untenable([2]).

The late Sir W. D. Evans, in discussing the prerogative of the crown, well observes, that although it may be rather a matter of curiosity than one of practical utility, the examination of the nature and foundation of the right will certainly lead to the conclusion, that such right could have had no legitimate origin upon any principles of the common law at present acknowledged. It seems, indeed, that the only occasion on which the validity of any of these patents was fully considered in a court of law as between the public and the crown, it was decided against them.

SECTION II.

Of the Prerogative Copyright in Acts of State.

The works in which a prerogative copyright is still retained, (though with regard to some of them most inconsistently) are the following:—

1st. Acts relating to the *state*, namely, the statutes, the King's proclamations, the orders of Council.

2nd. Acts relating to the *church*, namely, the liturgical and other divine service, and the *English* translation of the Bible.

In some of these the crown maintains, by its own printer, a *sole* copyright; and in others it is exercised *conjointly* with the Universities, under their respective charters.

1st. *Of the Statutes.*

On grounds of political and public convenience, it is said, that the King, as executive magistrate, has the right of promulgating to the people all acts of state and government([3]).

Mr. Justice YATES. "The right of the crown to the sole and exclusive printing of what is called prerogative copies, is founded on reasons of religion or state. The only consequences to which they lead are of a natural and public concern, respecting the established religion or government of the kingdom.

---

(1) 4 Burr. 2329, 2401.   (2) Ib. 2315. 3 Pere Williams, 255.
(3) 2 Blac. Com. 410.

Lord MANSFIELD considered the existence of prerogative copies as merely a modification of the general and common right of literary property.

He discussed at length the position that crown copies were founded solely on *property*, and said, that in Basket's case([1]) they had no notion of the prerogative of the crown over the press, or of any power to restrain it by exclusive privileges, or of any power to control the subject matter upon which a man might write, or the manner in which he might treat of it. They rested upon property from the King's right of original publication. The copy of the Hebrew Bible, the Greek Testament, or the Septuagint, does not belong to the King—it is common ; but the English translation he bought, and therefore it has been concluded to be his property. His power rests in property. His sole right rests on the foundation of property in the copy by the Common Law. What other ground (said he) can there be for the King's having a property in the Latin grammar, (which is one of his most ancient copies) than that it was originally composed at his expence ?

The exclusive right of printing Acts of Parliament and other matters of state, has been looked upon more favorably than the other branches of the prerogative in question.

Lord CLARE, in the case of Grierson v. Jackson([2]), said he could very well conceive that the King should have a power to grant a patent to print the Statute Books, because it was necessary that there should be a responsibility for correct printing, and because copy can only be had from the Rolls of Parliament, which are within the authority of the crown.

Sir William D. Evans observes, that the legal right in this monopoly of the statutes, considered with relation to its origin, rests upon no juster principles than the exploded rights respecting the Latin grammar and almanacs. Previous to the invention of printing, the usual course was to send the statutes to be proclaimed by the Sheriffs. Then, as now, every subject was bound to have taken notice of the contents of them at his peril ; and there is not the slightest trace of authority for a restriction of the employment of making manuscript copies, which, to the lawyers and judges of that day, must have been essentially necessary, although in case of any question arising judicially with respect to the contents of a statute, the original record, or some duly authenticated copy, would of course be resorted to ; and the learned Annotator adds, that he cannot discern any legal principle upon which a discovery, that had the effect of facilitating the multiplication of copies, could limit and restrain that common right of producing such copies which previously existed. In fact (says he), this authority, originally claimed by the crown, had no particular

---

(1) 1 Bl. 105. 2 Burr. 661.   (2) Ridgway's Reports, 304.

relation to the benefit of affording to the public more
accurate information upon the ordinances of Parliament, than
could otherwise have been obtained; but was merely one
amongst many other instances of the application of that
general overwhelming system of monopoly, which is now
reduced to very circumscribed limits, and supported only
upon grounds and principles that in former times were never
thought of.

We conclude this part of the subject by referring to the
case of *Baskett* v. *The University of Cambridge,* which is always
quoted in support of the prerogative copyright; but it is
observable that the parties in this litigation were equally
interested in upholding the *general* prerogative, though they
had quarreled about its exercise in that *particular instance.*

In that case the plaintiffs, who were the King's printers,
brought a bill into the Court of Chancery to restrain the
defendants from printing or selling a book entitled, "An exact
Abridgment of all the Acts of Parliament relating to the
Excise on Beer, &c." It was sent into the King's Bench
for the opinion of the court upon the Acts of Parliament
and Patents.

Several letters patent were insisted on by the plaintiffs, the last
bore date in the 12th year of Queen Anne, by which the *sole* power
of printing all, and all sorts of abridgments of all and singular
statutes and Acts of Parliament, was given to the grantees, with a
prohibition against all others.

On the other hand, the defendants contended that by a patent
granted in the 26th year of Henry VIII. they might lawfully print,
within the University, all manner of books approved by the Chancellor and Vice-Chancellor, and three doctors, and might put them
to sale wherever they pleased; and that by a patent dated 3 Car. I. the
King confirmed that right to the University, *notwithstanding* any
grant or prohibition contained in the subsequent letters patent, or any
of them.

The case was argued four times during the space of six years,
and the following certificate was made by Lord Mansfield and the
other judges.

"Having heard counsel on both sides, and considered of this
case, we are of opinion that during the term granted by the letters
patent, dated the 13th of *October*, in the 12th year of the reign of Queen
Anne, the plaintiffs are entitled to the right of printing Acts of
Parliament, exclusive of all other persons not authorized to print the
same by prior grants from the crown.

"But we think that by virtue of the letters patent, bearing date
the 20th day of *July*, in the 26th year of the reign of King *Henry* VIII., and
the letters patent bearing date the 6th of February, in the 3rd year of
the reign of King *Charles* I. the Chancellor, Masters, and scholars of

the University of *Cambridge* are entrusted with a *concurrent authority* to print Acts of Parliament, and abridgments of Acts of Parliament, within the said University, upon the terms in the said letters patent(¹).

Of the Statutes published with Notes and Selections of the Statutes.

It seems to have been agreed that the privileged copies may be printed by others than those having the patent right, *if accompanied by bona fide notes.*

In the case of Baskett v. Cunningham(²), the defendant, in conjunction with several booksellers, was publishing in weekly numbers A Digest of the Statute Law methodized under alphabetical heads, with large notes from Lord Coke, and other writers on the law. He had contracted with Strahan and Woodfall, the proprietors of the patent for printing law books, to print this work, and it was printed at their press. Baskett, the King's printer (whose patent extended to all statutes), filed a bill for an injunction. It was urged that the book was not within the meaning of the letters patent, being a work of labor and industry, and the method entirely new.

The LORD CHANCELLOR, however, was of opinion, that the work was within the patent of the King's printer, and that the notes were merely collusive. But he would not interfere between the two contending patents in the summary method of injunction, but left them to adjust their respective rights in the course of law. He, therefore, ordered an injunction to issue to restrain the proprietors from printing at any other than at a patent press; which, as Woodfall and Strahan were strictly in league with Baskett, and were at that time jointly concerned in a new edition of the Statutes, was equivalent to a total injunction, the law printers finding means to elude their contract with Cunningham.

2nd.   Of Proclamations and Orders in Council.

Though it was decided in the case of Baskett v. The University of Cambridge(³), that the University had, under letters patent, a concurrent authority with the Crown to print Acts of Parliament, and abridgments of Acts of Parliament, within the University, it seems this authority has not been extended to the King's Proclamations, Orders in Council, and other State Papers. These latter Acts of State would, therefore, appear vested in the king's printer solely.

(1) Baskett v. University of Cambridge, 1 Bla. Rep. 105.   2 Burr. 660.
(2) 1 Bl. Rep. 370.   2 Eden, 137.   2 Evans's Stat. 622.
(3) 2 Burr. 661.   1 Blac. Rep. 105, cited page 105 *ante.*

SECTION III.

Of the Copyright of the KING *as head of the* CHURCH.

1st. *Of the English Translation of the Bible.*

The King's prerogative in the exclusive printing of the Bible, is confined to the *English translation;* which, it is said, he *bought,* and, *therefore,* it has been concluded to be his property([1]).

Mr. Justice BLACKSTONE rests the claim of the King on the ground as well of his being the Head of the Church, as of original purchase. " On these two principles *combined* (he says), the exclusive right of printing the translation of the Bible is founded([2])."

The assumption of the private purchase, however, being now altogether abandoned, and the claim depending entirely on the exercise of the prerogative, during a period insufficient to constitute a prescriptive right, it seems by no means clear that the patent could be sustained in a court of law.

There are conflicting authorities on the subject; and the only instances in which the prerogative has been apparently upheld, were on occasions of disputed title between rival patentees, neither of whom were competent to moot the general question upon the footing of the public interest.

Upon an application for an injunction against printing an edition of the Bible in numbers, with prints and notes, Lord CLARE, the Chancellor of Ireland, asked if the validity of the patent had ever been established at law? and said, he did not know that the Crown had a right to grant a monopoly of that kind.

In the course of the discussion he made the following observations. " I can conceive that the King, as the Head of the Church, may say that there shall be but one man who shall print Bibles and Books of Common Prayer for the use of churches and other particular purposes; but I cannot conceive that the King has any prerogative to grant a monopoly as to Bibles for the instruction of mankind in the revealed religion ; if he had, it would be in the power of the patentee to put what price he pleased upon the book, and thus prevent the instruction of men in the Christian religion." " If ever there was a time which called aloud for the dissemination of religious knowledge, it is this ; and, therefore, I should with great reluctance decide in favor of such a monopoly as this, which must necessarily confine the circulation of the book." " As to very particular purposes, I have no doubt that the patentee has an exclusive right to print Bibles and Prayer Books ; but unless I am bound down very strictly, I will not determine upon

(1) 4 Burr. 2405.   (2) 2 Comm. 410.

motion that no man but the King's printer has a right to print such works as these."

" In giving judgment he said, that the case which had been mentioned seemed to intimate that it never had been solemnly decided how far the prerogative extends to give a sole and exclusive right of printing Bibles. Many of the old cases upon the subject were determined upon the principle of the Licencing Act;" and the motion was refused(¹).

A contrary decision, however, was pronounced some years afterwards in the case of the Universities of Oxford and Cambridge v. Richardson(²), in which an injunction against the King's printer in Scotland (who had a patent for the sale of Bibles) was granted, restraining him from printing or selling them in *England*.

This took place on an interlocutory motion before the hearing of the cause, on the ground that possession, under color of title, was sufficient to warrant the injunction, until it was proved at law that there was no real title. In the course of the case it appeared that in the year 1718, Sir Joseph Jekyll, as Master of the Rolls, had granted an injunction in a similar case, which was supported upon appeal before the Lord Chancellor ; and also that a decree of the Court of Session had, in the year 1717, been reversed by the House of Lords in favor of the King's printer in England, confining the right of the Scotch printer to Scotland.

In this case, also, it is evident that the general principle could not be investigated between patentees who derived their title, if valid, from the same source.

Of the Bible in the Original Languages, and portions of the English Translation.

Neither the Hebrew Bible, the Greek Testament, nor the Septuagint, belong to the King. Lord MANSFIELD (as before referred to) pronounced them to be unquestionably in common; and added, that if any man should turn the Psalms, or the writings of Solomon or Job, into verse, the King could not stop the printing or the sale of such a work. It would be the author's work. " The King has no power or control over the subject matter—his power rests in property."

Neither has any attempt ever been made to prevent any person from publishing a translation of one book, or of a *part* of the Bible, from the original text, and enjoying a copyright in his production(³).

(1) Grierson v. Jackson, Ridgway's Rep. 304.   2 Evans's Stat. 620.
(2) 6 Vesey, 689.   (3) Godson on Copyright, 325.

2nd.   Of the Common Prayer Book, &c.

Upon the same principle as Head of the Church, the King has a right to the exclusive publication of Liturgical and other books of divine service.

In *Eyre* and *Strahan v. Carnan*, which was decided in the Court of Exchequer, a bill was filed to restrain the defendant from publishing a *form of prayer*, which had been ordered by His Majesty to be read in all churches.

The plaintiffs were the King's printers.   The grant which was read, imported to be a grant of the office of printer to His Majesty, and his successors, of (amongst other things) all Bibles and Testaments in the English language ; and of all Books of Common Prayer, and Adminis-trations of the Sacraments, and other Rites and Ceremonies of the Church of England ; in all volumes whatsoever heretofore printed by the King's printer, or to be printed by his com-mand ; and of all other books which he, his heirs or successors, should order to be used for the service of God in the Church of England.

The bill stated, that in December, 1779, a form of prayer was ordered by His Majesty to be used in all Churches and Chapels throughout England and Wales, upon the 4th of February, 1780 ; that it was printed by the plaintiffs, and a sufficient number thereof circulated for sale at sixpence each, which was a reasonable price, and at which they had been formerly sold ; that the defendant had printed and sold a great number of them.

The court held that the grant was founded on public convenience, was supported by long usage, and the injunction was accordingly continued(¹).

SECTION IV.

Of publishing Proceedings in Parliament and Courts of Justice.

1st.   Of Parliamentary Proceedings.

Both Houses of Parliament consider a publication of their proceedings as a breach of privilege.   By sufferance, however, the reports of the debates are allowed to appear in the diurnal and other periodical works.   Not only the speeches of the members, but copies of documents, printed at the direction of either House, are thus circulated for the information of the

(1) E. T. 1781.   5 Bac. Ab. 597.

public; and it seems that the Courts of Justice will not interfere to restrain such publications, even when the matter comprised in them is libellous, provided it be a true account of
the proceedings(¹).

Thus the same reasons which justify the publication of
judicial proceedings, were held to warrant those of the senate.

It is, said Mr. Justice LAWRENCE, of advantage to the public,
and even to the legislative bodies, that true accounts of their proceedings should be generally circulated; and they would be deprived of
that advantage if no person could publish the proceedings without
being punished as a libeller. Though the defendant in the case before
the court was not authorized by the House of Commons to publish
the report in question, yet as he only published a true copy of it, the
rule for a criminal information was discharged(²).

2nd. Of Judicial Proceedings.

The House of Lords, in its judicial capacity, exercises an
exclusive privilege in publishing its own proceedings as the
supreme court of judicature. The course usually adopted by
the House is to direct the Lord Chancellor to cause the publication of the proceedings, and to prohibit all other persons.

Lord BATHURST, in a case of Bathurst v. Kearsley, granted an
injunction in favor of the printer under his authority, of the trial of
the Duchess of Kingston(³).

Lord ERSKINE, upon the precedent of the last decision, ordered
an injunction, until the hearing in the case of Gurney v. Longman,
with respect to the trial of Lord Melville, at the same time intimating,
that unless he had a strong impression that at the hearing he should
continue of the same opinion, and should grant a perpetual injunction,
he would not then grant an injunction(⁴).

But on the day of his quitting office as Lord Chancellor, he
desired that he should be understood that he had not delivered any
judgment, further than by granting the injunction until the hearing
upon the precedent of the former case of Bathurst v. Kearsley, and
should therefore consider the question as open in any future stage.
A demurrer was afterwards put in, but was never argued, a compro-
mise taking place.

In the Court of Common Pleas, in the time of C. J. EYRE, an
action was brought by *Currie* against *Walter*, the proprietor of "The
Times," for publishing a supposed libel, which consisted in merely
stating a speech made by a counsel on a motion for leave to file a
criminal information.

The CHIEF JUSTICE, who tried the cause, ruled, that this was not a
libel, nor the subject of an action, it being a true account of what
had passed in court; and in this opinion the Court of Common Pleas

(1) 8 T. R. 296-7.   Godson, 253, 341.   But see 7 East, 503.
(2) 8 T. R. 298.   (3) Cited 13 Vesey, 493.   (4) 13 Vesey, 493.

afterwards, on a motion for a new trial, all concurred, though some of the judges doubted whether or not the defendant could avail himself of that defence on the general issue.

In a subsequent case in the Court of King's Bench, Mr. Justice LAWRENCE entered somewhat fully into the question, and said, the proceedings of courts of justice are daily published, some of which highly reflect on individuals. Many of these proceedings contain no point of law, and are not published under the authority or the sanction of the courts, but they are printed for the information of the public.

Though the publication of such proceedings (he continued) may be to the disadvantage of the particular individual concerned, yet it is of vast importance to the public that the proceedings of Courts of Justice should be universally known. The general advantage to the country in having these proceedings made public, more than counterbalances the inconveniences to the private persons whose conduct may be the subject of such proceedings([1]).

In a later case, Lord ELLENBOROUGH and Mr. Justice GROSE observed, that it must not be taken for granted that the publication of every matter which passes in a Court of Justice, however truly represented, is, under all circumstances, and with whatever motive published, justifiable ; but that doctrine must be taken with grains of allowance.

It often happens, said Lord ELLENBOROUGH, that circumstances necessary for the sake of public justice to be disclosed by a witness in a judicial inquiry, are very distressing to the feelings of individuals on whom they reflect : and if such circumstances were afterwards wantonly published, I should hesitate to say that such unnecessary publication was not libellous, merely because the matter had been given in evidence in a Court of Justice([2]).

It seems at all events clear, that the several Courts of Justice possess the power of restraining the publication of a trial *during its progress*.

Thus in the case of *The King* against *Clement*([3]), it was held, that a court of general gaol delivery has the power to make an order to prohibit the publication of the proceedings pending a trial likely to continue for several successive days, and to punish disobedience of such order by fine.

The facts were as follows : on the 17th of April, 1820, Arthur Thistlewood was put upon his trial at the Old Bailey, upon an indictment for high treason.

Lord Chief Justice ABBOTT, one of the justices, stated publically before the commencement of the trial, that as there were several persons charged with the offence of high treason by the same indictment, whose trials were likely to be

(1) 8 Term Rep. 298.   (2) 7 East, 503.   (3) 4 Barn. and Ald, 218.

taken one after another, he thought it necessary strictly to prohibit the publishing of any proceedings of that or any other day, until the whole trial should be brought to a conclusion, and that it was expected all persons would attend to the admonition.

This order was infringed by the *Observer* Newspaper, and the proprietor was fined £500 for a contempt of Court.

An appeal was subsequently made to the King's Bench, and a rule nisi obtained to remove the case by certiorari into that court. On the argument for a rule absolute, the following judgment was pronounced by the remaining judges of the court---the Chief Justice and Mr. Justice BEST (before whom the order was made) having briefly stated their adherence to their former opinions.

BAYLEY, J. As to the validity of the order, it was contended in argument, first, that the court had no power to make an order prohibiting the publication of these trials pending the proceedings. Now, in order to judge of that, it becomes necessary to consider what the nature of the proceedings was. An indictment had been found against a number of individuals for the crime of high treason, and they were then about to be tried. The whole trial of all these individuals constituted one entire proceeding; for if they had not severed in their challenges, the prisoners would have been tried all at once. In point of fact, however, they did sever in their challenges, and were tried seriatim. It could not, therefore, be said, that the whole proceedings was terminated until the last of those prisoners had taken his trial. Now the court before whom the trial was about to take place, was a court of general gaol delivery, and had authority to make any order which they might judge to be necessary, in order to preserve the purity of the administration of justice, in the course of the proceedings then depending before them, and to prohibit any publication which might have a tendency to prevent the fair and impartial consideration of the case. On the present occasion it occurred to the court that it would be of great importance, with a view both to the interest of the prisoners and that of the public, that a publication like the present should be prohibited until after the termination of all the trials ; and if upon the first trial one or more of the witnesses had been of doubtful character, it might have been of the utmost importance to keep them apart from the rest, and to examine carefully whether upon each successive trial they continued to give the same account which they did upon the first. Now all this would be prevented if by a publication like the present such persons were enabled to see a printed account of the trial, and to read over not only their own evidence, but also that of the other witnesses who had been examined. This would give them an opportunity of explaining those parts of their statement which might be at variance with the other facts proved in the case. But it is argued, that if the court have this power of prohibiting publication, there is no limit to it, and that they may prohibit altogether any publication of the trial. I think that does not follow. All that has been done in this case is very different ; for the prohibition here has only been until the whole trial was completed.

HOLROYD, J. This was an order made in a proceeding over which the court had judicial cognizance : the subject matter respecting which it was made, was then in the course of judicature before them. The object for which it was made was clearly, as it appears to me, one within their jurisdiction, viz. the furtherance of justice in proceedings then pending before the court ; and it was made to remain in force so long, and so long only, as those proceedings should be pending before them. Now I take it to be clear that a Court of Record has a right to make orders for regulating their proceedings, and for the furtherance of justice in the proceedings before them, which are to continue in force during the time that such proceedings are pending. It appears to me that the arguments as to a further power of continuing such orders in force for a longer period, do not apply. It is sufficient for the present case that the court have that power during the *pendency of the proceedings.* This order was made to delay publication only so long as it was necessary for the purposes of justice, *leaving every person at liberty to publish the report of the proceedings subsequently to their termination.* I am, therefore, of opinion that this was an order which the court had power to make.

SECOND PART.

OF THE LIBRARY TAX,

AND

REGISTRY AT STATIONERS' HALL.

CHAP. I.——ANALYSIS OF THE STATUTE 54 GEO. III. CAP. 156.

SECT. I.——*Of the Tax on Original Works.*

The first section of the act commences by reciting the statute of Anne, so far as relates to the delivery of nine copies of each book, on the best paper, for the use of the several libraries therein mentioned; and after also reciting the 41st Geo. III. cap. 107, in regard to the additional two copies for Ireland, it is then stated, that it is expedient that future copies of books should be delivered to the libraries therein mentioned, with the modifications provided by the act.

It then proceeds to repeal so much of the acts of Anne, and 41st Geo. III. as required the delivery of the copies.

The following is the preamble of the statute, and the enacting part of the first clause.

Whereas by an act, made in the eighth year of the reign of Her late Majesty Queen Anne, intituled An act for the encouragement of learning, by vesting the copies of printed books in the authors or purchasers of such copies, during the times therein mentioned, it was among other things provided and enacted, that nine copies of *each book* or books, *upon the best paper*, that from and after the tenth day of April, one thousand seven hundred and ten, should be printed and published as in the said act mentioned, or reprinted and published with additions, should, by the printer and printers thereof, be *delivered to the warehouse-keeper* of the Company of Stationers for the time being, at the hall of the said company, *before such publication* made, for the use of the Royal Library, the libraries of the Universities of Oxford and Cambridge, the libraries of the four Universities in Scotland, the library of Sion College in London, and the library of the Faculty of Advocates at Edinburgh; which said warehouse-keeper is by the said act required to deliver such copies for the use of the said libraries; and that if any proprietor, bookseller, or printer, or the said warehouse-keeper, should not observe the directions of the said act therein, that then he or they so making default in not delivering the said printed copies, should forfeit, besides the value of the said printed copies, the sum of five pounds for every copy not so delivered: And whereas by an act made in the forty-first year of the reign of His present Majesty, intituled *An act for the further encouragement of learning in the United Kingdom of* Great Britain and Ireland, *by securing the copies and copyright of printed books to the authors of such books or their assigns, for the time herein mentioned,* it is amongst other things provided and enacted, that in addition to the nine copies required by law to be delivered to the warehouse-keeper of the said Company of Stationers, of each and every book and books *which shall be entered in the register books* of the said company, two other copies shall *in like manner* be delivered for the use of the library of the College of the Holy Trinity, and the library of the Society of the King's Inns in Dublin, by the printer and printers of all and every such book and books as should thereafter be printed and published, and the title of the copyright whereof should be *entered* in the said register book of the said company : And whereas it is expedient that copies of books hereafter printed or published, should be delivered to the libraries herein-after mentioned, *with the modifications* that shall be provided by this act ; may it therefore please your Majesty that it may be enacted, and be it enacted by the King's most excellent Majesty, by and with the advice and consent of the Lords Spiritual and Temporal, and Commons, in this present Parliament assembled, and by the authority of the same, that so much of the said several recited acts of the eighth year of Queen Anne, and of the forty-first year of His present Majesty, as requires that any copy or copies of any book or books which shall be printed or published, or reprinted and published with additions, shall be delivered by the printer or printers thereof to the warehouse-keeper of the said Company of Stationers, for the use of any of the libraries in the said act mentioned, and as requires the delivery of the said copies by the said warehouse-keeper for the use of the said libraries, and as imposes any penalty on such printer or warehouse-keeper for not delivering the said copies, shall be, and the same is hereby, repealed.

In the second section it is enacted, that eleven printed copies of the whole of every book, upon the paper on which the largest impression shall be printed for sale, together with maps and prints, *on demand made in writing at the publisher's within twelve months,* shall be delivered to the warehouse-keeper of the Stationers' Company, within *one month* after such demand, for the use of the libraries following : videlicet,

The British Museum,
Sion College,
The Bodleian Library at Oxford,
The Public Library at Cambridge,
The Library of the Faculty of Advocates at Edinburgh,
The Libraries of the four Universities of Scotland,
Trinity College Library, and
The King's Inns Library, at Dublin.

And the warehouse-keeper is required, within *one month* after such deposit, to deliver the same for the use of the libraries.

We here present so much of the second section as relates to the preceding analysis.

II.   And be it further enacted, that eleven printed copies of the *whole* of every book, and of every volume thereof, upon the paper upon which the *largest number* or impression of such book shall be printed for sale, together with *all maps and prints* belonging thereto, which, from and after the passing of this act, shall be printed and published, *on demand* thereof being made in writing to, or left at the place of abode of, the publisher or publishers thereof, at any time *within twelve months* next after the publication thereof, under the hand of the warehouse-keeper of the Company of Stationers, or the librarian or other person thereto authorized by the persons or body politic and corporate, proprietors or managers of the libraries following, *videlicet*, the *British Museum, Sion College*, the *Bodleian Library* at *Oxford*, the *Public Library* at *Cambridge*, the library of the *Faculty of Advocates* at *Edinburgh*, the libraries of the four Universities of *Scotland, Trinity College Library*, and the *King's Library* at *Dublin*, or so many of such eleven copies as shall be respectively demanded on behalf of such libraries respectively, shall be delivered by the publisher or publishers thereof respectively, within *one month after demand* made thereof in writing as aforesaid, to the warehouse-keeper of the said Company of Stationers for the time being; which copies the said warehouse-keeper shall, and he is hereby required to, receive at the hall of the said Company, for the use of the library for which such demand shall be made, within such twelve months as aforesaid ; and the said warehouse-keeper is hereby required, within one month after any such book or volume shall be so delivered to him as aforesaid, to deliver the same for the use of such library.

SECTION II.

Of the Tax on Second and subsequent Editions.

By the third section it is provided, that no copy shall be demanded or delivered for the use of the libraries of any second or subsequent edition of any book, unless the same shall contain *additions or alterations*.

And such additions or alterations only, if printed in an uniform manner with the former editions of the book, may be delivered for the use of the libraries entitled to such former editions.

The following is the clause in full.

III.   Provided always, and be it further enacted, that no such printed copy or copies shall be demanded by or delivered to or for the use of any of the libraries herein before mentioned, of the second edition, or of any subsequent edition of any book or books so demanded and delivered as aforesaid, unless the same shall contain additions or alterations : and in case any edition after the first, of any book so demanded and delivered as aforesaid, shall contain any addition ar alteration, no printed copy or copies thereof shall be demanded or delivered as aforesaid, if a printed copy of such additions or alterations only, printed in an uniform manner with the former edition of such book, be delivered to each of the libraries aforesaid, for whose use a copy of the former edition shall have been demanded and delivered as aforesaid.

SECTION III.

Of Periodical Publications.

In the case of magazines, reviews, or other periodical publications, it is provided that it shall be sufficient to make such entry in the register book of the Company, within *one month* next after the publication of the first number or volume of such magazine, review, or other periodical publication(¹).

SECTION IV.

Of Maps and Prints and the quality of Paper.

All maps and prints belonging to the works delivered, must accompany them(²).

The copy of every book that shall be demanded by the British Museum, (according to the third section) must be delivered of the *best paper* on which such work shall be printed.

The copies for the other public libraries are directed to be upon the paper on which the largest number or impression shall be printed for sale(³).

SECTION V.

Of the Registry of Books at Stationers' Hall.

In order to ascertain what books shall be from time to time published, it is by the fifth section enacted, that publishers shall enter them at Stationers' Hall, within *one calendar month* after the day on which they shall be first sold, published, advertised, or offered for sale within the *bills of mortality,* or within *three* calendar months for books published in any other part of the United Kingdom, and one copy on the best paper to be delivered for the use of the British Museum.

The payment for each entry in the register book of the Stationers' Company, is two shillings, and it may be inspected

(1) Section V. 54 Geo. III.   (2) Section II. Ib.   (3) Ib.

at all seasonable times on the payment of one shilling to the warehouse-keeper.

A certificate of the entry may also be obtained on paying one shilling.

The clause thus far referred to, is as follows:

V.   And in order to ascertain what books shall be from time to time published, be it enacted, that the publisher or publishers of any and every book demandable under this act, which shall be published at any time after the passing of this act, shall, within one calendar month after the day on which any such book or books respectively shall be first sold, published, advertised, or offered for sale, within the bills of mortality, or within three calendar months if the said book shall be sold, published, or advertised in any other part of the United Kingdom, enter the title to the copy of every such book, and the name or names and place of abode of the publisher or publishers thereof, in the register book of the Company of Stationers in London, in such manner as hath been usual with respect to books, the title whereof hath heretofore been entered in such register book, and deliver *one copy, on the best paper as aforesaid, for the use of the British Museum;* which register book shall at all times be kept at the hall of the said company; for every of which several entries the sum of two shillings shall be paid, and no more; which said register book may at all seasonable and convenient times be resorted to and inspected by any person; for which inspection the sum of one shilling shall be paid to the warehouse-keeper of the said Company of Stationers; and such warehouse-keeper shall, when and as often as thereto required, give a certificate under his hand of every or any such entry, and for every such certificate the sum of one shilling shall be paid.

SECTION VI.

Of the Duty of the Warehouse-keeper.

The sixth clause enacts, that the warehouse-keeper of the Company shall, without any greater interval than three months, transmit to the libraries correct lists of the books entered, and on request of the libraries call on the publishers for the copies to be demanded.

The wording of the clause is as follows:

VI.   And be it further enacted, that the said warehouse-keeper of the Company of Stationers shall from time to time, and at all times, without any greater interval than three months, transmit to the librarian or other person authorized on behalf of the libraries before mentioned, correct lists of all books entered in the books of the said company, and not contained in former lists; and that on being required so to do by the said librarians or other authorized person, or either of them, he shall call on the publisher or publishers of such books for as many of the said copies as may have been demanded of them.

SECTION VII.

Of the Penalties for non-registration.

In case the titles of books are not duly made in the Stationers' Registry within the period prescribed, the publisher is liable to forfeit five pounds, together with eleven times the price at which the book shall be sold or advertised, to be recovered, with full costs, by the party injured, in any Court of Record.

The words of the clause are the following :

And in case such entry of the title of any such book or books shall not be duly made by the publisher or publishers of any such book or books, within the said calendar month, or three months, as the case may be, then the publisher or publishers of such book or books shall forfeit the sum of five pounds, together with *eleven times the price* at which such book shall be sold or advertised, to be recovered, together with full costs of suit, by the person or persons, body politic or corporate, authorized to sue, and who shall first sue for the same, in any Court of Record in the United Kingdom, by action of debt, bill, plaint, or information, in which no wager of law, essoign, privilege, or protection, nor more than one imparlance, shall be allowed([1]).

SECTION VIII.

Of the Place of delivering the Books.

If any publisher be desirous of delivering the copies at the libraries entitled to them, he is authorized to do so under the 7th section, which is in the following terms :

VII. Provided always, and be it further enacted, that if any publisher shall be desirous of delivering the copy of such book or volume as aforesaid, as shall be demanded on behalf of any of the said libraries, at such library, it shall and may be lawful for him to deliver the same at such library, to the librarian or other person authorized to receive the same (who is hereby required to receive and to give a receipt in writing for the same) ; and such delivery shall, to all intents and purposes of this act, be held as equivalent to a delivery to the said warehouse-keeper.

SECTION IX.

Of the Penalties for non-delivery.

Publishers or the warehouse-keeper making default in not delivering or receiving the copies, are liable by the second section to forfeit the value of the printed copies, and five pounds for each copy not delivered, with full costs of

---

(1) Sec. V. 54 Geo. III. c. 156.

suit, to be recovered by the party injured, who is authorized to sue in any Court of Record.

The conclusion of this clause of the act is as follows :

And if any publisher, or the warehouse-keeper of the said Company of Stationers, shall not observe the directions of this act therein, that then he and they so making default in not delivering or receiving the said eleven printed copies as aforesaid, shall forfeit, besides the value of the said printed copies, the sum of five pounds for each copy not so delivered or received, together with the full costs of suit ; the same to be recovered by the - person or persons, or body politic or corporate, proprietors or managers of the library for the use whereof such copy or copies ought to have been delivered or received ; for which penalties and value such person or persons, body politic or corporate, is or are now hereby authorized to sue by action of debt or other proper action, in any Court of Record in the United Kingdom.

It is provided by the fifth section of this act, that no failure in making any entry, shall in any manner affect any copyright, but shall only subject the person making default to the penalty under the act.

For the other clauses of the act regarding the duration of copyright, we refer to the first part of this book(¹).

CHAP. II.

OF THE CONSTRUCTION OF THE ACT.

SECT. I.——*Of Works included in the Act.*

It does not appear that any case has been authentically reported since the passing of the act relating to its judicial construction, until the commencement of the present year.

The only previous occasion on which the claim of the public libraries was brought into litigation, was in the year 1812, when it was decided that the copies must be delivered, though the work should not have been entered at Stationers' Hall. This solitary decision, pronounced in the absence of one of the judges(²), we have fully stated in the first book(³).

In addition to which, it may be here observed, that the University of Cambridge claimed, in that case, to be entitled to a copy of the book on the *best paper ;* and it is stated in the margin of the report(⁴),

(1) Page 55, *ante.*   (2) Mr. Justice *Grose.*   (3) Vide page 55, *ante.*
(4) 16 East, 317. The Chancellor, Masters and Scholars of the University of *Cambridge v. Bryer.*

That the 8th Anne, c. 19, section 5, makes it necessary for the printer of a book, composed after the passing of the act, and published for the first time after the composition, which book is printed and published with the consent of the proprietor of the copyright, to deliver a copy, *upon the best paper*, to the warehouse-keeper of the Company of Stationers, for the use of the library of the University of Cambridge, notwithstanding the title to the copy of such book, and the consent of the proprietor to the publication, be not entered in the Register Book of the Company.

Though the *result* of the decision is thus quoted by the reporter, it does not appear that the quality of the paper was any where noticed in the judgment pronounced by the court.

The first section, however, of the 54th Geo. III. cap. 156, has set this question at rest. The clause in the statute of Anne, relating to the delivery of copies, is thereby expressly repealed, and in the second section the eleven copies are directed to be delivered "upon the paper on which the *largest number* or impression shall be printed for sale," with the single exception of the *British Museum*, which, under the third clause, is entitled to a copy on the *best paper* on which the work shall be printed ; and this National Institution seems to have been so far justly preferred to the other public libraries, that a copy is directed to be delivered at Stationers' Hall, at the time of the entry of the book, prior to the publication. The copies for the other libraries are not deliverable, unless demanded, within twelve months. If demanded, they must be supplied in the course of a month.

Maps and prints published without letter-press, are not liable to the tax ; but it seems that if the smallest imaginable quantity of letter-press should accompany the maps or prints, it will bring them within the range of this legislative method of encouraging literature and the fine arts, and entitle the libraries to sweep away eleven copies, maps, prints, letter-press and all !

<hr />

SECTION II.

Of Works not included in the Act.

Where the publication of a work in parts or numbers was commenced prior to the statute, and is still in progress, published at uncertain periods, it has been recently held, in a case between the *British Museum* and Messrs. Payne and Foss, the publishers, that the libraries are not entitled to the copies, either of the past or continuing numbers: the book being considered as one entire work, and part of it having been published before the act, and the remainder not yet completed, it is not comprised within the provisions of the statute.

The following is an account of the case referred to, as stated in a respectable periodical work:

The LORD CHIEF BARON of the Court of Exchequer lately pronounced judgment in an important literary question, The British Museum v. Payne and Foss, Booksellers and Publishers, which had been elaborately argued for some days in that court. The Trustees of the British Museum claimed a copy of a number of a splendid publication entitled *Flora Græca*, got up entirely by subscription, and no more copies printed than those subscribed for. The claim was resisted on the ground, that a publication for private circulation did not come under the operation of the act giving a copy of every work to the library of that national establishment. The court pronouncèd unanimously against the claim of the Trustees, *on the ground of its being only a portion of the work, and not a complete volume*(¹).

Since writing the above, we have obtained an authentic report of the judgment of the court, sitting in the Exchequer Chamber, on an appeal by way of writ of error, the substance of which it may be necessary to set forth.

The following is stated in the margin of the report, as the *result* of the case:

A *part* of a work *published at uncertain intervals*, of which thirty copies only were printed, twenty-six of which were subscribed for, the principal costs of publication being defrayed by funds devised by a testator for that purpose, is not a book demandable by the public libraries under the 54th Geo. III. c. 156.

It was contended on behalf of the publishers,

1st. That the work in question was not a work of profit within the contemplation of the act.

2nd. That the publication having been commenced originally before the act, it was not within the meaning of the clause for the infraction of which the penalty was sought to be recovered.

3rd. That this *fasciculus* was not a *book*, and need not therefore be entered at Stationers' Hall.

The judgment of the court seems to have proceeded on the last ground only, which is the one most general and advantageous to the interests of literature.

Lord Chief Baron ALEXANDER delivered the judgment of the court.—This was an action brought by the British Museum against the defendants in error, for penalties given

(1) Gent. Mag. Feb. 1828.

by the 54th Geo. III. c. 156, section 5, which act is for the encouragement of learning, and respects literary property. The fifth section of that statute requires that the publisher of every book demandable by force of it, shall enter the title of such book, with the name and residence of the publisher, at Stationers' Hall; and endeavours to enforce obedience to that requisition by imposing a penalty of five pounds, with eleven times the price of the book. The present action is brought for the recovery of those penalties.

The first count of the declaration avers, that the defendants in error were on the 10th of January, 1825, the publishers of, and did then publish, a certain book entitled *Flora Græca*. Then follows the title of the book, which it is not necessary for the purposes of this judgment to state. It avers the book to have been first published at the time mentioned at the price of £12. 12s. The count then avers it to be a book demandable by the act of 54th Geo. III., and charges the defendants with neglecting to enter the title to the copy of the book, and their names as publishers, at Stationers' Hall. There are many other counts in the declaration, but as the opinion of the court does not turn upon the form of the pleadings, it is not necessary to pursue the pleadings further. The defendants in error pleaded the general issue. Upon the trial a verdict was found in their favor, and upon that occasion a bill of exceptions was tendered to the learned judge who tried the cause.

The result of the evidence, as it appears from the bill of exceptions, is, that the publication in question is part of a considerable work, prepared by the late Doctor *Sibthorpe*, and by his will directed to be printed; that funds to a certain extent were by the same will given to carry on the undertaking; that some of the numbers were published before the act in question, that is, before July, 1814; that the defendants have of late years been the publishers; and that the number which is the foundation of this action is called No. 9, being the first part of the fifth volume.

In the view which this court takes of the question, these are the material facts. Mr. Justice Bayley, before whom the cause was tried, stated to the jury his opinion to be, that the defendants were publishers, within the true intent and meaning of the act, of the number called No. 9; but that this No. 9 was not a book demandable by force of the statute 54 Geo. III., and, therefore, that the evidence produced by the defendants was sufficient to bar the action. This opinion is excepted to by the plaintiffs in their bill of exceptions. It avers, that the No. 9 was a book demandable by virtue of the Act of Parliament, and whether it be or be not, is the question which this court is to decide upon the present occasion. Now, whether that which is confessedly not a book, nor even a volume, but a part only of a volume, be demandable, depends upon the second section of the act. This section, so far as it is necessary to state, enacts, " that eleven printed copies of the whole of *every book,* and of every *volume* thereof, and upon the paper upon which the largest number or impressions of *such book* shall be printed for sale, together with all maps and prints belonging thereto, which, *from and after the passing of this act,* shall be printed and published, on demand thereof being made in writing to, or left at the place of abode of, the publisher or publishers thereof, at any time within twelve months next after the publication thereof, under the hand of the warehouse-keeper of the Company of Stationers, or the librarian or other person authorized by the managers of libraries, shall be delivered by the publisher or publishers thereof respectively, within one month after demand made thereof in writing." By this provision, the thing required to be delivered on demand is the whole of every book, and of every volume thereof, and of which, the nonfeasance is made penal.

This Court is of opinion, with the learned judge who tried the cause, that the persons for whose benefit this provision was intended, have no right, by force of a provision so expressed, to demand from the publishers that which is *neither a book nor a volume,* but only a *part* of a volume. We are of opinion that we are to understand the legislature as having in this clause employed the words in their *common accepted sense,* and that we have no right, by a questionable subtilty, to extend the construction of the words beyond their usual and natural import.

No inference favorable to the plaintiffs, as it appears to us, can be collected from the fifth clause, on which this section is immediately founded, and which requires the entry. So for as it respects publications of this kind, it is general, and speaks of *book* or *books* only. And when the two clauses are combined, the act appears to mean that a volume would come within the word " book," but that a *fasciculus* cannot be said to be a volume.

We are, as I understand, all clearly of opinion, that this is not a periodical publication within the proviso which respects works of that description. The previous acts, the 8th Anne, 15th Geo. III., and 41st Geo. III., have been referred to as illustrating the clauses in question, and tending to sustain the view taken by the plaintiffs of this case. These acts have been looked into, and do not appear in any manner to warrant the construction contended for.

It has been asked, if this *fasciculus* is not demandable, nor required under a penalty to be entered, has the author any copyright in it? I answer, that is a different question, and whichever way it may be answered, would not rule that which is now before the court.

It has been also asked, if not now, will this *fasciculus* ever be demandable? I answer again, that question is properly left to be decided when it shall occur; but that, be that as it may, this No. 9, part of the fifth volume, was not demandable, nor required, upon the true construction of the statute, to be entered at the time when this action was brought.

We are all of opinion that there should be judgment for the defendants, and consequently the judgment will be affirmed(¹).

(1) 2 Younge and Jervis, 166.

THIRD PART.
OF PIRATING COPYRIGHT.

CHAP. 1.——OF PIRATING THE COPYRIGHT IN PRINTED BOOKS.

SECT. I.——*Of Original Works.*

It would, perhaps, be unreasonable to expect, that any full and precise definition should have been made of the extent to which a writer may lawfully quote or extract from the works of his predecessors. The courts have generally confined themselves to the decision of the mere point in litigation. The general principle, however, may be collected to be, that extracts made in a bona fide manner, are justifiable. According to some authorities, however, they must not be so extensive as to injure the sale of the original work, even though made with no intention to invade the previous author; nor must they be speciously or colorably adapted from the original into a form differing only in appearance and manner of composition.

The identity of a literary composition, says BLACKSTONE, consists entirely in the sentiment and the language. The same conceptions, clothed in the same words, must necessarily be the same composition : and whatever method be taken of exhibiting that composition to the ear or the eye of another, by recital, by writing, or by printing, in any number of copies or at any period of time, it is always the identical work of the author which is so exhibited(1).

Where labor, judgment, and learning, however, have been applied in adapting existing works into a new method, and the composition has been evidently made with a fair and honest intention to produce a new and improved work, it seems that the law will justify the publication, although the abridgment or compilation should injure the sale of the former works.

Lord ELDON, in the case of a *rival magazine,* protested against the argument that a man is not at liberty to do any thing which can affect the sale of another work of the same kind, and that because the sale was affected, therefore, there was an injury which the court was called upon to redress(2).

(1) 2 Comm. 405·
(2) Hogg v. Kirby, 8 Vesey, 221. For a further consideration of this point, vide the subsequent sections on *abridgments* and *compilations.*

In the case referred to, an injunction was granted against the defendant from publishing a number of the magazine in question, which was so printed as to appear a continuation of a work published by the plaintiff, and from selling any other publication as or being a continuation of the plaintiff's work or of the defendant's work, which had been published as such continuation.

The case was partly argued upon the ground of a breach of contract by the defendant, who had been the original publisher of the work of the plaintiff; but the court seemed to admit the general principle, that a person cannot publish a work professing to be, and handed out to the world as, the continuation of a work published by another. It was said in argument to have been determined, that property exists in a newspaper, and that an action lies for publishing under the same title.

In the course of his judgment the Lord Chancellor said, I do not see why, if a person collects an account of natural curiosities and such articles, and employs the labor of his mind in giving a description of them, that it is not as much a literary work as many others that are protected by injunction and by action. It is equally competent to any other person, perceiving the success of such a work, to set about a similar work, *bona fide* his own. But it must be in substance a new and original work, and must be handed out to the world as such.

My opinion is, that the defendant was at full liberty to publish a work really new. But the question is, whether he has not published this work, not as his own original work, but as a continuation of the work of another person.

Most of the cases have been, not where a new work has been published as part of the old work; but where, under color of a new work, the old work has been republished, and copies multiplied.

The question is, whether the regulating principle of these cases can be applied to this.

It is impossible not to say, (until it is better explained) an intention does appear both as to the transaction of the fifth number, and the other circumstances—in some degree upon the appearance of the outside, in a great degree upon the first page, the index, and the promised contents—to state this as a continuation of the former work, though in a new series.

The injunction, however, must operate upon nothing but the publication handed out to the world as the continuation of the plaintiff's work, and as to these numbers, the plaintiff shall bring his action:

I am anxious that nothing in the injunction shall imply that reviews, magazines, and other works of this species, may not be multiplied.

Of Notes and Additions.

Great talents, ingenuity, and judgment, (says Mr. Godson) are in general required to compose good notes or additions to the established work of an author of reputation([1]). To which may be added, that the annotator should possess great industry and habits of research, of arrangement or classification, and powers of analyzing and condensing the masses of new materials which recent times have produced. Hence it is justly said, when these notes or additions (brought down through a considerable lapse of time) are made on a book which is already in the power of any one to reprint, reason and justice say, that they ought to confer a copyright, as much as a separate and distinct work.

In the case of *Gray's Poems,* which had been for many years published, and were afterwards collected by Mr. Mason, and reprinted with tho *addition* of several new poems, though he had not a property in the whole book, yet the defendant having copied the whole, the Lord Chancellor, granted an injunction against him as to the publication with the additional pieces([2]).

So Lord HARDWICKE in another case([3]) granted an injunction to restrain the defendants from printing Milton's Paradise Lost, *with Dr. Newton's notes,* although there was no doubt that the original work, without the notes, might have been published.

The bill stated that the defendants had advertised to print Milton's Paradise Lost, with his life by Fenton, and the notes of all the former editions, of which Dr. Newton's was the last. The bill derived a title to the *poem* from the author's assignment in 1667. It was published about 1668, and it derived a title to his *life* by Fenton, published in 1727 ; and to *Bentley's* notes, published in 1732 ; and Dr. *Newton's* in 1749. The answer came in the 12th December, 1751, in which the defendants insisted they had a right to print their work in numbers, and to take in subscriptions.

It was intended to take the opinion of the court solemnly. The searches and affidavits which were thought necessary to be made occasioned a delay, and no motion was made till near the end of April, 1752.

The injunction was moved for on Thursday the 23rd of April. Lord Mansfield argued it. It was argued at large, upon the general ground of copyrights at common law.

---

(1) Godson, 242.   (2) Mason v. Murray, cited 1 East, 360.
(3) Tonson v. Walker, cited 4 Burr. 2325.

The LORD CHANCELLOR directed it to proceed on the Saturday following, and to be spoken to by one of a side. Afterwards it stood. over, by order, till Thursday, the 30th of April, when it was argued very diffusely.

The case could not possibly be varied at the hearing of the cause. The notes of the last edition (Dr. Newton's) were within the time of the act. But an injunction as to them only would have been of little avail ; and it did not follow that the defendants should not be permitted to print what they had a *right* to print, because they had attempted to print *more*. For in the case of Pope v. Curl, Lord Hardwicke injoined the defendant only from printing and selling the plaintiff's letters. There were a great many more in the book which the defendant had printed, which the plaintiff had no right to complain of. . If the inclination of Lord HARDWICKE's own opinion had not been strongly with the plaintiff, he never would have granted the injunction to the whole, and penned it in the disjunctive ; so that printing the poem, *or* the life, *or* Bentley's Notes, without a word of Dr. Newton's, would have been a breach of the order.

In Cary v. Longman, Lord KENYON said the plaintiff had no title to that part of his book which he had taken from the previous author ; yet it was as clear that he had a right to his own *additions and alterations,* many of which were very material and valuable, and the defendants were answerable at least for copying those parts in their book([1]).

Lord MANSFIELD, in another case, said, the question is, whether the *alteration* be colorable or not? There must be such a similitude as to make it probable and reasonable that one is a transcript of the other, and nothing more than a transcript. Upon any question of this nature, the jury will decide whether it be a servile imitation or not([1]).

SECTION III.

Of Abridgments.

An abridgment of a voluminous work, executed with skill and labor, in a bona fide manner, is not only lawful in itself, and exempt from the charge of piracy ; but is protected from invasion by subsequent writers. It seems, however, from the import of the word, as well as the reason and justice of the thing, that the abridgment should really be " an epitome of a large work contracted into a small compass."

A real and fair abridgment, said Lord HARDWICKE, may with great propriety be called a new book, because the invention, learning, and judgment of the author are shewn in it, and in many cases abridgments are extremely useful.

(1) 1 East, 360.   (2) Ib. 362.

The grounds of the decisions on this important subject, as reported in the law books, are not altogether consistent in principle. In some of them, it appears that the piracy occasioning, or obviously tending to, a *depreciation in the value* of the original work, is a fact on which much reliance has been placed in determining the question. In others, this circumstance has been altogether disregarded.

On the one hand it has been held, that a fair and bona fide *abridgment* of any book, is considered a new work; and however it may injure the sale of the original, yet it is not deemed a piracy or violation of the author's copyright([1]). On the other hand, in the case of the *Encyclopædia Londinensis,* in which a large part of a treatise on fencing was transcribed, though there might have been no intention to injure its sale, yet as it might serve as a substitute for the original work, and was sold at a much lower price, it was held actionable, and damages were recovered([2]).

There is, however, a clear distinction in the nature of these two cases, although the fact of *depreciation* might be in each the same. For the one was a case of *bona fide abridgment,* in which labor and judgment had been applied; and the other was a *wholesale compilation,* in which seventy-five pages were successively transcribed, without addition or alteration, and on which consequently no *skill or learning* had been bestowed, the exercise of which may be considered as the true criterion by which to determine the bona fide character of the abridgment or compilation([3]).

(1) Brown, C. R. 451. 2 Atk. 141.   (2) 1 Camp. 94.

(3) An abridgment, where the act of understanding is exercised in reducing the substance of a work into a small compass, by retrenching superfluities of language and circumstances, is a new work, useful and meritorious, and no violation of the author's property.

In the case of Mr. *Newbery's* Abridgment of Dr. *Hawkesworth's* Voyages, Lord Chancellor APSLEY, assisted by Mr. Justice BLACKSTONE, was of opinion, that to constitute a true and proper abridgment of a work, the whole must be preserved in its *sense,* and then the act of abridgment is an act of the understanding, employed in carrying a large work into a smaller compass, and rendering it less expensive, and more convenient both to the time and use of the reader, which made an abridgment in the nature of a new and meritorious work.

This had been done by Mr. Newbery, whose edition might be read in a *fourth part* of the time, and all the substance preserved and conveyed in language as good, or better, than in the original, and in a more agreeable and useful manner.

His Lordship had consulted Mr. Justice BLACKSTONE, whose knowledge and skill in his profession were universally known, and who, as an author himself, had done honor to his country. They had spent some hours together, and were agreed, that an abridgment, when the understanding is employed in retrenching unnecessary and uninteresting circumstances, which rather deaden the narration, is not an act of plagiarism upon the original work, nor against any property of the author in it, but an allowable and meritorious work : and that this abridgment of Mr. Newbery falls within these reasons and descriptions.—*Anon.* Lofft's Reports, 775. Mich. 1774.

The following cases and decisions will further elucidate the rules which govern this part of the subject.

The assigns of Dr. *Johnson* instituted a suit against the publisher of " The Grand Magazine of Magazines," for publishing *the Prince of Abyssinia,* a tale, which they had abridged, leaving out all the reflections.

The MASTER of the ROLLS observed, that the court had protected books which did not so well deserve it, as *Hoyle's Games of Whist,* &c.

The next question was, whether there had been any infringement of property ? It was said to be a piracy, and not a fair abridgment;—1st. From the quantity of it which was printed. 2nd. Because it was done in such a way as not to recommend the book, but the contrary; by printing only the narrative, and leaving out all the moral and useful reflections.

But, 1st., it does not appear that one tenth part of the first volume had been abstracted.

2nd. I cannot enter into goodness or badness of the abstract. It may serve the end of an advertisement. In general, it tends to the advantage of an author, if the composition be good ;—if it be not, it cannot be libelled. The plaintiffs had before published an abstract of the work in the London Chronicle, and therefore this work could not tend to their prejudice.

If I were to determine this to be elusory, I must hold every abridgment to be so(¹).

In the case of Gyles v. Wilcox (in 1740), a bill was filed to stay a book entitled *Modern Crown Law,* which it was alleged was colorable only, and borrowed from Sir Matthew Hale's Pleas of the Crown,---the repealed statutes being left out, and the Latin and French quotations translated into English.

Lord HARDWICKE said, where books are colorably shortened only, they are undoubtedly within the meaning of the Act of Parliament, and are a mere evasion of the statute, and cannot be called an abridgment.

But this must not be carried so far. If I should extend the rule to restrain all abridgments, it would be of mischievous consequences, for the books of the learned, *les Journals des Scavans,* and several others that might be mentioned, would be brought within the meaning of this Act of Parliament.

In the present case it is merely colorable, some words out of the

In *Bell v. Walker and Debrett,* regarding " Memoirs of the Life of Mrs. Bellamy," passages were read to shew that the facts, and even the terms in which they were related, were taken frequently *verbatim* from the original work.

The MASTER of the ROLLS said, if this were a fair *bona fide* abridgment of the larger work, several cases in that court had decided, that an injunction should not be granted; but he had heard sufficient read to entitle the plaintiff to an injunction until answer and further order.   1 Brown, C. R. 451.

(1) Dodsley v. Kinnersley, Amb. 403.

Historia Placitorum Coronæ are left out only, and translations given instead of the Latin and French quotations that are dispersed through Sir Matthew Hale's works ; yet not so flagrant as in the case of *Read v. Hodges,* for there they left out whole pages at a time([1]).

In a more recent case (in 1801), an injunction was applied for to restrain the defendant from selling a work entitled *An Abridgment of Cases argued and determined in the Courts of Law,* &c.

It was stated that the work was by no means a fair abridgment ; that, except in colorably leaving out some parts of the cases, such as the arguments of counsel, it was a mere copy *verbatim* of several of the reports of cases, and among them of the Term Reports, of which the plaintiff is proprietor ; comprising not a *few* cases only, but all the cases published in that work ; the chronological order of the original work being artfully changed to an alphabetical arrangement under heads and titles, to give it the appearance of a new work.

In support of the motion, *Bell v. Walker* was cited([1]).

LORD CHANCELLOR. I have looked at one or two cases, with which I am pretty well acquainted, and it appears to me an extremely illiberal publication.

An injunction was accordingly granted([2]).

SECTION IV.

Of Compilations.

It is difficult to define the exact limits to which a compiler is confined in his extracts or quotations from original authors, or from abridgments or previous compilations. In each case the peculiar circumstances attending it must be ascertained and considered.

A compilation, in a legal as well as a literary sense, is " a collection from various authors into one work ;" and as the law allows this to be done, and even establishes a copyright in the compilation itself, it evidently follows, that in the exercise of the right, very considerable latitude must be granted. It seems a necessary consequence of the legality of a compilation, that the law must also sanction its being done in a complete manner, and to effect this object, the quotations must generally be both full and numerous.

Yet reasonable bounds must be set to the extent of transcripts. If an article in a general compilation of literature and

-----

(1) 2 Atkyns, 141.

(2) Butterworth v. Robinson. 5 Vesey, 709. Yet a selection of what is material from a large body of Reports, commodiously arranged, whether alphabetical or systematic, seems an original work. Indeed the right is undisputed of selecting passages from books and reports (including entire judgments) in treatises on *particular* subjects. 2 *Evans' Coll. Stat.* 629.

science copies so much of a book, the copyright of which is vested in another person, as to serve as a substitute for it, though there may have been no intention to pirate it, or injure its sale,—this is a violation of literary property for which an action will lie to recover damages.

In the case of Roworth v. Wilkes, Lord ELLENBOROUGH said : This action is brought for prejudice to a work vested in the plaintiff, and the question is, whether the defendant's publication would serve as a substitute for it ? A *review* will not, in general, serve as a substitute for the book reviewed ; and even there, if so much be extracted that it communicates the same knowledge with the original work, it is an actionable violation of literary property. The intention to pirate is not necessary in an action of this sort ; it is enough that the publication complained of is in substance a copy, whereby a work vested in another is prejudiced. A compilation of this kind may differ from a treatise published by itself, but there must be certain limits fixed to its transcripts ; it must not be allowed to sweep up all modern works, or an *encyclopædia* would be a recipe for completely breaking down literary property. Here seventy-five pages have been transcribed out of one hundred and eighteen, and that which the plaintiff sold for half a guinea, may be bought of the defendant for eight-pence([1]).

In the case of Mr. Wilkins's *Antiquities of Magna Græcia,* an injunction was granted against " An Essay on the Doric Order of Architecture," in which various extracts from the former work had been made ; and an action directed to try whether the work was original, with a *fair use* of the other by *quotation and compilation,* which in a considerable degree was admitted.

The LORD CHANCELLOR said, there is no doubt that a man cannot, under the pretence of quotation, publish either the whole or part of another's work, though he may use, what is in all cases very difficult to define, *fair quotation.*

Upon inspection of the different works, I observe a considerable proportion taken from the plaintiff's, that is *acknowledged;* but also much that is *not;* and in determining whether the former is within the doctrine upon this subject, the case must be considered as also presenting the latter circumstance. The question upon the whole is, whether this is a legitimate use of the plaintiff's publication in the fair exercise of a mental operation, deserving the character of an original work([2]).

It was urged in one of the cases by *Sir Samuel Romilly,* that in a work consisting of a selection from various authors, two men might make the same selection ; but, said the LORD CHANCELLOR, that selection must be made by resorting to the original authors, not by taking advantage of the selection already made by another([3]).

(1) 1 Camp. 98.   (2) Wilkins v. Aikin, 17 Vesey, 422.   (3) 16 Vesey, 271.

In Trusler v. Murray, which was an action for pirating a *Book of Chronology*, it was proved, that though some parts of the defendant's work were different, yet in general it was the same, and particularly it was a literal copy, for not less than fourteen pages in succession.

Lord KENYON was of opinion, that if such were the fact, the plaintiff must recover, though other parts of the work were original. He referred to the publication of some original poems by Mr. Mason, together with others which had been before published. And the like with respect to an abridgment of *Cook's Voyage* round the World. The main question here was, whether in substance the one work is a copy and imitation of the other, for undoubtedly in a chronological work the same facts must be related. The parties having received his Lordship's opinion, it was agreed to refer the consideration of the two books to an arbitrator, who would have leisure to compare them(¹).

Though copyright cannot subsist in an *East India Calendar*, as a general subject, any more than in a map, chart, &c. it may in the individual work; and where it can be traced that another work upon the same subject is---not original compilation, but a mere copy with colorable variations, the former will be protected by injunction.

Lord Chancellor ERSKINE said, if a man by his station having access to the repositories in the India House, has by considerable expense and labor procured with correctness all the names and appointments on the Indian Establishment, he has a copyright in that individual work. I have compared the books, and find, that in a long list of casualties, removals, and deaths, there is not the least variation, even as to the situation in the page. I am bound to continue the injunction(²).

In the case of the *Imperial Calendar*, in which a motion was made to dissolve an injunction,

The LORD CHANCELLOR said, the question before me is, whether it is not perfectly clear that in a vast proportion of the work of the defendant, no other labor had been applied than copying the plaintiff's work. From the identity of the inaccuracies, he said, it was impossible to deny that the one was copied from the other *verbatim et literatim*. To the extent, therefore, in which the defendant's publication has been supplied from the other work, the injunction must go; but I have said nothing that has a tendency to prevent any person from giving to the public a work of this kind, if it be the fair fruit of original labor, the subject being open to all the world; but if it be a mere copy of an original work, this court will interpose against that invasion of copyright(³).

In King v. Read, the plaintiff had published a work

(1) 1 East, 363.   (2) 12 Vesey, 276.
(3) Longman v. Winchester, 16 Vesey, 269.

entitled *Tables of Interest*, giving calculations for one hundred days, which was extended by a second part to one hundred and eighty-four days. The defendant afterwards published a work under a similar title, but upon a more extensive plan, containing calculations for every day of the year.

The plaintiff moved for an injunction, alleging, that though the plaintiff could not claim any copyright in the calculations which had been previously published, nor in those which went beyond his calculation, yet he was entitled to restrain the intermediate calculations ; that as to these, the piracy was evident from the circumstance that errors were followed which could not be the effect of miscalculation ; for instance, an error to the amount of ten shillings, in a column of sums increasing regularly by very small fractions; and that copyright must exist in such a work upon the same principle that protects books of logarithms and calculations for the purpose of navigation.

For the defendant it was insisted, that a particular subject cannot be occupied'; that his work was produced by original calculation ; that the calculation for the extended period would be useless unless commencing with the beginning of the year ; and supposing both calculations accurate, the results for the same period must be the same, as in the cases of maps and surveys.

The LORD CHANCELLOR directed the plaintiff to bring an action([1]).

In Cary v. Faden([2]), the plaintiff published a *Book of Roads* of Great Britain, comprising Patterson's book, to the copyright of which the plaintiff was not entitled, with improvements and additions, made by actual survey and otherwise.

The LORD CHANCELLOR said, upon my inspection they are very different works. Patterson's is the original work. Corrections, improvements, and alterations have been made upon that from time to time. The plaintiff has taken a different line, having had a survey made for that purpose, to which he is very well entitled. He has made a very good map, with which it is very pleasant to travel. I think it is fair they should try their weight with the public. But what right had the plaintiff to the original work ? If I was to do strict justice, I should order the defendants to take out of their book all they have taken from the plaintiff, and reciprocally the plaintiff to take out of his all he has taken from Patterson.

In another case of a *Book of Roads*, Lord KENYON, in addition to the remarks already quoted([3]), said,

That the defendants had pirated from the plaintiff's book, was proved in the clearest manner at the trial. Nine tenths at least of the alterations and additions were copied verbatim. The printed work itself was made use of by the defendants at the press, some of it clipped with scissars, with a few slips of paper containing MS. additions inter-

(1) 8 Vesey, 223.   (2) 5 Vesey, 24.   (3) page 129 *ante*.

spersed here and there, and some of these merely nominal and color-able. The Courts of Justice (said his Lordship) have been long laboring under an error, if an author have no copyright in any part of a work, unless he have an exclusive right to the whole book.

Of Translations.

On the same principle which governs abridgments and compilations, that they constitute a species of new work, produced by *the labor and abilities of the writer*, it appears that TRANSLATIONS are also within the scope of the legislative provisions, and are protected for the same period of time.

In the case already referred to, a translation was distinguished from a reprinting of the original work, on account of the translator having bestowed his care and pains upon it[1]; but the decision on that occasion turned on another point, namely, the immortality of the book.

The LORD CHANCELLOR, in the case of Wyatt v. Barnard[2], observed, that translations, if original, whether written by the plaintiff, made at his expense, or given to him, were protected like other works by the statutes.

The plaintiff in the latter case was the proprietor of a periodical work called "The Repository of Arts, Manufactures, and Agriculture." He claimed the sole copyright of the work, containing, amongst other articles, translations from the foreign languages. The defendants were publishers of another periodical work, which contained various articles copied or contracted from the plaintiff's work, without his consent, being translations from the *French* and *German* languages, &c.

The defendants, by their affidavit, stated the usual practice among publishers of magazines and monthly publications, to take from each other articles, translated from foreign languages, or become public property, as having appeared in other works.

They relied on the custom of the trade, and contended, that neither of the works was original composition, both being mere compilations; that it was never decided that a translator has a copyright in his translation, supposing (what was not proved) that these translations were made by the plaintiff himself.

The LORD CHANCELLOR said, the custom among booksellers could not control the law.

An affidavit was afterwards produced, stating, that all the articles were translated by a person employed and paid by the plaintiff, and were translated from foreign books, imported by the plaintiff at considerable expense. Upon that affidavit an order was pronounced for an injunction[3].

(1) Burnett v. Chetwood, see page 89, *ante*.   (2) 3 Ves. and B. 77.
(3) See also Longman v. Winchester, 16 Vesey, 269. Wilkins v. Aikin, 17 Ves. 422.

CHAP. II.

OF PIRATING COPYRIGHT IN MANUSCRIPTS.

SECT. I. ——*Of unpublished Manuscripts in general.*

Manuscripts were always protected by the common law as the property of the author, and are also comprised in the provisions made by the legislature.

In the case of Donaldson v. Beckett, the first question put to the judges was,

Whether at common law the author of any literary composition had the sole first right of printing and publishing the same for sale, and could bring an action against any person for publishing the same without his consent?

Mr. Baron EYRE held, that "the *thinking faculty* being common to all, should likewise be held common, and no more be deemed subject to exclusive appropriation than any other of the common gifts of nature. I am, therefore, said he, clearly of opinion, as to the first question, that at common law the author of a literary composition hath *no* right of printing and publishing the same for sale."

The reason given for this conclusion is evidently falacious : no author claims a property in "the thinking faculty"—he claims the *fruits* of the labor of his own mind only.

Not less than *eleven* of the judges of the land (including those who decided against some of the claims of authors) were clearly of opinion, that by the common law the author of any literary composition had the sole right of printing and publishing the same for sale, and might bring an action against any person for publishing it without his consent.

The following extracts are made in their own language, and shew the unanimity of these learned personages on this interesting point of literary property.

Nares, J. It is admitted on all hands that an author has a beneficial interest in his own manuscript.

Ashurst, J. If a man lends his manuscript to a friend, and his friend prints it, or if he loses it, and the finder prints it, an action would lie.

Yates, J. Admitted this doctrine.

Blackstone, J. When a man, by the exertion of his rational powers, has produced an original work, he has clearly a right to dispose of it as he pleases.

Willes, J. I declare it as my opinion, that an author hath an indisputable power and dominion over his manuscript.

Aston. J. An author hath a natural right to the produce of his mental labor.

Perrot, B.   An author certainly hath a right to his manuscript; he may line his trunk with it, or he may print it.

Gould, J.   I agree that an author hath a right at common law to his manuscript.

Smyth, L. C. B.   The cases prove, and it is allowed, that literary property *is property* previous to publication.

De Grey, L. C. J.   There can be no doubt that an author has the sole right to dispose of his manuscript as he thinks proper.

Lord Mansfield.   It is just that an author should reap the pecuniary profits of his own ingenuity and labor.

There are several early cases in which the Court of Chancery restrained the printing and publishing of the manuscript works of authors without their consent.

One of these was that of Mr. Webb, who had his *Precedents of Conveyancing* stolen out of his chambers and printed. Another instance was that of Mr. Forester, whose *notes* had been copied by a clerk to the gentleman to whom he had lent them, and which were printed. In both cases the parties were prohibited from printing and publishing the works.

According to a recent decision of the Court of *King's Bench*, the 54th Geo. III. c. 156, does not impose upon authors, as a condition precedent to their deriving any benefit under the act, that the composition should be *first printed;* and therefore an author does not lose his copyright by selling his work in manuscript before it is printed.

Thus in the case of *White v. Geroch,* it appeared that the plaintiff was the author of a musical composition, of which he had sold several thousand copies whilst in manuscript, a year before it was printed. Upon this it was objected, that by the previous sale in manuscript, the plaintiff had lost the benefit conferred by the statute.

On the trial of the cause, Mr. Justice BAYLEY directed the jury to find a verdict for the plaintiff, with liberty for the defendant to move to enter a non-suit. And subsequently, on a motion being made for that purpose,

ABBOTT, C. J. said the object of the legislature was to confer upon authors, by the act in question, a more durable interest in their compositions than they had before. I am of opinion that the author does not lose his copyright by having first sold the composition in manuscript, for the statute 54th Geo. III. c. 156, must be construed with reference to the 8th Anne, c. 19, which it recites, and which, together with the 41st Geo. III. c. 107, were all made in pari materia for the purpose of enlarging the rights of authors. The 8th Anne, c. 19, gave to authors a copyright in works, not only composed and printed, but composed and *not printed;* and I think that it was not the intention of the legislature either to abridge authors of any of their former rights, or to impose upon them as a condition precedent, that they should not sell their compositions in manuscript before they were printed([1]).

The *Court of Chancery*, also, has lately exercised its power by restraining the use of manuscripts surreptitiously obtained.

Thus in the case of *Stephens* and *Sherwood* (Michaelmas Term, 1826). Mr. *Horne* applied for an injunction to restrain the publication of a work, which the defendant Stephens claimed as his property. His client, the plaintiff, was a Mr. Sherwood, a Parliamentary Agent, who, in the course of his business, had made various observations and notes, which he had observed in the passing of private bills through the Houses of Parliament. His clerk, *Thomas Ebbes*, who had access to these MSS. purloined large portions of them, together with many of Mr. Sherwood's opinions upon practice, &c., and published them, with certain trifling and colorable alterations, in a work entitled "Practical Instructions upon passing Private Bills through Parliament, by a Parliamentary Agent." Mr. Sherwood afterwards determined to publish a book upon the subject himself, for which purpose he wrote many notes and observations, which *Ebbes* also transcribed for the purpose of a second edition of his own work. Ebbes published his second edition, but sold the copyright to Mr. Butterworth. Stephens moved for and obtained an injunction against Butterworth. It was established by that injunction, that for all purposes of publication the first and second editions were the same.

Mr. Wright for the defendant said, he had nothing to do with Ebbes. He had only to shew that Sherwood was not entitled to the book. Ebbes might have learned all that it contained from his practice as a clerk. Sherwood's observations were not original. Three parts of the book consisted of rules and orders. There was also a book on the same subject by Mr. Ellis, in which he had no doubt he should find the source of most of Sherwood's observations. Sherwood had allowed twenty months to elapse before he applied for the injunction.

Mr. HORNE said, Stephens had published the book on condition that Ebbes should receive half the profits.

The LORD CHANCELLOR. If that fact had been stated in the case where Stephens, Ebbes, and Butterworth were concerned, there would have been no ground for the injunction. When the motion for an injunction against Mr. Butterworth was made, it stated that Stephens gave Ebbes seventy pounds for the copyright of the work, and he therefore thought that there could never be a clearer case in which an injunction might be granted. The fact, however, that Ebbes was to divide the profits with Stephens, introduced an entirely new feature into the case; and although during the present motion he was strongly impressed with the idea, that by permitting twenty months to expire, the plaintiff had abandoned his right, yet he was so impressed under the supposition that the work had been purchased by Stephens. All objections, however, were removed by the proof of this compact respecting the work between Ebbes and Stephens. The injunction must be granted.

(1) 2 Barn. and Ald, 293.

SECTION II.

Of the Manuscripts of Deceased Persons.

The manuscripts of the deceased seem in some respects to be placed on a different footing from the manuscripts of the living. The distinction has been pointed out by *Sir William D. Evans.*

During the life of a writer, the publication (he observes) may be deemed a *personal injury;* but after his death, several material questions may arise with respect to the claim of his representatives. It is taken for granted in Millar v. Taylor, that the injunctions were founded upon clear *property.* Now an executor can only bring an action on the case for some *damage* which reduces the assets, and to the extent of which assets he is accountable. But the right to prevent any person having a manuscript of the deceased, from publishing it, is no " property," which can constitute part of the *assets,* in respect of which alone he represents the deceased. The same observation will in some degree apply to the heir. Besides which, this kind of property is nowise analogous to any hereditament recognized by the law. The interpositions appear to be on behalf of the family of the writer. But it seems a legal anomaly to take notice of the family of a deceased person in any other manner than as connected with the property which constitutes real or personal assets.

The Court of Chancery, however, exercises its authority in restraining the publication of manuscripts of persons deceased. In the case of the Duke of Queensbury v. Shebbeare, before Lord Hardwicke([1]), an injunction was granted against printing the second part of *Lord Clarendon's History.*

Lord Clarendon, it was stated, let Mr. Francis Gwynn have a copy of his history. His son and representative insisted he had a right to print and publish it. The court was of opinion that Mr. Francis Gwynn might have every use of it, *except the profit of multiplying in print.* It was to be presumed (as Mr. Justice WILLES observed) that Lord Clarendon never intended that extent of permission when he gave him the copy. The injunction was acquiesced under, and Dr. Shebbeare recovered before Lord Mansfield a large sum against Mr. Gwynn for representing that he had a right to print. Mr. Justice WILLES adduces this case as an argument for the general right of literary property, in which he is followed by Lord Mansfield, who observes, that Mr. Gwynn was entitled undoubtedly to the paper of the transcript of Lord Clarendon's History, which gave him the power to print and publish it after the fire at Petersham, which destroyed one original. That copy might have been the only manuscript of it in being. Mr. Gwynn

(1) Cited in Millar v. Taylor, 4 Burr. 2330.

might have thrown it into the fire had he pleased. But at the distance of near a hundred years, the *copy* was adjudged the property of Lord Clarendon's representatives, and Mr. Gwynn's printing and publishing it without their consent, was adjudged an injury to that property, for which, in different shapes, he paid very dear([1]).

SECTION III.

Of Private Letters, Literary and General.

There is a material distinction between *literary* and *general* letters---the former being protected as the subject of copyright, whilst the publication of the latter is restrained on the ground only of *breach of contract* or *confidence*, or when they tend to the injury of private *character*, or are calculated to wound private *feelings*.

The earliest case on this subject is that of Pope v. Curl (in 1741), in which a motion was made to dissolve an injunction obtained by Mr. *Pope* against the bookseller, for vending a book called " Letters from Swift, Pope, and others."

Lord HARDWICKE. I think it would be extremely mischievous to make a distinction between a book of *letters*, which comes out into the world either by the permission of the writer or receiver of them, and *any other learned work*.

The same objection may hold against *sermons*, which the author may never intend should be published, but are collected from loose papers, and brought out after his death.

It has been objected, that where a man writes a letter, it is in the nature of a gift to the receiver.

But I am of opinion it is only a special property in the receiver ; possibly the property in the paper may belong to him ; but this does not give a licence to any person whatsoever to publish them to the world, for at most the receiver has only a joint property with the writer.

It has also been insisted on, that this is a sort of work which does not come within the meaning of the Act of Parliament, because it contains only letters on familiar subjects, and inquiries after the health of friends, and cannot properly be called a learned work.

But it is certain that no works have done more service to mankind, than those which have appeared in this shape upon familiar subjects, and which perhaps were never intended to be published; and it is this makes them so valuable, for I must confess for my own part, that letters which are very elaborately written, and originally intended for the press, are generally the most insignificant, and very little worth any person's reading.

The injunction, however, was continued by the Lord

---

(1) Millar v. Taylor, *per Lord Mansfield.*

Chancellor only as to those letters which are under Mr. Pope's name in the book, and which are written *by him,* and not as to those which are written *to him*(¹).

In the case of *Lord Chesterfield's* Letters, an injunction was obtained till the hearing by his Lordship's executors against the widow of Mr. Stanhope.

Lord APSLEY, according to the report, recommended it to the executors to permit the publication, in case they saw no objection to the work upon reading it, and having copies delivered to them(²). It is said, that by the register's book it does not appear that an injunction was actually granted(³). It is well known that the publication did appear, but whether upon the judgment of the executors, that they saw no objection to the work, or upon what other ground, we are not informed.

In the case of the Earl of Granard v. Dunlein(⁴), the executors of Lady Tyrawley obtained an injunction in the first instance against the defendant publishing *Letters to Lady Tyrawley* from different correspondents, and which he had got possession of by being permitted to reside in her house, and continuing to do so after her death.

Another case of private letters was heard by the Lord Chancellor in private, in which an injunction was granted, restraining the publication of *Letters from an Old Lady,* of a nature that made it very important to prevent the publication; but the defendant in that case, as stated by the Vice Chancellor in his judgment, had received a sum of money not to publish the letters, and the attempt to publish them was therefore a *violation of contract*(⁵).

In the case of the late *Dr. Paley,* who left certain manuscripts to be given to his own parishioners only, a bookseller, having obtained possession of them, was restrained from publishing(⁶).

But this principle does not extend to letters which are not of a literary kind. Thus in the case of Lord and Lady Percival v. Phipps and Mitford, it was stated by the bill, that *Lady Percival* had written to the defendant Mitford several letters of a private nature, upon the confidence that he would not part with them, or communicate the contents to any person, nor publish, or permit them to be published;---that Mitford had communicated them to Phipps, who had published one, and announced an intention to publish others, and on these facts an injunction was prayed. On the other hand, Phipps by his answer stated, that Mitford was confidentially employed by

(1) 2 Atk. 342.   (2) Ambler, 737.
(3) 2 Ves. and B. 21.   (4) 1 Ball and B. 207.
(5) ——— v. Eaton, 13th April, 1813. 1 Ves. and B. 27.
(6) Cited 2 Ves. and B. 23.

Lady Percival to publish authentic information relative to a subject which very much engaged the public attention,---that Phipps desired Mitford to offer his newspaper as a channel for communicating such information. This offer, it was alleged, was accepted, and the letter in question delivered to the defendant for publication, and various paragraphs were also delivered from time to time for the same purpose. Subsequently, a statement was inserted in the *News*, (which was the title of the paper) conveying intelligence as communicated by Lady Percival, which it appeared was false, and which was disavowed by her. The letters in question were written to Mitford upon similar subjects, materially tending to shew that the intelligence did come from Lady Percival, and that as she had denied being privy to the former publication, the character of Phipps, and the value of his paper, were in danger of falling into discredit with the public.

The VICE CHANCELLOR.—An injunction, restraining the publication of private letters, must stand upon this foundation, that letters, whether of a private nature, or upon general subjects, may be considered as the subject of *literary property;* and it is difficult to conceive in the abstract, that they may not be so. A very instructive and useful work may be put into that shape, as an inviting mode of publication.

Admitting, however, that private letters may have the character of literary composition, the application of that as an universal rule, extending to every letter which any person writes upon any subject, appears to me to go a great way; including all mercantile letters, all letters passing between individuals, not only upon business, but on every subject that can occur in the intercourse of private life. If in every such instance the publication may upon this doctrine be restrained, as a violation of literary property, whatever may be the intention, the effect must frequently be to deprive an individual of his defence by proving agency, orders for goods, the truth of his assertion, or any other fact, in the proof of which, letters may form the chief ingredient.

" This is the naked case of a bill to prevent the publication of private letters, not stating the nature, subject, or occasion of them, or that they were intended to be sold as a literary work for profit, or are of any value to the plaintiff. Upon such a case, it is not necessary to determine the general question, how far a Court of Equity will interfere to protect the interest of the author of private letters. The interposition of the court in this instance is not a consequence from the cases that were cited; upon which I shall merely observe, that though the form of familiar letters might not prevent their approaching the character of a literary work, every private letter upon any subject to any person, is not to be described as a literary work, to be protected upon the principle of copyright. The ordinary use of correspondence by letters, is to carry on the intercourse of life between persons at a distance from each other, in the prosecution of commercial or other business, which it would be very extraordinary to describe as a literary work, in which the writers have a copyright. Another class is the correspondence between friends or relations upon their private concerns, and it is not necessary here to determine how far such letters, falling into the hands of executors, assignees of bankrupts, &c. could be made public in a way that must frequently be very injurious to the feelings of individuals. I do not mean to say that would afford a ground for a Court of Equity to interpose to prevent a breach of that sort of confidence, independent of contract and property."

Although there may be a joint property in letters of correspondence between the sender and receiver, it does not seem, by any means necessarily to follow that one of several *joint owners in a literary composition* may not exercise the right of publication. Supposing different persons to be possessed of manuscript copies of a given composition, in which no other has a paramount claim to restrain the publication, it cannot be supposed that any of them individually could prevent the publication by the others(').

SECTION IV.

Of Written Lectures.

The means of diffusing knowledge, and the modes of instruction, vary at different periods of society. It is observable that of late years the custom has increased of communicating information by public lectures, and it seems fitting, therefore, in a work devoted to the examination of the laws relating to the protection of the fruits of intellectual labor, that a proportionate degree of attention should be paid to the questions which may arise out of the respective rights of lecturers and pupils, as well as the public generally. We shall, therefore, avail ourselves of the elaborate judgments which from time to time were delivered by the late LORD CHANCELLOR in the celebrated litigation between *Mr. Abernethy* and the proprietors of *The Lancet*, in which all the questions suggested at that time were minutely and fully considered, and which his lordship enumerated as follow :

The first question is, whether an oral lecture is within the protection of the law? Now, as far as my recollection goes, that has not yet been the subject of determination. On the other hand, if there be a lecture apparently oral, but which is nevertheless delivered by the assistance of a very good memory from a written composition,

(1) 2 Evans's Coll. Stat. 625.

the question then will be, if it could not be made out in point of law that an oral lecture or an oral sermon was within the protection of the law, whether protection is due to the written composition? Another question will be, whether this court would interfere before notice had been given that that apparently oral lecture was the delivery of matter from a written composition? And a farther question will be, whether if the oral lecture is to be protected by the fact that it is, in truth, the delivery of a written composition, it does not lie on those who insist that that circumstance gives the protection of the law to that which appears to be orally delivered, to produce and shew that written composition, in order to make out their case.

We shall take the liberty of separating the luminous judgment of his lordship into two parts---the 1st, on the copyright in lectures which were either *read* from a written composition, or delivered from the *recollection* of it; the 2nd, on the copyright in lectures *orally* delivered, of which no manuscript existed.

First, then, of *written* lectures.

Where the court is called upon to restrain a publication on the ground that it is a piracy of a composition which has been substantially reduced into writing, it is the duty of the court to see that the plaintiff produces his written composition.

The LORD CHANCELLOR.—The very early part of this case turned entirely upon the question of property; and indeed it can be viewed only in two ways---either as a question of *property*, or a question of *trust*. In the first place, I have nothing to do with all the considerations that have been pressed on me with respect to the benefit which the public may receive from the publication, even of such lectures as those which so distinguished a man as Mr. Abernethy might publish, or other persons might publish for him; and in the next place, I have nothing to do with the moral question of how far the editor of this work has righteously possessed himself of the means of publishing it. When I say with the moral question, I mean to qualify the expression; because if I can collect that those means have been obtained either by a *breach of trust*, or by *fraud*, this court *will* have something to do with it.

In the present case, Mr. Solicitor General has viewed it, with respect to its connection with writing, in these two ways. He says, that Mr. Abernethy has a composition which one would call a copy or a writing, and which contains the whole of what this defendant has published. And then he says, if he have not such a copy, yet he delivered it AS *from writing*; and, therefore, he must be understood as having some notes, which were to suggest to him from time to time what sentiments to deliver orally to the persons who attended his lectures.

Now with respect to either of those views of the case, I apprehend when this court is called on to enforce a legal right, by giving a remedy beyond that which the law gives, it is the bounden duty of this

L

court, be the case what it may, to see that the plaintiff *produce his written composition,* and therefore, if this case be to be put at all on the right which Mr. Abernethy is supposed to derive from his having a full and correct copy; there must be an original, or a writing which contains all that has been published in this book, or he must have a writing which is such in its nature as that, coupled with what he orally delivered, it may be taken that he has *substantially* a written composition as well as that which he delivered orally. When this court is called on to give a remedy beyond the remedy which the law gives to persons who have a legal right, *the court must know what it is proceeding on*; and if the case be put on this ground, either that there is a writing of one character or a writing of another character, *that writing must be produced,* so that the court may know what it is doing. If that writing be not produced, I must then look at the motion as an application made to me merely on the ground of an oral publication ; and then the question of property will arise, coupled as it may be with the doctrine of *trust* and with the *doctrine of fraud*([1]).

It is said that Mr. Abernethy is not to be looked on as holding the same character with reference to a subject of this kind as a clergyman of the church, or a professor in a University; for as I understand the affidavit which has been filed on the part of the defendant, Mr. Abernethy is represented, not only as a surgeon, but as a person *appointed* by the governors and guardians of this hospital to give lectures :---" and this deponent saith" (such is the language of the affidavit) " that the surgeons and lecturers for the time being of such hospital, are appointed by the governors of the said hospital."

Now if a professor be appointed, he is appointed for the purpose of giving information to all the students who attend him, and it is his duty to do that ; but I have never yet heard that any body could publish his lectures ; nor can I conceive on what ground Sir William *Blackstone* had the copyright in his lectures for twenty years, if there had been such a right as that ; we used to take notes at his lectures ; at Sir Robert *Chambers's* lectures also the students used to take notes ; but it never was understood that those lectures could be published ;--- and so with respect to any other lectures in the University, it was the duty of certain persons to give those lectures ; but it never was understood, that the lectures were capable of being published by any of the persons who heard them([2]).

SECTION V.

Of Oral Lectures.

An injunction will not be granted to restrain an alleged piracy of lectures delivered *orally,* when no written composition substantially the same with these lectures is produced.

---

(1) On these points see the next section.   (2) 3 Law Journal, 209.

But persons attending an oral lecture have no right to publish it for profit.

An action upon the implied contract will lie against a pupil attending an oral lecture, who caused it to be published for profit.

The court will grant an injunction against third persons publishing lectures orally delivered, who must have procured the means of publishing those lectures from persons who attended the oral delivery of them, and were bound by the implied contract(¹).

The Lord CHANCELLOR, in delivering his judgment in the case in which the preceding doctrine was held, commenced his observations as follows :

With regard to the question of literary property, I have no right to interfere by injunction, unless I have a very strong opinion that the legal right is with the plaintiff. Now looking at all that has passed with respect to literary property, and particularly with respect to the case of *Millar v. Taylor*, which was first before the Court of King's Bench, and afterwards before the House of Lords (though there was a vast deal of argument on the question of what sort of property a man may have in his unpublished ideas or sentiments, or the language which he uses), yet I do not recollect in the course of those proceedings (particularly in the House of Lords) that any question was put to the judges that did not adapt itself to the case of *a book* or *a literary composition* ; for of the questions which were there put to the judges, the first was, " whether at common law an author of any book or literary composition had the sole right of first printing and publishing the same for sale, and might bring an action against any person who printed, published, and sold the same without his consent ?" The next question was, " if the author had such a right originally, did the law take it away upon his printing and publishing such book or literary composition, and might any person afterwards reprint and sell for his own benefit such book or literary composition against the will of the author ?" The third question was, " if such an action would have lain at common law, was it taken away by the statute of Anne, and was an author by that statute precluded from any remedy except on the foundation of the statute, and on the terms and conditions prescribed thereby ?"

On these questions the judges of the land differed. On the first question, one of them was of opinion that at common law an author of any book or literary composition had not the sole right of first printing and publishing the same for sale, and that he could not bring an action against any person who printed, published, and sold the same, unless such person had obtained the copyright by fraud or by violence. So that although this judge was of opinion that at law the author was not the party who had the sole right of first printing

---

(1) Abernethy v. Hutchison, Knight and Lacey.

and publishing a composition for sale, yet he was also of opinion, that to give him a right of action against those who first printed and published the same for sale, it was necessary to shew, in order to maintain an action, that the person who had first printed and published had gotten it either by *violence or fraud.*

Now if, said his Lordship, it can be made out, as matter of contract between Mr. Abernethy and those who attend his lectures, that they should *not* be at liberty to print or publish the same, I should say then, that supposing notes of all that he delivered in his lectures to be taken, and supposing it to be a proper thing for the use of the students that that should be done, yet I never would permit a third person to make use of the delivery of those notes to that third person, for the purpose of doing that which the person delivering those notes would not himself be permitted to do. I should call that, in the sense in which a court of equity uses the word, *a gross fraud.*

If this injunction be applied for, not on what was done in *Millar v. Taylor,* but on the reasoning to be found in that case, it becomes a judge in equity to look about him before he ventures to decide the legal question. That legal question, in the shape in which it is now put, namely, with respect to an oral delivery of ideas and sentiments, has occasioned much abstruse learning ; and as in the case which I have alluded to, the judges of the land in the first instance, and the House of Lords in the last instance, avoided giving any opinion upon it when it was discussed ; certainly it becomes me to know what opinion a court of law would give in such a case as this, before I grant the injunction in unqualified terms.

There is another difficulty which belongs to a case of this kind, even supposing that there is the right which is contended for—I mean the difficulty there must be nine times out of ten in sustaining an action for want of proof; for if a lecture be published which has been delivered orally, and that can form the subject of an action, how is it possible, unless the court is to be satisfied with something like the substance of what was said, to prove that the printed publication was parcel of the oral publication. In this case, however, there is no difficulty on that point, which is another reason perhaps that ought to induce the court to be a little cautious in what determination it comes to. Because this editor has, in the most distinct manner, admitted in his publication—and what is admitted in his publication must be taken in this court to be true against himself---he has admitted in the publication that what he has published was orally delivered by Mr. Abernethy. The difficulty of proof, therefore, to which I have alluded, is not found to exist in this case.

At the same time *it is one thing to contend that it has not been established that a person who orally delivers lectures, has that species of property in them which may enable him to bring an action,* and after having succeeded in the action, to apply for an injunction here, either with or without an account to be kept in the mean time of the profits of the work ; and *it is another thing to say, that a person who has possessed himself of the means* of publishing what another has delivered in lectures, which are afterwards to be put into writing, and which the author (if I may so call him) may, or may not mean to publish, *has himself the copyright* of what he does so publish. That it may not be supposed I sanction that doctrine, I beg to have it understood, that I do not give any such opinion.

On the other hand, if the editor of the Lancet be not only himself at liberty to publish 5000 copies of this work, but 5000 other persons (notwithstanding his pretence of having the copyright of this publication called the Lancet) may likewise publish the work, that would go directly to destroy the value of any property which Mr. Abernethy may have in the subject. These are all the views of the case, as far as they go to the question of literary *property*.

With respect to the question of *trust*, a good deal of that must depend, not only on the nature of these lectures, and so on, and the rights and obligations abstractedly considered which those persons are under to whom they were delivered; but it must depend also (indeed very materially) on the affidavits that have been actually filed.

On a subsequent day, Mr. Abernethy made an additional affidavit, stating, " that he has given his lectures as most lecturers do, orally, and not from a written composition; but that previously to the delivery of such lectures, he had from time to time committed to writing notes of such, his said lectures, which have been increased and transposed until a great mass of writing has been collected, written in as succinct a manner as possible, with a view to exhibit the arrangement he has formed, and the facts he has collected together, with his opinions relative to certain subjects of surgery: that a considerable portion of such notes have been by, or under the direction of this deponent extended and put into writing, with a view to publication, which writings he is ready to submit to the inspection of any respectable and competent person, as a test of this deponent's accuracy in the statement made to the court in his former affidavit, and that such writings are in his possession; that at the time of delivering his said lectures, he did not read or refer to any writing before him, but that he delivers such, his lectures, orally, and from recollection of such notes and writings, and that the lectures so delivered by him, though not verbatim the same as his notes and writings, yet are in substance, arrangement, and statement of the facts substantially the same: that such lectures vary from time to time both in the language and arrangement according to circumstances, and from any new matter that may have occurred to him, by way of illustration or otherwise: that on a comparison of the written notes or lectures with those so orally delivered by him, they will, and must necessarily vary, and in like manner they will be found to vary from the lectures pirated, or alleged to be pirated, by the defendants in the publication

called the Lancet : that the composition of the said lectures
so reduced into writing have cost him much time and study
for a long series of years : that his duties as a surgeon to St.
Bartholomew's Hospital and lecturer are entirely distinct, and
that it is not a part of his duty as such surgeon to deliver
lectures, but that the same are in the nature of private lectures,
and are not attended by any persons unless by his permission,
and are not in any way open or accessible to the public."

The case was again argued.

The LORD CHANCELLOR. If Mr. Abernethy had produced in
court the writings from which he says his lectures were really delivered,
so that I might myself have exercised a judicial opinion upon those
writings, and have seen that his lectures, though orally delivered, were
delivered from what I should say was *a literary composition*, I should
have had no difficulty in the case. If on the other hand in comparing
what is said to have been orally delivered, and what has got into this
book called the Lancet, with the notes, I could not accurately have
referred the publication to those notes as being the same.—(I mean
with those trifling literary distinctions which must exist in such cases.)
I should then have known what to have done, by not applying myself
to any thing but a reference to authorities.   But I apprehend, that if
those notes are not produced and made, (substantially made,) part of
the case before me, the court has but two ways of proceeding left to it:---
the court must either refer it to the master, to enquire whether what is
admitted to have been published in this book is the same as the notes,
or it must decide the case by calling upon the lecturer to deliver the
notes to the court itself, that the court may see whether they are the
same.   And it may be very inconvenient to produce those notes; so
much so, that I should not be surprised if a gentleman such as Mr.
Abernethy would rather suffer himself to go out of this court without
a judgment, than produce the notes.   But if he had gone to the
master, which would have been the more private way, the master must
have reported to me, and if there had been an exception taken to his
report, there must afterwards have been a public production in this
court.   The consequence of all this is, that *I am compelled to look at
the present case as that of a lecture delivered orally*.   In Millar and
Taylor, there is a great deal said with respect to a person having a
property in sentiments and language, though not deposited on paper ;
but there has been no decision upon that point; and as it is a *pure
question of law*, I think it would be going farther than a judge in
equity should go, to say upon that, that he can grant an injunction
upon it, before the point is tried.

There is another ground for an injunction, which is a ground
arising out of an *implied contract*.   I should be very sorry if I thought
that anything which has fallen from me should be considered to go to
the length of this---that persons who attend lectures or sermons, and
take notes, are to be at liberty to carry into print those notes for their
own profit, or for the profit of others.   I have very little difficulty on that
point.   But that doctrine must apply either to *contract* or *breach of*

trust. Now with respect to contract, it is quite competent for Mr. Abernethy, and for every other lecturer, to protect himself, in future, against what is complained of here. There is a contract expressed and a contract implied ; and I should be very sorry to have any man understand that this court would not act as well upon a contract implied, as upon a contract expressed, provided only the circumstances of the cause authorize the court to act upon it. I have not the slightest difficulty in my own mind that a lecturer may say to those who hear him, "you are entitled to take notes for your own use, and to use them perhaps in every way except for the purpose of printing them for profit; you are not to buy lectures to sell again : you come here to hear them for your own use, and for your own use you may take notes." In the case of *Lord Clarendon's* work, the history was lent to a person, and an application was made for an injunction to stay the publication ; it was said there, that there was no ground for the injunction ; and it was proved on affidavit that my Lord Clarendon's son said, " there is the book, and make what use you please of it ;" the *Chancellor*, however, of that day said, that he could not mean he was to print it for his profit. So with respect to letters, my Lord *Hardwicke* says in one case, that the person who parts with letters, still retains a species of property in them ; and that the person who receives them, has also a species of property in them. He may do what he pleases with the paper, he may make what use he pleases of the letters, *except print them.* There he puts his jurisdiction on the ground of *property.* In other cases we find it put upon the ground of *breach of a trust*---that the letter is property, part of which *I* have retained, and part I have given to you ; you may make what use of the special property you have in it you please, but you shall not make use of my interest in it ; therefore you shall not print it for profit. Now if there be an express contract---for instance, if Mr. Abernethy say " Gentlemen, all of you who attend and pay five guineas for attending my lectures, may take notes of what I say, but let it be understood, that you shall not print for profit;" then in that case I should not have the least difficulty in saying, if any student afterwards did think proper to publish for profit, that there is hardly a term which this court would think too harsh for him, and it would restrain him. There is another ground, which is, whether, looking at the general nature of the subject, it is not very difficult to say, that there is not a contract which would call upon the court to restrain the parties who hear the lectures, from publishing the notes they may have taken. They may make whatever use of them they please, but they ought not to publish them. If an express contract exists, or if any contract is to be implied, either contract would be the ground of an action for a breach of contract.

With respect to trust, the question here would be, whether there is not an *implied trust* with respect to the student himself? One thing is quite clear, that if those lectures have been published from short-hand writer's notes, they have been published from short hand writer's notes taken by some student, or from short hand writer's notes taken by some intruder into the lecture room ; for I do not see how it is possible that they could have been taken otherwise. If there is either an implied contract on the part of a student, or a trust, and if you can, make out that the student has published, I should not hesitate to grant the injunction. With respect to the stranger, if this court is not to be told (and certainly it has no right to compel the parties to tell) whether the power of giving the oral lectures to the : public was derived from a student or not, I think it very difficult to tell me that that should not be restrained which is stolen, if you would restrain that which is a breach of contract or of trust.

Upon the whole, taking this case as it now stands as a case simply of oral lectures, it must be tried whether it is legal to publish them or not. Upon the question of property in language and sentiments, not put into writing, I give no opinion, but only say that it is a question of mighty importance. At present, therefore, I must refuse the injunction : but I give leave to make this very motion on the ground of breach of contract or of trust.

Afterwards the bill was amended by the introduction of allegations, that no persons had a right to attend the lectures, except those who were admitted to that privelege by the lecturer: that it had always been understood by him, and those who preceded him in the office, and those who attended the lectures, that the persons who so attended did not acquire, and were not to acquire, any right of publishing the lectures which they heard : but that the plaintiff and his predecessors respectively had and retained the sole and exclusive right of printing and publishing their respective lectures, for his and their own respective benefit: that there was an implied contract between the plaintiff and those who attended his lectures, that none of them¹ should publish his lectures, or any part thereof: that the defendants had been furnished with the copy of the lectures which they had printed, through the medium of some person who had attended the lectures under Mr. Abernethy's above-mentioned permission ; and that it was a breach of contract or trust in such person so to furnish the copy, and in the defendants, to print and publish the same.

These allegations being verified by the affidavit of the plaintiff, the subject underwent further discussion.

LORD CHANCELLOR. Without deciding the question of literary property in this case, but merely excluding it, the point to be determined was, whether there was such a violation of contract as to sustain an action ; if not, whether an injunction could be asked for. No evidence was given to shew—first, whether the defendants attended as pupils, or secondly, whether they received their report from a person guilty of a breach of trust; or thirdly, whether a short hand writer not being a pupil, gave them a copy of the lectures. It was therefore a question, whether a stranger not bound by contract could be enjoined. Various considerations would arise out of this ; for a Court of Equity would be called upon to say, whether the means by which the defendants were enabled to publish the lectures, might, or might not, be used. One view of the case which ought not be lost sight of was, that supposing the lectures to have been taken down by a pupil who afterwards communicated them to the publishers, and you could not get at the pupil, you could not maintain an action. But in that case the publishers might come under the jurisdiction of the court, upon the ground of having made a fraudulent use of that which had been communicated to them, by one who had committed a breach of trust.

The LORD CHANCELLOR on a subsequent day(¹) finally delivered his judgment.

He stated, that where the lecture was orally delivered, it was difficult to say that an injunction could be granted upon the same principle upon which literary composition was protected, because the court must be satisfied that the publication complained of was an invasion of the written work; and this could only be done by comparing the composition with the piracy. But it did not follow that because the information communicated by the lecturer was not committed to writing, but orally delivered, it was therefore within the power of the person who heard it to publish it. On the contrary, he was clearly of opinion that whatever else might be done with it, the lecture could not be published for profit. He had the satisfaction now of knowing, and he did not possess that knowledge when this question was last considered, that this doctrine was not a novel one, and that *this opinion was confirmed by that of some of the judges of the land.* He was therefore clearly of opinion, that when persons were admitted as pupils or otherwise to hear these lectures, although they were orally delivered, and although the parties might go to the extent, if they were able to do so, of putting down the whole by means of short hand, yet they could do that only for the purposes of their own information, and could not publish for profit that which they had not obtained the right of selling. There was no evidence before the court of the manner in which the defendants got possession of the lectures, but as they must have been taken from a pupil or otherwise, in such a way as the court would not permit, the injunction ought to go upon the ground of property and although there was not sufficient to establish an an implied contract as between the plaintiff and the defendants, yet it must be decided, that as the lectures must have been procured in an undue manner from those who were under a contract not to publish for profit, there was sufficient to authorise the court to say the defendants shall not publish. He had no doubt whatever that an action would lie against a pupil who published these lectures. How the gentlemen who had published them came by them he did not know; but whether an action could be maintained against them or not, on the footing of implied contract, an injunction undoubtedly might be granted : because if there had been a breach of contract on the part of the pupil who heard these lectures, and if the pupil could not publish for profit, to do so would certainly be what this court would call a

<hr/>

(1) June 17, 1825.

fraud in a *third* party. If these lectures had not been taken from a pupil, at least the defendants had obtained the means of publishing them, and had become acquainted with the matter of the lectures in such a manner that this court would not allow of a publication. It by no means followed because an action could not to be maintained, that an injunction ought not to be granted. One question had been, whether Mr. Abernethy, from the peculiar situation which he filled in the hospital, was precluded from publishing his own lectures for his profit; but there was no evidence before the court that he had not such right. Therefore the defendants must be enjoined in future.

The only question remaining was, whether the delay which has taken place in renewing the application, was a ground for saying that the injunction ought not to go to restrain the sale of such lectures as had been printed in the interim. His Lordship's opinion was, that the injunction ought to go to that extent, and should include the lectures already published([1]).

CHAP. III.

OF PIRATING COPYRIGHT IN DRAMATIC WORKS.

SECT. I.——*Of Unpublished Plays.*

Not only is the manuscript of a dramatic author protected by the law, like every other literary composition, but even after it has been represented on the stage, the poet still retains the exclusive right of printing and publishing it.

In the case of *Macklin v. Richardson*([2]), it appeared that the defendant had employed a short hand writer to take down the farce of *Love à la Mode,* upon its performance at the theatre and he inserted one act in a magazine; and gave notice that the second act would be published in the magazine of the following month.

Upon an application to LORD CAMDEN for an injunction, he directed the case to stand over until that of Millar and Taylor, which was then depending, should be determined, and after the determination, the injunction was, by the Lords Commissioners SMYTHE and BATHURST, made perpetual. *Smythe,* L. C .B. said, it has been argued to be a publication by being acted, and therefore the printing is no injury to the plaintiff, but that is a mistake; for besides the advantage of the performance, there is as much reason that he should be protected in that right as any other author. *Bathurst.* " The printing it before the author, is doing him a great injury."

(1) 3 Law Journal, 209.   (2) Amb. 695.

Of representing published Plays.

Although a represented and *un*published play is protected from piracy by *printing*, it seems that a different doctrine prevails in regard to the *representation* of published plays.

Hence an action cannot be maintained for the *penalties* under the statute for representing on the stage the production of an author which had been previously printed and published: it being held that such representation is not a publishing within the intent of the act.

Thus in Colman v. Wathen, an action was brought for the penalty under the statute 8th *Anne*, c. 19, for publishing an entertainment called the " Agreeable Surprise." The plaintiff had purchased the copyright from *O'Keeffe* the author, and the only evidence of publication by the defendant, was the representation of this piece upon his stage at Richmond. A verdict was given for the plaintiff with nominal damages, in order to raise the question, whether this mode of publication were within the statute(¹)?

ERSKINE contended that this was sufficient evidence for the jury to conclude that the work had been pirated, for it could not be supposed that the performers could by any other means have exhibited so perfect a representation of the work. Besides, if this were not held to be a publication within the statute, all dramatic works might be pirated with impunity, as this was the most valuable mode of profiting by them.

Lord KENYON, C. J. There is no evidence to support the action in this case. The statute for the protection of copyright only extends to *prohibit the publication of the book itself* by any other than the author, or his lawful assignees. It was so held in the great copyright case by the House of Lords. But here was no publication.

BULLER, J. Reporting any thing from memory, can never be a publication within the statute. Some instances of strength of memory are very surprising, but the mere act of repeating such a performance, cannot be left as evidence to the jury that the defendants had pirated the work itself.

It is observable in this case that the party sought redress for the injury he had sustained, not by an action for damages, but for the *penalties given by the statute*, and consequently he was bound by the express provisions it contained, which in a penal action were of course construed strictly.

In a later instance (1822), that of *Murray v. Elliston*, the LORD CHANCELLOR sent a case for the opinion of the Court of King's Bench, in which the manager of a theatre had represented Lord BYRON's tragedy of *Marino Faliero, Doge of Venice* (altered and abridged for the stage), without the

(1) 5 T. R. 245.   (1) June 17, 1825.

consent of the owner of the copyright, who had previously
caused the tragedy to be printed and published.

The COURT of King's Bench certified its judgment in
the usual form to the Lord Chancellor, without stating the
reasons on which it was founded. It will be necessary,
therefore, to introduce the arguments of counsel.

SCARLETT, for the plaintiff. This question is quite different from
that in *Colman v. Wathen*(¹). There it turned upon the words of the
statute, 8 Anne, c. 19, and the point determined was, that the acting
a piece on the stage was not a publication of it within that statute.
Here the question is different, for it depends not on the statute, but on
the *right of property* which the plaintiff has in this work. The moment
such a right is established, the consequences must follow, that any
injury done to the property is the subject of legal redress. This is
only one mode in which it may be injured. Unfair and malicious
criticism is another, and for that an action will lie(²). Suppose this
play failed of success when represented, the sale of the work would
thereby be damaged. Besides, the curiosity of the public would be
thereby satisfied, and so the plaintiff would be injured in the sale of
the work. And whether the right of property arise from the common
law, or from the statutes relative to it, is in this case immaterial. For
if the statute makes a literary work property, the common law will
give the remedy for the invasion of it. The only question is, whether
the representation of this piece for profit, may not injure the copyright? If so, the plaintiff is entitled to the judgment of the court.

ADOLPHUS contra. In *Donaldson v. Beckett*(³), the majority of
the judges were of opinion that the action at common law was
taken away by 8th Anne, c. 19, and that the author was precluded from
every remedy except on the statute, and on the terms and conditions
prescribed thereby. The claim by the plaintiff on this occasion is at
variance with this decision. For here he contends for a far more
comprehensive security, and one co-existing with that given by the
statute, and restraining the public in points of which the statute takes
no notice. The case of *Macklin v. Richardson*(⁴) was very different.
There the farce of Love á la Mode had never been published, and the
defendant having employed a short hand writer to take it from the
mouths of the actors, published it, and it was held that he could not
do so. But when in Colman v. Wathen the converse of this was
attempted, the court held that the action would not lie. This decision
was plainly founded on the nature of copyright, the property in which
is exactly the same as if but one book existed which the author permitted individuals to read on payment of a certain sum. The injury
then which an author sustains by the violation of his copyright, is this;
that a stranger without permission disposes of the use and possession
of his book, and thereby receives the profit to which he the author
is justly entitled. If then the book be not in all reasonable strictness

(1) See page 155 *ante*.　　　　(2) Carr v. Hood, 1 Camp. 355.
(3) 4 Burr. 2408.　　　　(4) Page 154 *ante*.

such as may be called the author's own book, as if it be a bona fide abridgment, the case of *Gyles v. Wilcox*([1]) shews that the author has no remedy. Now in the present case a theatrical exhibition falls within the principle above laid down. Persons go thither not to read the work or to hear it read, but to see the *combined effect of poetry, scenery, and acting.* Now of these three things, two are not produced by the author of the work, and the combined effect is just as much a new production, and even more so, than the printed abridgment of a work. There are many instances in which works published have thus, without permission of their authors, been brought upon the stage. The safe rule for the court to lay down is, that an author is only protected from the piracy of his book itself, or some colorable alteration of it : and in that case the defendant is entitled to the judgment of the court.

The COURT afterwards sent the following certificate :

We have heard this case argued by counsel, and are of opinion, that an action cannot be maintained by the plaintiff against the defendant for publicly acting and representing the said tragedy, *abridged* in manner aforesaid, at the Theatre Royal Drury Lane, for profit([2]).

CHAP. IV.
OF PIRATING UNREGISTERED BOOKS.

Although the fifth section of the statute 54 Geo. III. c. 156, requires that all books should be entered at Stationers' Hall within certain times after their publication, it is expressly provided, at the close of that section, that *no failure in making any such entry shall in any manner affect any copyright,* but shall only subject the person making default to the penalty under the act.

It may not be unimportant to state, that prior to this statute, the judges of the Court of King's Bench unanimously held that an action for damages might be maintained for pirating a work before the expiration of twenty-eight years from the first publication, although the work was not entered at Stationers' Hall, and although it was first published without the name of the author affixed([3]).

Lord KENYON. All arguments in support of the rights of learned men in their works, must ever be heard with great favor by men of liberal minds, to whom they are addressed. It is probably on that account that when the great question of literary property was discussed, some judges of enlightened understanding went the length of main-

(1) 5 T. R. 245.
(2) *Quere* whether an *exact* representation would be permitted ?
(3) Beckford v. Hood, 7 T. R. 620.

taining, that the right of publication rested exclusively in the authors and those who claimed under them for all time; but the other opinion finally prevailed, which established that the right was confined to the times limited by the Act of Parliament. And that, I have no doubt, was the right decision. Then the question is, whether the right of property being vested in authors for certain periods, the common law remedy for a violation of it does not attach within the times limited by the Act of Parliament. Within those periods the act says that the author "shall have the sole right and liberty" of printing &c. Then the statute having vested that right in the author, *the common law gives the remedy* by action on the case for the violation of it. Of this there could have been no doubt made, if the statute had stopped there. But it has been argued, that as the statute in the same clause that creates the right, has prescribed a particular remedy, *that* and no other can be resorted to. And if such appeared to have been the intention of the legislature, I should have subscribed to it, however inadequate it might be thought. But their meaning in creating the penalties in the latter part of the clause in question, certainly was to give an *accumulative remedy* ; nothing could be more incomplete as a remedy than those penalties alone, for without dwelling upon the *incompetency of the sum,* the right of action is *not given to the party grieved,* but to any common informer. I cannot think that the legislature would act so inconsistently as to confer a right, and leave the party whose property was invaded without redress. But there was good reason for requiring an entry to be made at Stationers' Hall, which was to serve as a notice and warning to the public, that they might not ignorantly incur the forfeitures or penalties before enacted against such as pirated the works of others ; but calling on a party who has injured the civil property of another for a remedy in damages, cannot properly fall under the description of *a forfeiture or penalty.* Some stress was attempted to be laid on the acts passed for preserving the property of engravers in their works in which a special provision is made to meet such a case as the present and to give the same right of action as is here contended for. But it is well known that provisions of that kind are frequently inserted in Acts of Parliament pro majori cautelâ, and no argument can be drawn from them to affect the construction of other Acts of Parliament. On the fair construction of this act, therefore, I think it vests the right of property in the authors of literary works for the times therein limited, and that consequently the common law remedy attaches if no other be specifically given by the act; and I cannot consider the action given to a common informer for the penalties which might be pre-occupied by another, as a remedy to the party grieved within the meaning of the act.

ASHURST, J. In the case alluded to, of Donaldson v. Becket in the House of Lords, I was one of those that thought that the invention of literary works was a foundation for a right of property, independently of the act of Queen Anne. But I shall not enter into the discussion of that point now, as the question in the present case is much narrowed. And upon the construction of that act I entirely concur with my Lord, that the act having vested the right of property in the author, there must be a remedy in order to preserve it. Now I can only consider the action for the penalties given to a common informer as an additional protection, but not intended by the legislature to oust the common law right to prosecute by action any person who infringes this species of property, which would otherwise necessarily attach upon the right of property so conferred. Where an Act of Parliament vests property in a party, the other consequences follow of course, unless the legislature make a special provision for the purpose, and that does not appear to me to have been intended in this case. I am the more inclined to adopt this instruction because, the supposed remedy is wholly inadeqate to the purpose. The penalties to be recovered may indeed operate as a punishment upon the offender, but they afford no redress to the injured party; the action is not given to him, but to any person who may get the start of him and sue first. It is no redress for the civil injury sustained by the author in the loss of his just profits.

GROSE, J. The principal question is, whether within the periods which the exclusive right of property is secured by the statute to the author, he may not sue the party who has invaded his right for damages up to the extent of the injury sustained, and of this I conceive there can be no doubt. In the great case of Millar v. Taylor, Mr. Justice *Yates* gave his opinion against the common law right contended for in authors, but he was decidedly of opinion that an exclusive right of property was vested in them by the statute for the time limited therein. No words can be more expressive to that effect than those used by him. But it is to be observed, that the penalties given by the act attach only during the first fourteen years of the copyright, and during that time only is the offender liable for such penalties if he invade the author's right; but he is liable during the whole period prescribed by the act to make good in an action for damages any civil injury to the author. If this construction were not to prevail during the last fourteen years of the term, the author would be wholly without remedy for any invasion of his property. But there must be a remedy, otherwise it would be in vain to confer a right. I was at first struck with the consideration that six to five of the judges who delivered their opinions in the House of Lords in the case of Donaldson v. Beckett were of opinion, that the common law right of action was taken away by the statute of Anne; but upon further view it appears that the amount of their opinions went only to establish that the common law right of action could not be exercised beyond the time limited by that statute.

LAWRENCE, J. I entirely concur with the opinions delivered by my brethren upon the principal point, and the case of Tonson v. Collins([1]) is an additional authority in support of it; for there Lord MANSFIELD said, that it had been always holden that the entry in Stationers' Hall was only necessary to enable the party to bring his action for the penalty, but that the property was given absolutely to the author, at least during the term.

(1) 1 Black. Rep. 330.

CHAP. V.

OF PIRATING THE COPYRIGHT IN ENGRAVINGS, ETCHINGS, PRINTS,
MAPS, CHARTS, AND PLANS.

SECT I.——*Of Engravings, Etchings, and Prints.*

It has been well expressed by Mr. *Godson,* that upon the
same principles, and for the same reasons, that the legislature
have protected the SCHOLAR in the enjoyment of the fruits of
his knowledge and industry; so it has provided that the
ARTIST shall not exert his skill and ingenuity without a hope
of reward from the result of his labors([1]).

There would appear to be a greater difficulty in detecting
the piracy of an engraving or print, than in that of the language and sentiments of a literary composition, and the means
of concealing the piracy appear somewhat easier in the
former than the latter case. Still the subject is capable of
ascertainment. And it is clearly decided, that where a print
is a copy *in part* of an original, by varying in some trifling
respects only from the main design, the vendor is liable to an
action by the proprietor of the original; and this liability exists,
although the vendor did not know it to be a pirated copy.

Thus in the case of *West* v. *Francis,* it appeared at the trial that
the plaintiff was the proprietor of the prints described in the declaration; and that the defendant, who was a print-seller, had sold copies
of the same, all varying from the original in some respect, but preserving generally the design of the original. There was no evidence to
shew that the defendant knew the prints he sold to be copied from the
plaintiff's prints. It was objected for the defendant, that the action
was not maintainable under the 17th Geo. III. c. 57, for merely selling
a varied copy of a print. The Lord Chief Justice reserved the point,
and the plaintiff having obtained a verdict, a rule nisi was obtained for
entering a non-suit. On the motion to make it absolute, the court
pronounced the following judgment.

ABBOTT, C. J. This Act of Parliament was intended to preserve
to artists the property of their works. The question is, what is the
meaning of the word " copy" of a print? Now in common parlance
there may be a copy of a print where there exist small variations from
the original; and the question is, whether the words are used in that
popular sense in this Act of Parliament. That is to be collected from
looking at the whole clause, by which it is provided, that if any one
shall engrave &c., or in any other manner copy in the whole or in part,
by varying, adding to, or diminishing from, the main design, or shall
print, or reprint, or import for sale, or publish, or sell, or otherwise dispose of any copy of any print, he shall be liable to an action. Now
if the selling of a copy with colorable variations is not within the Act

(1) Godson, page 287.

of Parliament, the printing or importing for sale such copies will not be prohibited. The whole must be taken as one sentence; and the sale of any copy of a print, although there may be some colorable alteration, is within the Act of Parliament. The case of Gahagan v. Cooper proceeded upon a different Act of Parliament. In this case I am satisfied the verdict is right, and therefore this rule must be discharged.

BAYLEY, J. I am of the same opinion. The provisions of the 8th Geo. II. c. 13, are entitled to great weight in the construction of this latter Act of Parliament. That act imposes first a penalty upon any persons who shall engrave, copy, and sell, or cause to be copied and sold, in the whole or in part, by varying, adding to, or diminishing from, the main design; and secondly, upon persons selling the same knowing the same to be so printed or reprinted. The act of the 17th Geo. III. c. 57, was passed to remedy the same mischief, and the words "knowing the same to be so printed" are omitted. It may therefore be fairly inferred that the legislature meant to make a seller liable, who did not even know that they were copies. The former part of the 17th Geo. III. c. 57, s. 1, applies to persons who actually make the copy, and who therefore must know that it is a copy. But the latter branch applies to all persons who shall import for sale or sell any copy of a print. Every person, therefore, who sells a copy which comes so near the original as this, is thereby made liable to an action. There can be no reason why a person should not be liable where he sells a copy with a mere collusive variation; and I think we should put a narrow construction on the statute, if we held such a collusive variation from the original, not to be a copy. A copy is, that which comes so near to the original, as to give to every person seeing it the idea created by the original. For these reasons I think the plaintiff is entitled to recover; and consequently that the rule must be discharged.

HOLROYD, J. I am of the same opinion. We should be careful not to give too extensive a construction to this Act of Parliament, but at the same time one sufficient to remedy the mischiefs intended to be guarded against. The question is, what is the meaning of the word "copy." Now in the preceding part of the clause, the legislature, have called that a copy which is not strictly so in all its parts, being one varying from the main design, and I think that the word must have the same construction in the latter part. Gahagan v. Cooper was decided upon another Act of Parliament, and Lord Ellenborough's judgment proceeded upon the particular mode in which the counts of the declaration were framed.

BEST, J. concurred.

In treating of the *duration* and *extent* of copyright(¹), we have already adverted to the "degree of originality," which entitles the inventor to the protection of the law.

In Blackwell v. Harper, it was held, that the statute was not confined merely to invention, as, for instance, an allegorical or fabulous representation, nor to historical only, as the design of a battle;

---

(1) Vide page 82, *ante*.

M

but it means the designing or engraving anything that is already in nature; even a print published of any building, house, or garden, falls within the act([1]).

A person *procuring* a drawing or design to be made is not entitled to protection.

Lord HARDWICKE said, the case is not within the statute, which was made for encouragement of genius and art. If it was, any person who employs a printer or engraver would be so too. The statute is in this respect like the one of new inventions. If there can be no claim of property, there can be no title to relief([2]).

SECTION II.

Of Pirating Maps, Charts, and Plans.

The general principles which regulate other kinds of copyright, are equally applicable to maps, charts, and plans. They are indeed expressly protected by the statute 7th Geo. III. cap. 38. Lord MANSFIELD, in a case tried before him in the year 1785, said, " the rule of decision in this case is a matter of great consequence to the country. In deciding it, we must take care to guard against two extremes equally prejudicial; the one, that men of ability who have employed their time for the service of the community may not be deprived of their just merits, and the reward of their ingenuity and labour; the other, that the world may not be deprived of improvements, nor the progress of the arts be retarded. The act that secures copyright to authors, guards against the piracy of the words and sentiments; but it does not prohibit writing on the same subject. In all these cases the question of fact to come before a jury is, whether the alteration be colorable or not? There must be such a similitude as to make it probable and reasonable to suppose that one is a transcript of the other, and nothing more than a transcript. So in the case of prints, no doubt different men may take engravings from the same picture. The same principle holds with regard to charts; whoever has it in his intention to publish a chart, may take advantage of all prior publications. There is no monopoly of the subject here any more than in the other instances; but upon any question of this nature the jury will decide whether it be a servile imitation or not.

The charts in question were four in number, which the defendant had made into one large map.

<hr/>

(1) 2 Atk. 93.   (2) Jeffery's v. Baldwin, Amb. 164.

It appeared in evidence, that the defendant had taken the body of his publication from the work of the plaintiffs, but that he had made many alterations and improvements thereupon. It was also proved, that the plaintiffs had originally been at a great expence in procuring materials for these maps. Delarochett, an eminent geographer and engraver, had been employed by the plaintiffs in the engraving of them. He said, that the present charts of the plaintiffs were such an improvement on those before in use, as made them an original work. Besides their having been laid down from all the charts and maps extant, they were improved by many manuscript journals and printed books, and manuscript relations of travellers: he had no doubt the materials must have cost the plaintiffs between £3000 and £4000, and that the defendant's chart was taken from those of the plaintiffs, with a few alterations. In answer to a question from the court, whether the defendant had pirated from the drawings and papers, or from the engravings? He answered, from the engravings. Winterfelt, an engraver, said he was actually employed by the defendant to take a draft of the Gulph Passage (in the West Indies) from the plaintiffs' map.

Many witnesses were called on behalf the defendant, amongst others a Mr. Stephenson and Admiral Campbell. Mr. Stephenson said, he had carefully examined the two publications; that there were very important differences between them, much in favor of the defendants. That the plaintiff's maps were founded upon no principle; neither upon the principle of the Mercator, nor the plain chart, but upon a corruption of both. That near the equator the plain chart would do very well, but that as you go further from the equator, there you must have recourse to the Mercator. That there were very material errors in the plaintiffs' maps. That they were in many places defective in pointing out the latitude and longitude, which is extremely essential in navigating. That most of these, as well errors in the soundings, were corrected by the defendant. Admiral Campbell observed that there were only two kinds of charts, one called a plain chart, which was now very little used, the other, which is the best, called the Mercator, and which is very accurate in the degrees of latitude and longitude. That this distinction was very necessary in the higher latitudes, but in places near the equator it made little or no difference. That the plaintiffs' maps were upon no principle recognized among seamen, and no rules of navigation would be applied to them; and they were therefore entirely useless.

Lord MANSFIELD, in addition to the general observation already quoted, said, " If an erroneous chart be made, God forbid it should not be corrected even in a small degree, if it thereby become more serviceable and useful for the purposes to which it is applied. But here there are various and very material alterations. This chart of the plaintiffs is upon a wrong principle, inapplicable to navigation. The defendant has therefore been correcting errors, and not servilely copying." And he directed the jury, if they thought so, to find for the defendant; if they thought it was a mere servile imitation and pirated from the other, they would find for the plaintiffs. A verdict was accordingly found for the defendant(¹).

In the case of a map of the island of St Domingo, made by Mr. Bryan Edwards, and which was pirated,

The LORD CHANCELLOR said, it might be asked, how is it possible to have a copyright in a map of the Island of St. Domingo? Must not the mountains have the same position, the rivers the same course? Must not the points of land, the coast connecting them, the names given by the inhabitants, every thing constituting a map, be the same? The answer was, that the subject of the plaintiff's claim was a map, made at great expence, from actual surveys : distinguished from former maps by improvements that were manifest : the defendants map was a servile imitation, requiring no expence, no ingenuity ; possessing nothing that could confer copyright(²).

CHAP. VI.

OF THE REMEDIES FOR PIRACY.

The statutes having vested the right of property in the author, there must be a remedy by the principles of the common law in order to preserve it. It is accordingly clearly settled, that the action for penalties given to a common informer as an additional protection to the copyright of an author, does not oust the common law right of property so conferred(³).

The modes of procedure in obtaining redress for injuries to copyright, are

1st. By action on the case for damages.
2nd. By action under the statute for penalties.
3rd. By a suit in Equity to restrain the publication, and compel an account of the profits.

SECTION I.

Of the remedy by action on the Case for Damages.

It is not deemed necessary to the completion of the design of this treatise, to enter upon the technical description of the *pleadings* either at law or in equity(⁴); but the general

---

(1) Sayre v. Moore, 1 East, 361, *note.*   (2) Cited, 12 Vesey, 274.
(3) Beckford v. Hood, 7 T. R. 620.
(4) For observations on the pleadings, vide 6 Petersdorff's Abr. 574.

nature of the EVIDENCE required at the trial, it will be material to point out.

For the PLAINTIFF it must of course be proved, if the action be brought by·him, that he is the author or proprietor of the work.

As the best species of evidence, he should produce the manuscript where the action is brought for pirating a book, and prove his hand writing, or the hand writing of his amanuensis. Hence it is always important to preserve the original.

If the manuscript should have been lost or destroyed, the fact of loss or destruction it should seem must be proved before evidence can be received of its composition by the author, or by his dictation.

In an action for pirating engravings, it is sufficient to produce one of the prints taken from the original plate—the production of the original itself not being required([1]).

Where the action is brought by the *assignee* of the author, he must, in addition to the proof of the original title of the author, deduce his own title by legal assignment from him([2]).

The same species of evidence will of course be required when the subject matter of the action consists of *notes* or *additions* to a former work.

It will next be necessary to produce a copy of the work complained of, and prove the injury sustained according to the specific allegations in the pleadings ; whether by printing and publishing, or by exposing to sale, or importing.

Proof is often given, that parts of the first work were used at the press when the second was printed, and that the alterations supplied in the MSS. were merely colorable. The prevalence of errors in the second work identical with those in the first, is likewise good evidence of piracy, since it can scarcely have happened that two persons would fall into precisely the same mistakes in repeated instances.

The extent of the damages may be proved by the number of copies sold by the defendant, or by any other facts incident to the nature of the work.

The allegations in the pleadings of the title of the book pirated, and the time (if set forth) of the first publications should be carefully made, lest the defendant avail himself of the error by shewing a variance from the fact

For the DEFENDANT, the evidence will of course vary according to the nature of the defence.

It may be shewn that the plaintiff is not the author of

(1) 5 T. R. 41.
(2) For the mode of transfer vide the next part of this book.

the composition alleged to be pirated, by proving who was the real author.

If the defence be a publication of the second work by the *consent* of the author of the first, such consent must be strictly proved, and in conformity to all the statutes it must be given in *writing*.

According to the statutes previous to the 54th Geo. III. c. 156, it was requisite that the consent in writing should be signed in the presence of two or more credible witnesses, but in the last act, this clause of attestation is omitted.

The transfer of engravings and sculpture must be attested by two witnesses.

The next question at the trial will be, whether the defendant's work is *substantially* the same as that of the plaintiff, so as to leave no doubt that, however varied in some particulars, it is a fraudulent imitation.

It would be competent for the defendant to shew that the work which he had published, was compiled from the original authorities, and entitled therefore to be considered as a new work([1]).

It would also be a good defence, as we have seen([2]), if the work of the plaintiff were of an illegal or immoral nature.

So also if the period limited by the statute for the protection of the copyright had actually expired, or the action were not commenced within the time prescribed by the statutes.

On the latter point it is material to observe, that for pirating the copyright of BOOKS, the proceedings must be commenced within *twelve* months. For the piracy of ENGRAVINGS, etchings, prints, maps, and charts, as well as original SCULPTURE, models, and casts, the remedy is limited to *six* months.

In all the instances, whether for pirating the copyright of books, engravings, or sculpture, the plaintiff, if he recover a verdict, is entitled to *double the costs of the suit*, whether in the English or the Scottish Courts.

If the action be discontinued or the plaintiff should be nonsuited, the defendant is entitled to the ordinary costs.

We have already adverted to the conflicting decisions

---

(1) It is not a piracy to make another engraving from the same original picture.

Where an artist was employed to make engravings of two pictures, and after he had completed them, made two sketches from the same original without using the engravings, and sold them for the use of the Sporting Magazine,

Lord Chief Justice ABBOTT said, it would destroy all competition in the art to extend the monopoly to the painting itself. After quoting the words of the statute, his Lordship added, "in this case the defendant's engraving was made from the original picture, and not from the plaintiff's print. *De Berenger* v. *Wheble*, 2 Staik, 548.

(2) Page, 89, *ante.*

relating to the date of the publication of engravings, &c(¹)·
In a late case, the Court of Common Pleas, after noticing
these opposite opinions, and looking through the statutes,
held, that it was the intention of the legislature that the
public should be protected against the continuance of the
monopoly beyond the prescribed term, which might be the
case if the date had not been required to appear on the face
of the prints(²).

But it was also held by the same court that the plaintiff
need not describe himself *as proprietor*.

The words on the print were *Newton, del.* 1*st May*, 1826, *Gladwin,*
sculp. The court said it was not usual, nor did they think it necessary
that it should be stated on the print, in terms, that a particular person
is the proprietor. The uniform practice is to place the names of the
designer and engraver alone, and a decision questioning its propriety
would have the effect of destroying much valuable property(³).

SECTION II.

Of the remedy by Penalties under the Statutes.

The author or proprietor of a work which has been
pirated, or *any other person*, may maintain an action of debt
to recover the penalties inflicted by the several statutes for
the protection of literary compositions.

The clauses containing the penalties have been already
stated. The following is a summary of their amount.

As to BOOKS.

1st. The forfeiture of pirated books, printed, published, or
exposed to sale, and every sheet thereof, to be delivered to the author
or proprietor, and by him (on the order of the court) forthwith
damasked or made waste paper of.

2nd. A fine of three pence for every sheet printed, published, or
exposed to sale, one moiety to the King and the other to the plaintiff.

Two penalties may be incurred on the same day for
selling books, the originals of which have been written and
published here, and afterwards reprinted abroad, and imported into this country, *if the acts of sale be distinct*(⁴).

As to ENGRAVINGS, &c.

1st. A forfeiture of the pirated plates and prints to the proprietor
of the original to be forthwith destroyed and damasked.

---

(1) Page, 82.   (2) Newton v. Cowie, 5 Law Journal, p. 161. Easter T. 1827.
(3) Ibid. In Thompson v. Symonds it was doubted whether in an assignment the
name of the inventor or the assignee should appear. 5, T. R. 41.
(4) Brooke v. Milliken. 3 T. R. 509.

2nd. A fine of five shillings for every print found in the defendant's possession, either printed or published, or exposed to sale: the one moiety to the King, and the other to the plaintiff.

As to SCULPTURE.

The remedy for pirating sculpture, models, and casts, seems confined to an action for damages, or a suit for an injunction and account. No penalties are specified in either of the acts on this subject.

It would seem that the EVIDENCE necessary to support an action for the penalties must be as complete in all respects as that which is required for the recovery of damages. Indeed it is reasonable that the informer should be held, if possible, to a stricter degree of proof than the party really injured ; and if the latter were to sue for the penalties, he must still be bound by the strict construction applicable to cases under penal statutes.

The LIMITATION of the time within which the penalties must be sued for, is the same as that prescribed for the commencement of an action for damages ; namely, in regard to the copyright of books, *twelve* months, and of engravings, sculpture, &c. *six* months.

Though it is still doubtful whether the name and date are essential to the recovery of damages in an action for piracy, it is clear they are both necessary in an action for *penalties* under the statute(¹).

SECTION III.

Of the remedy by Injunction in Equity.

The most usual and expeditious means of obtaining redress for piracy, and preventing the continuance of the injury, are to be found in a Court of Equity, where, by the preliminary process of injunction, justice is more readily administered than in a Court of Law, where the evil may continue until the final decision of the cause, and from the circumstances of the case may then be irremediable.

In order to obtain this summary relief, the title of the plaintiff must be founded on the possession of a legal copyright ; or at all events there must be a strong *prima facie* case of legal title. Where the plaintiff's right is doubtful, a Court of Equity will not interpose in the first instance, but

(1) 2 Atkins, 92. 5 T. R. 41. 1 Camp. 94.

leave the party to establish his right by an action at law. After which, he will of course be entitled to the additional aid of an injunction in equity.

The question regarding the date of engravings, has also occurred in the Court of Chancery.

In Harrison v. Hogg, the *Master of the Rolls* said, he was glad that he was relieved from determining upon the act, for *at present* he was inclined to differ from Lord Hardwicke. He must believe that it is essential to the plaintiff's right to insert the date. Many good reasons, which it was not then necessary to mention, require that the date should be upon the plate. But, he said, as Courts of Law have permitted plaintiffs to make this sort of general allegation (on the pleadings), it would be strange for Equity to be more strict([1]).

The *mode of procedure* to obtain an injunction, is simple and expeditious. A bill is filed by the proprietor, stating his title to the original work, the nature of the piracy, and the consequent injury.

The particular facts are next to be verified by affidavit, and a special motion may then be made to restrain the publication. The whole question may thus be brought before the court; and an injunction will either be granted forthwith, or an issue directed to try the question before a jury in a Court of Law, unless the work be apparently excluded from legal protection on the ground of its mischievous tendency, or for other reasons be of a description in which no legal proprietorship can exist; and then the plaintiff is left to seek such remedy as he may be entitled to in another court.

In injunction cases, it appears that no affidavit as to the title of an author or proprietor will be received after the defendant's answer has been filed, though affidavits in opposition to the answer may be read as to facts([2]).

Though it is clear that the proceeding by injunction is thus the most ready and effectual remedy which can be resorted to on the part of the plaintiff; a great degree of caution, in the application of that proceeding, in the first instance, is requisite for preventing injustice to the defendant, whose loss does not from the nature of it admit of reparation, if the injunction should, upon further investigation, be found to have been erroneously applied, and the judges in Courts of Equity have in many cases expressed a strong sense of the importance of this principle([3]).

(1) 2 Vesey, 327.
(2) Cited in Platt v. Button, 19 Ves. 448, and see Norway v. Rowe, ib. 144.
(3) 2 Evans's Coll. Stat. 630.

FOURTH PART.

OF THE TRANSFER OF COPYRIGHT, THE CONTRACTS OF AUTHORS AND BOOKSELLERS, AND OTHER INCIDENTS OF LITERARY PROPERTY.

SECT. 1.——*Of the Transfer of Copyright generally.*

The transfer of every kind of copyright, according to the several provisions in the statutes, must be *in writing.* There does not appear to be any reason for making a distinction between the copyright of books, and that of engravings, of maps, or of sculpture. But the last statute has made a distinction which it is necessary to point out.

The statutes of 8 Anne, c. 19 and 41 Geo. 3. c. 107, required the consent of the authors or proprietors for printing, reprinting, or importing books of which they possessed the copyright to be in writing, " signed in the presence of *two* or more credible witnesses." The 54 Geo. III. cap. 156, does not contain this requisition, and the mode of attestation, therefore, appears to be immaterial in giving effect to the transfer.

In the acts relating to engravings, etchings, prints, maps, and charts, it is required that there should be an " express consent of the proprietor or proprietors, first had and obtained *in writing*, signed by him, her, or them respectively, with his, her, or their *own hand* or hands, in the presence of, and attested by *two or more credible witnesses*(¹)."

In the case of *original sculpture, models, and casts,* the requirements of the act proceed still further, for though in the second section the same language is used as in the case of engravings, &c. ; in the 4th section it is provided, that persons who purchase the right or property in original sculpture, &c. from the proprietors, expressed in a *deed* in writing, signed and attested as in the former case, shall not be subject to any action under the statute(²).

It would appear, therefore, that the right of exclusively printing and publishing books may be transferred by a con-

---

(1) The 7th section of 7 Geo. III. c. 38, by which the copyright in engravings, &c. is extended to twenty-eight years, gives no additional term in case the author survives that period.

(2) By the 6th section of 54 Geo. III. c. 56, the artist is entitled to a second term of fourteen years, if he survives the first, but it does not continue during his life beyond he second period.

sent in writing, without attestation---the right of publishing prints and maps by a consent in writing, attested by two witnesses---and for the right of making models and casts, the consent must be given by deed, also attested by two witnesses.

SECTION II.

Of particular Contracts between Authors and Booksellers.

Although the transactions between authors and booksellers must evidently be very numerous, and greatly diversified in their nature, there are few cases reported in the authentic law books of any disputes which have existed between them.

We shall presently refer to the particular points which have undergone judicial investigation, but have previously to notice a peculiar species of literary property which has become of vast importance to its proprietors in recent times. We allude to the articles or *contributions* supplied *to periodical works and encyclopedias.*

Some distinction appears to exist between *entire works* completed by the author, and sold to the publisher, and those *partial contributions* which are composed at the request of the proprietor, and originally intended to form part of larger works under the editorship of a person distinct from the author. There seems here some analogy to the principle by which an exception is allowed in the law of debtor and creditor; for although no one is answerable for the debt of another, unless the engagement be in writing, yet an original credit may be given to one person, and the goods supplied to another. So here, it may be said, the bookseller is the *proprietor of the work at large,* and engages different persons to supply different portions of the undertaking. When these are delivered, they appear to be the property of the owner of the general work, more especially as the several articles are wrought into their appropriate form by the literary agent of the proprietor. They seem thus to lose their separate identity after leaving the hands of the author.

Transactions of this kind between publishers and authors resemble contracts for so much work and labor towards a general undertaking, and are different from the sale of a complete copyright, which requires an assignment in the exact terms of the act—as there may be various engagements (all verbal) with the several artificers to the building of a house; but the edifice itself cannot be conveyed on account of the *land* on which it is situated, unless the transfer be in writing.

It may also be urged, that a composition of this sort is *not a book* in the language of the statute, *nor any volume thereof,* and cannot be comprised within its provisions. All contracts therefore, relating to such compositions, can be limited only by the ordinary principles of law, and a *verbal* agreement, (distinctly proved,) would be sufficient to pass all the interest which an author can possess in such works. This view of the subject, is somewhat supported by a very recent decision in the Appeal Court of the Exchequer Chamber, in which it was held that the public libraries are not entitled to copies of works which are not within the ordinary signification of a " book" or a " volume," and that *parts* of a volume published at uncertain intervals, are not within the meaning of the act([1]).

On the other hand, it is evident from all the cases which have been decided on the subject of the transfer of copyright, that the interests of authors are favorably regarded, and the requirements of the statutes on their behalf strictly enforced. This rule of construction is important not only to authors themselves but to those who derive their title by assignment for them. We have seen, in treating of the extent of copyright, that the law protects it from piracy, however small or insignificant the composition may be. Every original work, though consisting merely of a single sheet of paper, or the music of a single song, has been considered a book within the meaning of the Act of Parliament([2]). And it is not improbable, therefore, that an express assignment would be held necessary to deprive the author of the right of republishing the article himself in a separate form, although evidently it would be a breach of contract to dispose of it again for the use of another compilation([3]).

The communications, however, from correspondents to the editors or proprietors of periodical publications, are said to be the property of the person to whom they are directed; and cannot be published by any other person, who by chance may have obtained possession of them([4]).

But these communications, it would appear, must be

---

(1) British Museum v. Payne and Foss, 2 Younge and J. 166. (2) Pages, 74-5-6.
(3) Supposing, that the proprietor of an encyclopædia, or periodical publication, possess such a property in the articles contributed for his work, that the author can make no other use of them without the consent of the proprietor, still it is questionable whether the right be *limited to the purpose for which the composition was written,* or may be extended, so as to enable the proprietor of the encyclopædia to publish it as a *separate book,* without a new agreement with the author. The copyright in such case would probably be considered as a *special* one---not *general* and unlimited ;---and for the purpose of separate publication a consent must be given by the author in writing, according to the terms prescribed in the Act of Parliament.   (4) 8 Vesey, 215.

such as are sent implied or expressly for the purpose of publication; but on the principle that an author has an absolute control over his manuscripts, it seems they may be reclaimed at any time before publication.

Under the *general* assignment by an author of all his right in a work, the assignee has the benefit of the resulting term for the life of the author, in case the latter should survive the twenty-eight years from the day of publication (¹).

It has been questioned whether, in the case of a *joint authorship*, the copyright would continue to the end of the life of the survivor, supposing both of them outlived the twenty-eight years from the day of publication? And whether there would be any resulting term, supposing one of the authors died within the twenty-eight years?(²).

It would appear, however, that so much as had been actually composed by the survivor, must evidently be protected to the end of his life. And we do not see how any part of the work could be safely pirated, unless the extent were precisely known of the contribution of the deceased author. It seems also that the benefit of the resulting term to the survivor could not depend on *both* of them outliving the twenty-eight years.

If an author engage to furnish a bookseller with a transcript, he must answer in damages for not fulfilling his contract(³).

And Lord ELDON held, that a covenant in articles of agreement, by which a dramatic writer undertook not to compose pieces for any other than the Haymarket Theatre, was a legal covenant(⁴).

But where a gentleman had contracted to supply a bookseller with reports of the cases argued in the Court of Exchequer upon certain terms, and afterwards sold them to another bookseller, the Lord CHANCELLOR would not grant an injunction to restrain the publication, and force him to report and give his manuscript to the bookseller, observing that he could not grant an injunction whereby *the person* of the defendant would not be at liberty(⁵).

It is not necessary for an author to put his name in the title page in order to preserve it(⁶).

Lord ELDON, however, on one occasion, doubted how far he could relieve the publisher of a work with a fictitious name(⁷), but he granted an injunction until answer or further

---

(1) 2 Brown, C. R. 80. (2) Godson, 311.
(3) Gale v. Leckie, 2 Stark, 107. (4) Morris v. Colman. 18 Vesey, 437.
(5) Clarke v. Price, 2 Wils. 157. (6) 4 Burr. 2367. (7) 8 Vesey, 226.

order to restrain the publication of a work in the name of
Lord Byron, who was abroad, upon an affidavit of his Lordship's agent of circumstances, making it highly probable that
it was not a work by his Lordship, and on the refusal of the
defendant to swear as to his belief that it was written by
him(¹).

In Storace v. Longman, the plaintiff was the composer of
a musical air, tune and writing, which was reprinted by [the
defendant within the fourteen years limited by the act.

Erskine for the defendant examined the plaintiff's sister,
to shew that the song was composed to be sung by her at the
Italian Opera, and that all compositions so performed were
the property of the house, not of the composer. But,

Lord Kenyon said, that this defence could not be supported; that the statute vests the property in the author, and
that no such private regulation could interfere with the public
right(²).

In *Power v. Walker*(³), at the trial before Lord Ellenborough, the plaintiff, in order to establish his title, proved,
that Mr. Moore, the author of a work entitled "A Selection of
Irish Melodies," of which this song was one, transferred the
copyright of the work by *verbal* agreement to R. Power of
Dublin, who agreed also by *parole* with the plaintiff that the
latter should have the exclusive right of publishing and
selling the work in England, reserving to himself the right of
selling it in Ireland. It was objected for the defendant, first,
that by stat 8th Anne, c. 19, every assignment of copyright
must be in writing, and secondly, that the right conveyed to
the plaintiff by Power, (supposing it to be well conveyed) did
not amount to an assignment of the copyright, such as would
sustain this action, but was a mere *licence* to the plaintiff for
the publication and sale in England.

Lord Ellenborough said, that the statute having
required that the consent of the proprietor, in order to
authorize the printing or reprinting of any book by any other
person, shall be in writing, that the conclusion from it seemed
almost irresistible, but that the assignment, must also be in
writing, for if the licence which is the lesser thing must be in
writing, a fortiori, the assignment which is the greater thing
must also be so.

Dampier, J. expressed himself to the same effect, and

(1) Lord Byron v. Johnson, 2 Meriv. 29.
(2) 2 Camp. 27, *note.* But *quere,* as to the accuracy of this opinion, as authors
frequently dispose of MS. and copyright, and a general usage upon the subject may be
evidence of such a disposition. 2 Evans's Coll. Stat. 627.
(3) 3 Maule and S. 7.

said, that the assignment could only be under the statute, and therefore the plaintiff must shew that he was such an assignee as the statute required.

The construction of the statute is so strict, that though the author of a musical composition acquiesced for six years in the defendant's publication of it; this was held insufficient evidence of the transfer of his interest in the copyright.

Nor will a receipt given by the plaintiff for money received by him as the price of the copyright, preclude him from maintaining the action.

The facts were as follows : the piece of music in question " Le Retour de Windsor," had been composed by the plaintiff in the year 1801, and it appeared that in 1812, and previously, the defendants had sold copies bearing Latour's name as the composer, and that this had been done with his acquiescence. It was also proved, that ten years ago the plaintiff had given a receipt (which had since been destroyed) to the defendants for thirty guineas, as the consideration of the purchase of the copyright, but that there was no other writing than the receipt; and that the plaintiff had afterwards said that he ought to have had more for the copyright.

ABBOTT, J. was of opinion, that there had not been any assignment. In the case of *Moore v. Walker*([1]), the author had admitted that he had assigned his interest ; but here it appeared in evidence that there had not been any assignment such as the statute required. By the act of Anne, which was made for the encouragement of genius and learning, an exclusive right had been given to the author of any work for the term of fourteen years; and he might during that term assign his interest to another, and if he died without assigning his copyright, the interest would go to his executors. If he survived the term of fourteen years, he would be entitled to the enjoyment of the copyright for fourteen years more. A question might perhaps be made, whether an assignment within the first fourteen years would carry the contingent interest ; but here no such question arose, since there had been no assignment according to the mode pointed out by the statute([2]).

Where, however, a copyright in music was not asserted against violation by several persons for *fifteen years*, the Court of Chancery refused an injunction until the right should be established at law.

The LORD CHANCELLOR said, I admit this to be the

(1) 4 Camp. 9, *note*.   (2) Latour v. Bland, 2 Stark. R. 382.

subject of copyright. But the plaintiff has permitted several people to publish these dances, some of them for fifteen years: thus encouraging others to do so. That, it is true, is *not a justification;* but under these circumstances a Court of Equity will not interfere in the first instance. If, as is represented, some of them were published only last year, and one two months ago ; the bill ought to have been confined to those. You may bring your action, and then apply for an injunction(¹).

SECTION III.

Of the Bequest of Copyright.

We have seen that it was usual from the earliest period after the invention of printing not only to sell copyrights (at that time in perpetuity), but that they were made the subject of family settlements for the provision of wives and children(²); and where they were not included in such settlements, of course the proprietors disposed of them by their wills, or they passed to the administrator in the same manner as other goods and chattels.

It does not appear that there is any case reported in which the title to a copyright depended upon a bequest ; but there can be no doubt that an author has the power of bequeathing it. A patentee may bequeath his interest in a *patent*(³), and if he die intestate, it will be assets in the hands of his administrator(⁴). It must clearly follow, therefore, that the author or proprietor of a book may transfer his copyright by a testamentary disposition, and in the absence of which it will pass in the same way as other kinds of personal property. Its limited duration has naturally prevented the occurrence of many instances in which copyright has been *specifically* bequeathed. The only case reported on the subject is that of the interest in a *newspaper*. The property in question on that occasion, however, consisted rather in *printing* the work and the implements of trade necessary to conduct it, than in the copyright of the composition.

In Keene v. Harris, the printer of a newspaper, the *Bath Chronicle,* bequeathed to his widow the benefit of that trade, subject to the trust of maintaining and educating her family. Having formed an attachment for the person who had been employed as foreman in conducting that business, she assisted him in setting up the same paper giving him the use of the

(1) Platt v. Button. 19, Ves. 447.   (2) Page 16.
(3) Godson, 168.   (4) 1 Vesey, Jun. 118. and 3 B. and P. 573.

letter press, &c., on the premises.   A bill was filed by the executors, and an injunction was granted(¹).

SECTION IV.

Of the rights of Creditors, under an Execution or a Commission of Bankruptcy.

The unpublished *manuscript* of an author cannot, it seems, be taken in execution at the suit of creditors(²).   Such a seizure would be contrary to the established principle of law, that until an actual publication has taken place, the author has an uncontrolled right to, and dominion over his manuscripts(³).

It would also be contrary to the principle by which the instruments of a man's trade or profession, whilst in use, are protected from the process of distraint.   The *books of a scholar* are enumerated in the old authorities as exempt from distress; and *a fortiori*, if his books generally are protected, the manuscript on which he is at work, which being unpublished may be presumed incomplete, is that kind of property, which the policy of the law has wisely protected from seizure.

Neither are the assignees under a Commission of Bankruptcy, entitled to the manuscripts of an author, although the copyright of a book which has been printed and published will legally pass for the benefit of the creditors(⁴).

---

(1) Cited 17 Vesey, 338.   There is a distinction between the right to publish a similar work, or set up a similar trade, and the fraud of identifying it with the work or trade of another.   *Ib.* 342.

(2) 4 Burr. 2,311.   (3) Amb. 695.

(4) Longman v. Tripp, 3 New. rep. 67.   It is questionable whether a book not completely printed and consequently uupublished, could be claimed by the creditors.

N

BOOK III.

DISQUISITIONS

ON THE

PRINCIPLES OF THE LAWS.

AND THEIR

EFFECT ON LITERATURE.

BOOK III.

𝔒𝔫 𝔱𝔥𝔢 𝔓𝔯𝔦𝔫𝔠𝔦𝔭𝔩𝔢𝔰 𝔬𝔣 𝔱𝔥𝔢 𝔏𝔞𝔴𝔰.

FIRST PART.

OF THE LIMITATION OF COPYRIGHT TO TWENTY-EIGHT YEARS.

CHAP. 1.——THE OBJECTIONS TO A PERPETUITY IN COPYRIGHT CONSIDERED.

I. It has been objected that, although the invention and labor, by which literary compositions are produced, entitle the author to the exclusive use of his manuscript, *the right cannot be extended to* IDEAS, because they are not objects of property.

In the commencement of our historical view, we have considered the nature and foundation of the rights of literary property, and shewn that it was equally entitled with any other production whether depending upon *occupancy* or *labor,* to the full protection of the laws—that if it came not within the *literal* definition of "property," as laid down of old, it was assuredly within its *spirit*---that the general interests of society, as well as the comprehensive principles of justice, required the protection of copyright, and to exclude it would be a violation of the boasted maxim of the English Law, that *redress is provided for every injury.*

In further reply to this objection, "that there can be no *property* in ideas," it must be observed, that an author does not claim a copyright in the *subject* on which he has written, but in *the composition which he has produced* on that subject. In the cases which have been decided regarding the piracy of copyright, it is repeatedly laid down, that "the subject" of literary compositions is open to all writers ; but that no one must seize and appropriate to himself the labor bestowed by another. He may avail himself of it as a guide to the sources from whence the result was derived---to the mines where the raw material may be found, but he cannot lawfully take the manufactured article. A lively image has been used to explain the extent of the right. *The wells of literature are open to all, but no one has a right to use the bucket of another.*

The objection, indeed, resolves itself entirely into the supposed difficulty of ascertaining whether the later author has drawn his materials from the original sources, to which the first must have resorted, or has availed himself of his predecessor's ingenuity and labor, without exerting his own.

But the same difficulty prevails in the present limited state of legal protection. The same questions arise *within* the twenty-eight years, as would arise after they had expired. The argument, therefore, if it be worth anything, should lead to the abolition of all protection whatever.

II. It has also been urged, that as it is every man's natural right to follow a lawful employment, and printing and bookselling are of that kind, *every monopoly that would intrench upon these lawful employments, is a restraint upon the liberty of the subject.* And if the printing and selling of every book that comes out may be confined to a few, and for ever withheld from all the rest of the trade, it is asked, what provision will the bulk of them be able to make for their respective families ?

It is curious, that this objection should have occurred to the learned judge who advanced it; for, if it be well founded, then the holding of any kind of property exclusively and for ever is also a monopoly.

It is obvious there could be no monopoly in this case more then prevails in the possession of a plot of land or a herd of cattle. It is not a monopoly of *all* books, of all kinds —such as the prerogative claim was formerly made ; nor of all books upon *one subject*—it is the mere appropriation of the property in *one book*, the produce of *individual* invention and labor. Not only is every subject of literature open to the exertion of the talents and industry of all ; but every trader in literary works has the same opportunity as others to purchase the existing copyright of authors, by offering a sufficient price, or of engaging literary men to write new works on the same or on other subjects, of which there is a boundless and exhaustless number.

Further, this objection to a supposed undue restraint on plagiarists and pirates, like the former one, should extend, if it be tenable, to the abolition of the law altogether, and therefore annihilates itself.

III. But it said---*others, may arrive at similar conclusions.*

It would be difficult to a ascertain the right owner, and inconveniently increase litigation.

There is here an unfounded assumption: No two minds being alike, it is impossible for any two men to compose a work precisely similar. They may arrive indeed at the same " conclusions"—Thinking upon the same subject, the truth may be apparent to both ; but each will proceed by different methods, and those who are skilled in criticism would have no difficulty in determining which of the two was the plagiarist, and an intelligent jury, aided by competent witnesses and the learning of the bar, and the experience and wisdom of the bench, would surely be able to determine whether the work was colorably pirated from another, or an original and *bona fide* production.

But, admitting that there might be occasional *difficulty in identifying* the works of one author from another. Such cases would be rare. Are we to abandon the property in general because it sometimes may be troublesome to ascertain it ? There is frequent difficulty in identifying other species of property—nay, even, of identifying persons; but no one has yet been wild enough to propose the abolition of the laws of property or personal protection, because the evidence of ownership and identity is sometimes doubtful. We do not conceive the difficulty would be greater in this than in many other kinds of property, There are no insuperable obstacles in identifying a literary work within the time already limited by the statute, and the same rules might be applied if the time were extended.

That *it will give rise to litigation* so long as men are dishonest cannot be doubted ; but the same occasional evil prevails in every kind of property. He who prints and publishes another man's copy, or makes such voluminous extracts from it as to injure its sale, knows as well as the depredator of any thing else, that it is not his own, and if he has no sense of rectitude, he should be taught by the law that it is wrong, and punished either in purse or person for his transgresssion. There would be no greater degree of litigation than in proportion to the number of violations of the law of copyright, and the inclination of the injured to seek redress. Let the experiment be tried and there will be no difficulty in providing remedies for any evil that may casually arise in the execution of the law.

IV. *The composition is the property of the writer whilst in manuscript, but the act of publishing gives it to the world.* If there be any force in mere *legal* reasoning, in this objection, there is, none in reason or common sense. By the publication the author *gives* nothing whatever. He *sells* each copy for its price, and the purchaser may do what he pleases with the copy *except* printing other copies. He may make use of the language and sentiments it contains in any way he thinks proper, *except* to the injury of the author. He may quote or abridge passages to improve his own works, provided his extracts be not of unreasonable length, and have the effect of injuring the sale of the original. He may also lend or sell his copy, and may make a profit by the loan or sale. But he cannot appropriate to himself the profit derivable from the sale of *other copies* the right to print which was never sold. The purchase he has made is for his own use, not the use of the public, and he must abide by the reasonable conditions of his bargain. It may be compared to the case of a proprietor of a theatre, who grants for a certain price a ticket of admission, which, if transferrable, the purchaser may lend or let on hire ; but whoever supposed, that he had a consequent right to multiply copies and sell them to the injury of the proprietor? So, in the instance of a public Water Company, the contract includes the unlimited use by the person who pays for it, but conveys no right to vend the smallest portion. By analogy, therefore, to other kinds of limited sales ; as well as from the reason of the case, it is clear that the act of publishing is no dedication to the public, so as to make the property common to all.

V. Another objection is, that the *Patentees of Mechanical inventions possess but a limited term*, and therefore, that the authors of literary or scientific works should be satisfied with the same measure of legal protection.

We shall not enter into the argument of the distinction between the nature of new machinery and that of literary compositions, for we are not entirely satisfied that it is well founded([1]). But we rest on this, if there is a distinction, in fact, we are glad the patentees suffer less wrong : If not, they are common sufferers, and should take part in seeking redress. It is a proof of the straits to which our opponents are driven when they excuse one act of injustice by another.

VI. It is objected that it would prolong the power of the owner to deal with the public as he chose, and that he might *either suppress a valuable work or put an exorbitant price upon it ;* in both of which events the public would be injured.

The fear of *suppression* may be easily provided against. If the proprietor does not re-print the work when required within a reasonable time, there would be no injustice in con-

---

(1) The best comment on this point seems to be made by Mr. *Hargrave.*—vide NOTES.

sidering the copyright as abandoned. It is replied, that there
would be a difficulty in proving an abandonment. We do
not perceive the difficulty, at least, in the majority 'of
instances, and regulations which experience would suggest,
might be adapted to circumstances. Generally speaking, if
it were worth while to reprint a work, the copies of which
were exhausted, it would not be abandoned. Where it was
out of print, notice might be given to the last publisher and
entered in the registry of the Stationers' Company, and if at
the expiration of a certain length of time (perhaps proportioned to the magnitude of the work) it were not reprinted, it
might then become common property.

    There is no probability that the *price* of literature will be
enhanced more than the price of land. Some ages ago a
large price might have been required, and as the demand was
then limited, a higher price was not unjustifiable. But since
the development of the true principles of trade, there can be
no apprehension of such a result. Every publisher now
knows that the cheaper he sells his books, the greater is the
sale, and a small profit, upon a rapid and extensive sale is in
the result more advantageous, than a larger profit upon a slow
and limited one. The more generally useful the work, the
cheaper it might be sold, on account of the greater number
of purchasers. It is only of works which are little demanded
that a high price could be necessary. So that the evil cures
itself, and both the cause of literature and the interest of the
public, would be promoted by enabling the proprietors of
this kind of property to deal with it as unreservedly as with
any thing else. And surely, if the principle of free trade
should any where be acted upon, it ought to prevail in favor
of the press—that great instrument of national knowledge
and improvement, and by which all other improvements are
so much extended and promoted.

    Besides the price might be restrained by a jury. Com-
pensation for property is settled on many occasions under
Acts of Parliament for roads and canals. It would be competent for an author or proprietor to prove the *capital* invested
and learned men might be called to estimate the *skill*, and
publishers to prove what would be a fair or liberal remune-
rating price.

    But then it is said, if there be an actual *right*, it is im-
proper to restrain it. Now we have no wish that it should be
restrained : we do not apply for the restraint. We think it
not only *needless* but *objectionable* and unjust.—We conceive
that every man's own interest will be the best protection to

the public for the fair exercise of the right. It is so in all other
arts and trades and why should it not be the same in those of
printing and publishing?   But if we cannot have the right
without the restraint, we will submit to it.—It is an odd
objection that denies a right, because if exercised without
the restraint it may be injurious, and then rejects the restraint
because all restraints are reprehensible.

VII. The advocates of *limited* copyright further contend,
that "*glory is the reward of science, and those who deserve it,
scorn all meaner views.*" It was not for gain that Bacon, Newton,
Locke, &c. instructed the world. There are various unan-
swerable replies to this piece of rhetoric.

First, the question is not what are the motives of an
author—Glory or Gain—but what is due in justice from
the public to those who have conferred benefits upon it?
What is *right?* If the benefit be perpetual, why should not
the reward? If Shakespeare has left us volumes of intellectual gratification which can die only (nay, not even then) with
the language in which they are written, why should not his
decendants (long reduced to poverty) derive the benefit
which justice demands, and which gratitude would cheerfully
pay.   Granting that Nelson and Wellington were stimulated
to their immortal exertions by glory alone, do we owe them
nothing, because they have received their reward? Were the
titles and the wealth that were bestowed upon them needless?
Besides, it may be asked, how do the national rewards of
substantial property act in the way of excitement upon the
conduct of others. Has the perpetual entailment of Blenheim
had no influence upon the minds of subsequent warriors?

2ndly. Different men possess different propensities and
feelings. The objection supposes all men alike, and that they
are alone influenced by the predominant passion of ambition.   It is an objection founded in utter ignorance of human
nature. A very large class certainly are desirous of renown.
But there are *other classes besides the ambitious.* Many men
love their parents, wives, children, and kindred, and to that
intense degree that they will exert their powers more
eminently for them than for the empty buzz of strangers or
of distant posterity. Do these lawyer-like reasoners suppose that all men of warm affections are deficient in ingenuity,
and that the stern and cold man of ambition is the only
inheritor of genius and greatness? Now a man of this kindly
nature may care but little for "gain," so far as he is
personally concerned; but for the sake of those who are
dearer to him even than "glory," he may bestow more labor

than the mere ambitious man, and wherefore should not he be permitted to receive that, which the public would readily and gladly pay? Who is there that has read the " Paradise Lost," that would not be delighted whilst paying its price to know, that he had contributed his mite to avert the penury in which had died the last descendant of its author?

It is any thing but philosophical to talk of men, in general, as exerting themselves *disinterestedly*, and " scorning all mean views." Small must be the knowledge of human nature which ventures upon such declamation. There are men of the strictest integrity, who far surpass the generous and the ambitious in acts of justice, and yet are influenced by motives of gain. Are all men, who desire to be paid for the services they perform, " mean?"

Authors are not a peculiar race of men---able to live on the air, " glory crammed." Neither we suspect were those who reasoned with such loftiness able to live on the renown, either of framing or administering the laws with impartiality.

There is yet another class of men, the most numerous of all, who are not actuated by any *single* predominant motive, to whom neither glory, nor gain, are master passions; but who are influenced by mixed motives, and who would bestow greater exertions, if their social, as well as selfish feelings were equally gratified. Why should we not use all the means which justice permits, to excite men to the exertion of their best faculties?

He who can, by his works, obtain not only the prospect of future fame, but the substantial advantage of immediate recompense, with a provision for his family after his death, will labor with greater diligence than those who are incited only by the desire of posthumous renown.

The reward of glory may, indeed, stimulate the production of works of pure genius, and the more especially as the exercise of the imagination is so peculiarly delightful; but this cannot be the case, in an equal degree, in the department of philosophy. Great, persevering, and often painful labor, is necessary to the accomplishment of many works of science, and therefore every possible inducement should be added, instead of being diminished, that may tend to encourage the prosecution of such labors.

Besides, an author, who wished for no other reward than renown, might still exercise his liberality, and either present his labors gratuitously to the public, or bestow them on some meritorious object. He can do so now in favour of the Uni-

versities ; and the glory of the bequest would be the greater
because it would be more rare and generous.

CHAP. II.

ON THE INJUSTICE AND IMPOLICY OF THE LIMITATION.

In the previous part of the work we have considered the
reasons and foundation on which the claim to an extension of
copyright depends, and the unlimited protection to which it
is entitled, under the general laws which apply to all kinds
of *property*. It will not be necessary in this place to enter
into an examination of the subtilties, by which it was attempted to exclude literary compositions from the guardianship of
our courts of justice. In the *Introductory Dissertation*, and the
sections on the nature and *definition of literary property*, and its
claim to a perpetuity by the *common law*, which commence
the Historical View, we have endeavoured to establish a foundation for the property in question, which we conceive to be
consistent, equally with the laws of civilized communities in
general, and with those of this country in particular.

Referring to those previous parts of the Treatise, for the
preliminary consideration of the basis on which the right is
founded, we shall proceed, in this place, to discuss the *policy*, as well as the *justice*, of extending to the Scholar and the
Artist the provisions which guard the property of all other
classes of the community.

It is one of the most indisputable principles of justice,
that THE LAWS SHOULD BE EQUAL.

This golden rule is violated in the distinction created between the copyright of individual authors, and the copyrights
held by the Crown and the Universities, in both of which instances it endures without limitation.

The several cases reported in the law-books, for violating
patents for printing prerogative copies, after the expiration of
the period limited by the statute, prove that a copyright was
acknowledged by the common law : since if the king had not
the right, he could not grant it to the patentee. It is clear that
the king, by his prerogative, has no power to *restrain* printing, which is a trade and manufacture ; or to grant an *exclusive* privilege of printing any book whatsoever, *except* as a subject might; by reason of the copyright being his property.
It is now clearly settled, that the king is owner of such books
or writings only, as he had the sole right originally to publish,

consisting of acts of parliament, orders of council, proclamations, English translations of the Bible, and the Common Prayer-Book. These are his *own* works, as he represents the state, and, according to the constitution, is head of the church.

There seems to be no principle on which the exclusive privilege thus established in favour of the Crown, should be denied to private authors. If there be any sufficient reason for appropriating the acts of state and the ordinances of the church, the same reason would extend to the case of all other copyright;---if it be thought necessary, in order to secure correct copies of the statutes and ordinances, that no one but the king's printer should be permitted to publish them ; it is in a comparative degree important, that the author of a literary work should retain the superintendence of its publication; since it may otherwise be incorrectly printed, or he may be deprived of the power of amending or improving it--- of correcting errors on the one hand, or extending the illustration of truths on the other.

So far, indeed, from there being any solid reason for the exercise of the prerogative, whilst the ordinary rights of property are denied to individuals, it is manifest that here there ought to be no copyright whatever, beyond the printing of such copies as are necessary for judicial proof, or other public purposes. For all other objects there ought to be no restraint, since it must be the interest, as it ought to be the duty of government, to diffuse a knowledge, as extensively as possible, of the regulations both of church and state; and there is a sufficient guarantee, that the unofficial copies of these acts of state will be adequately faithful, for any blunders in them would be soon detected, and the publication which came recommended by its accuracy, would be the most extensively circulated.

The other instance in which the right claimed by authors has been granted to others, whilst it was denied to them, is that of the *Universities* of England and Scotland, and the *Colleges* of Eton, Westminster, and Winchester, and that of Trinity-College, Dublin.

It is difficult to conjecture any reason for allowing to these public institutions a copyright in literary compositions, which does not, in a far stronger degree, belong to the individuals by whom this intellectual property was produced.

Without exhausting conjectures on the foundation of this privilege, we may resort to the Act of Parliament by which it is created, and where the basis of the claim is thus described :—

Authors, it is said, may give or bequeath the copies of books to these respective Universities and Colleges, and may direct the profits to be applied for the advancement of learning; lest, therefore, such useful purposes should be frustrated, the sole printing is secured to them in *perpetuity*.

Now, it is manifest, that if the Universities, as *the legatees of authors*, are entitled to this extended protection, the authors themselves are still better entitled to it. Admitting that the Universities are in possession of no more than their just rights, it is evident that private individuals, not merely for their own sakes, but for the interests of science and literature, are, at least, *equally*, if not in a higher degree, entitled to legal protection.

The Universities, in their corporate capacity, can establish no pretensions on which the exemption can be justly founded. They are not, collectively, in advance of the literary and scientific world; nor have they accelerated the progress of modern improvement It is, indeed, often urged, that these institutions rather impede than assist the extension of science; that they follow, at no inconsiderable distance, rather than lead forward the human intellect to new fields of inquiry. Without discussing this invidious view of the subject, it may be assumed, without much fear of injustice, that the personages who compose these learned associations, have achieved nothing in their *official* character, which can justify the peculiar exemptions they possess. The distinguished writers who, in their *private and individual* capacity, have conferred honor by their works on the seats of learning to which they belonged, cannot but make common cause with their literary brethren.

It is worth observing, also, that the privilege of the Universities cannot be upheld on the ground of necessity;--- they cannot plead that it is granted in commisseration for their *poverty*, for they are unquestionably better able to bear the wrong which the laws inflict on individuals, but which the Colleges possess such effectual power to prevent. Indeed, were there any foundation for such a pretension, it would be infinitely better for the sake of justice, and the example of an equal administration of its sacred principles, that they should receive a parliamentary grant, than that so flagrant an anomaly should be permitted to exist.

THE EVASION OF THE LAWS is always a great evil, for there is not only the immediate injury to justice of the specific violation; but a general weakening of the salutary reverence which is entertained for national institutions when founded on principles of reason and equity.

Now both the authors and the publishers to whom they

have assigned their works, have a strong feeling that the limitation of copyright to the period of twenty-eight years is inconsistent with the regulations of all other arts and professions, at variance with the commonest principles of free trade, and equally injurious to authors and publishers without any correspondent benefit to the public. It is natural, therefore, that every effort should be made to elude the consequences of an arbitary and irrational infringement of their own rights and of the property of their families—of a patrimony often earned at the expence of health, and of the abridgment of life. And whilst acting under such feelings, there are few, even of the coldest-hearted legislators, who would visit with much censure, the plan of ingenuity and contrivance which has been resorted to by the parties interested, in saving themselves, as much as possible, from injury or diminishing its magnitude.

The proprietor of the copyright prior to its expiration takes care to prepare a new edition *with notes*, and though the original work becomes common property, the notes are protected on the ground of their constituting an original composition. By a sort of combination also amongst the principal booksellers, these renewed editions " with notes," receive a preference over others. The interpretation which the judges have put on this mode of republication is exceedingly liberal, but if it be right that publishers should resort to these expedients to protect their property, the law should allow it to be done openly instead of surreptitiously: an honorable man must revolt against a system which subjects him to lose his property or to practice devices and evasions which out of respect to the laws of his country he must dislike. And although by these means the mischief is somewhat practically diminished, much of it unavoidably remains. The work may not really require any notes either of explanation or addition or they may be such as the humblest talents can supply. There are, it is true, some subjects which are undergoing continual change and the publications which treat of them require proportionate alterations. But if not so, the work is incumbered with useless comments, or the name of some eminent author is appended to a new edition which an ordinary writer might equally well supply.

Not only individual publishers would gain by the extension, but it would promote the interest of publishers in general, if the property in a work were vested perpetually in the author and his assigns. Suppose that the moment a valuable book were published, every one had a right to pirate it, the effect would be, that a general scramble would ensue to

reprint cheaper editions than the original. A great number
of persons would be engaged in doing the same thing. The
market would be over stocked. None would be sufficiently
remunerated and all would be more or less injured. It would
be analagous to permitting the land of a deceased person to
be retained by any one who could by stratagem or force
obtain posession. A riot would then succeed the death of
every landed proprietor. Now something of the same kind
must take place, though in a less degree, at the expiration of
the statutory period, and although the evil is partially sub-
dued by the evasions and combination before adverted to,
still it cannot be generally avoided.

It has been urged by those who maintain the sufficieney of
the present system, that the extension of the term would produce *no good* to the public. But the question ought to be,
what evil will it occasion? For if there be no evil, there ought
to be no restraint. It is happily clear that right and expediency are as inseparable in this as in all other cases, for by the
extension of the term the public would receive superior and
cheaper publications. Authors are at present discouraged
from executing works of a standard nature because such
works demand the labor of a life. It is evident that talent
may be more profitably employed in the attention to works
of temporary excitement. The fashion of a particular age or
season is consulted instead of the general and enduring interest
of the community. The question with an author who is about
to select the sphere of his literary labor is not determined by
any opinion of what will be beneficial to mankind at large, or
ultimately ensure his own reputation, but what will sell the
best in the literary market.

It is not easy to estimate the labor and expence of a
work of superior utility and importance. It demands a
degree of research and care which can scarcely be bestowed
whilst the law continues in its present state. Besides the
works which are costly in their embellishments, the scientific
and literary labor which many of them demand, can only be
encountered where there is no apprehension of restraint. Thus,
in works of great historical scope—the investigation of ancient as well as modern manuscripts and records—of scarce
documents, ill-digested and repulsive works—of conflicting
evidence—all these demand not only great judgment and
accuracy in the winnowing of large masses of materials,
but superior skill in adopting the best arrangement, and
selecting the most appropriate language and illustration—
and without the devotion of much time and leisure, the

greatest talents cannot execute the work in a manner proportioned to its magnitude and importance.

Again, in works of a philosophic and scientific character—should they comprise subjects of striking originality : the invention of a new system—the task of experiment and induction may require a still wider range of exertion and longer continued perseverance, which it is vain to suppose will be often bestowed without superior recompense. It is not reasonable to expect that the public can render immediate justice to works of an entirely novel description. For whatever is at variance with established opinions and received theories is naturally liable either to neglect or opposition. Perhaps it is the safer course for the public that it should be so. There is less danger in adopting a system after it has been subjected to every kind of ordeal, than if it were favorably received upon its first hasty and insufficient investigation. But whilst the public enjoy this immunity, let no needless injustice be done to the sons of genius. If the reward of their splendid discoveries cannot be bestowed in the age they live in,—if the authors of new and ingenious systems cannot reasonably expect that justice will be done to their meritorious labors during the span of their own brief existence, let them at least possess the consolation of looking forward to that day, however distant, when posterity will make amends to their surviving family or to some future descendant.

The evil it is evident must thus fall the heaviest on the most useful authors, whom it should be the policy of the legislature in the highest degree to protect, encourage, and recompense. It has often been remarked, that the best and most original works make the slowest advances in general circulation. *Smith's Wealth of Nations* passed through two editions only in eight years. *Hume's History* fell dead-born from the press ; and MILTON's immortal poem remained for many years in almost total obscurity.

It is a fact, proved by indisputable evidence before a Committee of the House of Commons, that many important works of an expensive nature have not been published owing to the hardships imposed by the law. A great part of that hardship is attributable to the heavy tax of the eleven presentation copies for the public libraries (which we shall presently examine) but much also of disadvantage arises, even as regards these costly publications, from the limitation of time, because the splendid engravings, which occasion the chief expence of many of these works are equally doomed to common depredation after the end of twenty-eight years.

It must be recollected that, authors are generally dependent on circumstances of a very uncertain nature for the notice their productions receive from the public. A great name will often do much and so may a great subject. Reviewers also are able to accomplish not a little in favor of a new publication, yet criticism is not infallible nor always well intentioned. It may suit the taste or the interest of the critic to cry down the subject, or to affix the "branding iron," upon the author. Malice may purposely condemn and prejudice, or ignorance blunderingly censure.—Thus "the whole ear" of the reading public may be "abused."

It is obvious, that if the period were extended, a higher remuneration might be afforded for works of superior importance on account of the enduring nature of the property in them. The profit it is true might not be rapid but its unlimited continuance would generally in the result compensate for the advance of a larger amount of capital. We might illustrate this fact by reference to the nature of leasehold and freehold property. For all ordinary purposes, to the great bulk of mankind, long leasehold property is really as useful as freehold, and endures as long as the lives of any for whom they feel an interest, yet we may perceive that such is not the general feeling, for the price in the market is exceedingly different: men are content with about three per cent when it is ensured to them in perpetuity, but they expect seven or eight in the other case, though it may last out three generations.

The cheapness of a work would thus obviously be promoted by the just extension of the period of its protection, because the proprietor would not depend upon any sudden return of his capital, but would proportion his gain to the extent of its duration. As he would ultimately receive a better remuneration he could afford to diminish its present amount. The calculation is now made upon an immediate return : if that does not take place, the work is supposed to be condemned—no matter what may be its intrinsic merits, no further efforts are made to bring them before the notice of the public.—The legal period being so short, it is not deemed worth while to keep open the account, and it is closed as soon as possible.

It may be said, however, that this extension of copyrgiht would not produce any very perceptible difference in the immediate price to the public of literary works. And undoubtedly to effect a sufficient reduction, corresponding with the sale of books on the Continent, the tax in favour of the public libraries, the imposts upon paper, and the duty on advertisements should be duly moderated if not removed. It must, however, be apparent, that great good would be done by the extension of the copyright, and it would be an earnest of future improvements, that would give a great impulse to the best kind of literary undertakings.

SECOND PART.

OF THE LIBRARY TAX OF ELEVEN COPIES
OF EVERY BOOK.

———

CHAP I.——THE GROUNDS OF THE LIBRARY CLAIM EXAMINED.

Having brought before the reader the state of the law
with reference to the contracted period during which the
rights of authors are protected, and animadverted upon the
monstrous injustice of permitting the productions of intellectual labor to become the object of common plunder after
twenty-eight years, whilst the fruits of ordinary industry
were wisely secured in perpetuity; we now turn to the consideration of the next feature of oppression in these statutes
"for the encouragement of learning." After curtailing the
duration of the right of literary property, from a perpetuity to
the brief term of twenty-eight years (in return for which
restraint, it might have been anticipated that some splendid
boon was intended to be conferred) the Acts of Parliament
proceed to impose *a tax of eleven copies* on every publication,
whether the most rare and expensive, or the cheapest and
most insignificant.

Although the statutes impose a penalty of three pence
per sheet for pirating copyright, the old mode of redress by
an action at law for damages, or an injunction and an
account in equity has always been and is still preferred. So
that, in truth, the statute has practically left the remedy just
where it was, and in consideration of the three pence per
sheet (which is rarely if ever sued for) cut down the perpetuity of right to the short span of twenty-eight years; and
in return for these services to literature, this protection of
learned men and their families, (which closely resembles the
protection afforded by the vulture to the lambs)—the legislature imposed a new tax of six copies, and revived an old
one of three others which had been levied in the time of
Charles II. but had expired soon after the revolution. Thus
we perceive, that the mild literary imposts of the Stuarts
were not deemed sufficient in that æra which has somewhere
been denominated the Augustine Age of English Literature!

The two remaining copies, which complete this measure
of "encouragement," were imposed so late as the year 1802.
The purpose for which these last copies are professedly de-

signed, might be considered, at first sight, as mitigating, in
some degree, the quantum of injustice, for they are imposed
for the benefit of Ireland—constituting, it may be supposed,
some little compensation for the evils to which that ill-fated
province was subjected, and realizing part of the high expec-
tations which were so flatteringly held out to its patriotic
feelings, that the union of the two parliaments would be followed by the happiest effects.

Thus, for the paltry consideration of these miserable
copies, wrung from the hard pittance of the ingenious men of
this country; the gifted sons of Ireland, who have so long
shed a lustre upon the literature of the empire, are in their
turn mulct,—not in *two* copies only, but in *eleven!* Such are
the notions of equal laws and equal justice, which have
hitherto prevailed on this important subject.

In treating of the origin of this tax, we examined the
legal pretensions on which it was attempted to be maintained([1]).
It was formerly contended that the art of printing had been
introduced at the expense of the king, and therefore that he
was entitled to impose such terms as he pleased, in granting
a license for its exercise. The agreement was also adduced
by which the Stationers' Company engaged to furnish a copy
of every book to the University Library at Oxford. These
pretensions having been exploded, we have now to examine
the *general and more popular grounds,* on which the advocates
of the Universities still contend for the continuance of the
tax.

I. That *the law is beneficial to the Universities* need not be
disputed. These gratuitous contributions to their several
libraries save their funds. But is the saving necessary or
just? Have they not sufficient means to purchase every useful publication? Do they really make use of the current literature of the age? These are questions which cannot be answered, except in the negative. It cannot be requisite that
every work that issues from the fertility of the press should
be deposited in all the libraries. The works which are esteemed in these ancient colleges are those which have long maintained their rank as standard productions. The great bulk of
modern publications are not introduced, and cannot, perhaps,
with propriety be introduced into the course of study pursued
at the Universities. A large part of the system of education
is confined to ancient authors, and to subjects which do not
admit of modern improvement. Indeed, the general plan of
instruction is opposed to whatever is novel and speculative.

Nothing is adopted but that which has been long tried and established, and we cannot conceive, therefore, why the heads of colleges require those valuable but modern works, which they do not permit to be used.

Even were it necessary to the welfare of the Universities, that each should possess a copy of every publication, it is iniquitous to exact them at the expense of individual authors or proprietors. The colleges of which they are composed are in general richly endowed, and if each college could not afford to possess itself of the modern publications, their united funds would certainly be amply sufficient. It may be true, that some of the Scottish colleges have but little surplus wealth to dispose of in the purchase of every kind of publication ; but whatever may be thought to the contrary, we are persuaded that the intelligent people of Scotland, in general, possess too much just pride to plead the *poverty* of their Universities as a ground for unjust exactions.

II. It is said that *the Universities cannot purchase the splendid editions* of great and expensive works, and yet they are works of which they stand in the greatest need : *they give a University dignity and respectability.* And in some departments of liberal education, accurate drawings and engravings are essentially requisite.

Now, however agreeable to the eye are splendid editions, and however suited to the taste of the affluent, we exceedingly question their utility, not only to the student, but to the professed author. Fine plates and bindings are adapted to the literary idler and looker-on, but can scarcely stimulate any one to intellectual exertion. These splendid trappings are for holidays, and not for days of learned labor. They tend, like great luxuries in general, more to enervate than invigorate.

That the welfare of a college is at all dependent on splendid editions we, therefore, altogether deny. If they should be rich enough to purchase these luxuries there can be no objection, for though not necessary to the real student and man of letters, they are no doubt agreeable subjects for literary relaxation.

The "respectability" of the establishment surely cannot be promoted by robbing an author of any portion of his fair-earned reward, and drawing down upon itself the odium of the whole republic of letters. And its " dignity " can scarcely be increased by any other means than the opportunity it affords to attain sound, comprehensive, and accurate knowledge, in the highest departments of philosophy and literature. It is beneath its real dignity to owe any of its attractions to the splendid decoration of its library, in which, indeed, there should be as little as possible addressed to the external sense, and every thing adapted to excite the intellect.

It is true that the student may be assisted in his pursuits by occasional engravings, but those which are useful are of a very different class to the splendid drawings which render many works so costly. Even in architecture, we apprehend it is not necessary that the plates for purposes of study, should be very costly, and besides, it is not in a college that the education of an architect can be completed. Antiquarian works are of course expensive, but we are not aware that the Universities profess to induct their pupils in the knowledge of antiquities, the study of which may safely be left to the Antiquarian Society. So also botany and zoology may be effectually studied without the aid of magnificent plates, which, indeed, are rather calculated to excite a taste for drawing, and to encourage a love of show and splendour, than to induce philosophical and studious habits. We can see no advantage to public education in attracting the pupil to quit the hard study, which can alone render him eminent in society, for the purpose of gratifying his taste in examining splendid folios, and admiring the productions of the arts of drawing and engraving.

III. But the law is said to be beneficial to general literature, by *affording to men of literary talents and industry the means of information*, and enabling them to accomplish works of the highest merit and utility.

This is too barefaced an excuse for injustice : it is robbing Peter, not to *pay* Paul, but to enable him dishonestly to live at the expense of Peter. The men of " literary talents and industry," who *have* accomplished works of merit and ability, are to be deprived of a large part of their profit, where any exists, in order that others may avail themselves of the results of their industry gratuitously. Surely, the fellows of these learned Universities, who favor the world with their collegiate lucubrations, and who set their own price upon them, should stand on the same footing as other literary men, and purchase the materials which they require in the course of their labors. It may be very convenient, but it cannot be just, that by the aid of these Universities a writer should possess himself of the property of his predecessors, for which no remuneration whatever has been made. And after all, there is not the plea of *necessity* in favor of the injustice ; for it is the common practice of an author who is engaged on a work, in the preparation of which he has occasion to refer to a variety of books, to obtain them from his publisher ; and it is part of the understanding between them, that all the books which are necessary shall be lent him.   Of course there is, of all others, the least difficulty in supplying the modern publications.   And we presume, no one who is tolerably acquainted with the history and circumstances of literature, can believe that it has been, or is likely to be, benefited or improved by the doctrine, for the first time laid down in 1812, that the Universities are entitled to copies of every publication.   We may venture to say, that if not the *best* authors of the present age, at least, as good as any others, are unconnected with the Universities, and derive no advantage whatever from the accumulations which have been made in their libraries, either since 1812, when *every* book has been supplied, or prior to that time, when the registered books only were delivered.   Indeed, it is absurd to suppose that the intellect of the country is to be advanced by such paltry means, and the true friends of academical learning are no doubt as much ashamed of the folly of such an argument, as of the dishonesty of its principle.

Supposing, however, all these considerations set aside, let us inquire what is really the use of the single copy given to any one University ?   In general, the books are of no use whatever to any one in any of the colleges. Of the far greater portion, not a single page is ever read.   It either is utterly useless, or is so considered for all collegiate purposes.   Indeed, how can it be otherwise, when the libraries indiscriminately demand their copies of every publication---of all the trash, folly, and obscenity, which find their way out of the press.

But, suppose the work to be really valuable, either for its profound philosophy or learning, or for the popularity of the subject and the talent it indicates.   Then every one becomes desirous to read it.   Thousands of students apply for it ; and what is the consequence ?   As but few can possibly obtain it, the work is either purchased or borrowed from the common circulating libraries, and the copy in each of the eleven libraries has precisely the effect of preventing purchases from the author, for the sole benefit of a few individuals, who can either do without the book, or afford to pay for it.

IV. Another benefit of the law, however, is said to consist in *preserving the books from the danger of loss,* some of which are valuable, and others will to future times prove curious.

The really valuable works there is no probability will ever be destroyed. The art of printing has disposed of all reasonable apprehension of that contingency, and we think it bad morality, on the coldest application of the doctrine of expediency, to do an act of positive injustice, for the sake of preserving something which may become *curious*. Certainly, many a production, intrinsically worthless, may, from its extreme rarity or antiquity, obtain an artificial value in the estimation of those who are pleased with such things; but it is not politic, (to say nothing of honesty,) to injure and discourage the writers of the present age, in order that a biblical antiquary may, some centuries hence, feed his idle vanity with the possession of a specimen of unique absurdity!

To meet, however, the object of preserving a copy of every kind of publication, whether the offspring of the talented or the foolish, the moral or the vicious, it would be sufficient to deposit a single copy in the British Museum as the *National Library*. To this, we are sure, no author or publisher would offer an objection, and this copy, so deposited, would serve the purpose, and render unnecessary the extra copy which every printer, by the 39th Geo. III. c. 79, sec. 27. 29, is obliged to reserve of every work he prints.

CHAP. II.

OF THE EFFECT OF THE TAX ON LITERATURE.

After having thus considered the nature of the claim of these favoured libraries, and the grounds on which it rests, we proceed to notice the evils which must necessarily attend its continuance.

The law has the effect of preventing the publication, both of valuable and expensive works; of those which require in their composition great learning and talent, and those which demand expensive illustrations and embellishments. The costliness of a work necessarily diminishes the number of its purchasers, and consequently the copies published are proportionally of a limited amount. It is well known, also, that the scarcity of a book increases its value in the literary market, and it is consequently material that as accurate a calculation as possible should be made of the expected demand. The skill and capital which are embarked in these expensive undertakings, cannot be rewarded without placing a high price upon each copy, and the exaction of eleven

copies out of fifty or 100, generally absorbs the whole profit.
In some instances, the eleven copies amount to a tax of upwards of 40 per cent.; in others of 20; and in a very large
proportion of cases, to 10 per cent.

Even in the most ordinary publications, the tax is sufficiently oppressive. The proprietor of the work, whether author or publisher, of course, forms the best estimate in his
power of the probable extent of the sale. The custom of the
printing-trade, it is well known, is to make the charge on each
250 copies, and the loss on eleven copies is exactly the price
for which they would sell, or if that number of extra copies
were printed, the loss would be equal to the printing of 250
copies, exclusive of the expence of paper. It is futile to say,
that the printer might make his charge in a different manner
—the custom of the trade has [been long established, and
we are not aware that the printer's remuneration is higher
than it ought to be, or that it can possibly be reduced.
On the contrary, we understand that journeymen taylors
receive higher wages than the compositors in a printing
office.

We have heard it argued, that where the work is
popular and the sale extensive, the exaction becomes a mere
trifle and is scarcely perceptible. Further, that when the
work does not sell, the eleven copies may as well be placed
in the public libraries as in the lumber-room of the publisher.

In considering this point, it must be borne in mind, that
the majority of publications are not sufficiently successful to
pay their expence, and although the publisher might afford
to pay the tax on a work which met with great good fortune,
yet it is only by these occasionally successful speculations
that he is enabled to bear the frequent losses which he must
necessarily sustain by other publications. This tax like
every other, should be imposed according to general principles and in conformity with the rights and interests of the
community at large. It is the language of heartless despo-
tism to tell an author that if his book is not sold he may as
well place it in a library as a lumber-room. Would this
cruel mockery be endured by other classes of the community?
If a man has more corn than he can sell, may the surplus be
seized? Is the manufacturer liable to this sort of confiscating
process when he cannot find a market for his wares? Can
the land of the lordly proprietor be taken possession of when
no profitable tenant can be found? Many of our monied men
have larger incomes than they think proper to consume,
and more capital than they can usefully employ—may we lay

hands upon a certain proportion of the surplus ? We suppose not—yet wherefore should the unsold productions of an
author be subjected to a different rule ? Though not saleable
now, they may sell at some future time, and if not at the price
demanded at a lower one.—At all events they will fetch their
weight as waste paper.

It may be observed also, that if the work is to be estimated as mere lumber, it cannot be valuable to the Universities,
unless indeed (as we have heard it hinted) those patrons and
promoters of learning increase their sufficiently ample
revenues by selling the books which they do not think proper
to dignify with a place on their shelves. We may classify
works into good and bad, doubtful and indifferent. Those
which are really valuable are not exceedingly numerous, and
the Universities ought to pay for them. They used to do so,
prior to the year 1812, when it was for the first time decided
that they were entitled to a copy of every publication, whether
entered at Stationers' Hall or not. Of works which are
worthless, these great preceptors of the rising generation,
surely need no copies ; and such as are of a doubtful or
indifferent character they ought not to require. Life is
short—the season of youth is brief, and should not be wasted
in the perusal of idle or questionable productions. Looking
at the ample endowments of many, if not all, of the Colleges
which constitute the several Universities, one should think
that their funds could not be better employed than in bestow-
ing part of them in the encouragement of valuable works,
upon the publication of which, indeed, depends that great
object of intellectual improvement, for the furtherance of
which, the Colleges themselves were established.

Amongst other arguments, or rather pretences, in support
of the policy, if not the justice, of the law, it has been
strangely contended that the sale of valuable publications is
favored by an opportunity being afforded by seeing such
works in the public libraries, and thus awakening a relish for
them ! Nothing can exceed the puerility, untruthfulness, or
misapprehension of such a suggestion. We take it, that, if
the knowledge of the public with respect to new publications,
were restricted to such information as they could obtain from
their deposit in the libraries named in the Act of Parliament, very few of them would find purchasers. Indeed, a
single advertisement or notice in a periodical work of extensive circulation, will evidently effect more in behalf of the
work, than if it were bestowed upon every College in the
Empire. We may be sure there is no lack of inclination to
purchase able and useful publications, and if the supply

could be made at a cheap rate, it is scarcely possible to estimate the extent of the demand. It is perfectly childish to talk of the excitement produced by seeing books in a public library, when compared with the effect of their exhibition in the shops of the booksellers. In London there is one copy deposited in the British Museum, and another, for the benefit of the clergy in Sion College : compare the number of persons who look at books of any kind in those two repositories, with those who are attracted by their exhibition in other ways, and we shall be satisfied of the fallacy of the notion. The fact is, that the British Museum (to which no one would object that a copy should be presented) is resorted to generally, not for the purpose of reading new publications, but to consult those which are old and scarce, and it is to the periodical press, and to the activity of publishers, that an author can alone look for "awaking a relish" for any production that can now be offered to the public.

Another supposed reason in excuse of the exaction, is, that it cannot affect authors or proprietors, because the amount either is, or may be, charged to the public. But in this hypothesis it is entirely forgotten, that literary works do not form a necessary of life, and especially that the higher class of them, which need the greatest encouragement, are required by comparatively a small part only of the community. The tax on the means of subsistence must be paid by the consumer, although, even in that instance, the quantity consumed varies according to the price, and when the tax is high, the tradesman, if he throws the whole amount on the consumer, necessarily suffers by the diminution of his custom. Literary works are of the class of luxuries and the smaller the price, the more extensive the sale. There is a certain quantum of money expended in articles of this class —a taste for literature is fashionable—it excites admiration and gratifies vanity, whilst it also exercises far higher and better qualities.—If the tax upon paper and advertisements, as well as this library imposition, were removed or reduced, and the period of copyright extended, so that books might be published and made known, as they should be, for two-thirds of the present expence, the sale of them would then increase, not only in the proportion of that third, which is now consumed in preliminary expenditure, but in a much greater degree; for not only the same sum would naturally be expended, which has hitherto been applied in the purchase of literary works, and therefore the sale increased upwards of 30 per. cent; but the reduced price would as naturally induce a still greater number to become purchasers, who are now deterred by its present heavy amount.

It has been contended, that the University and other libraries cannot purchase expensive books, and therefore the tax does not injure the sale. Whatever may be the case with respect to some of the minor colleges, it is certainly not so in the case of others. Several of them, prior to the new construction of the statute in 1812, were in the habit of subscribing for copies of costly publications : such as Dibden's Typographical Antiquities, Nichols's Leicestershire, &c. These instances of encouragement, formerly numerous, obviously tended to increase the number of such undertakings, but the present law has clearly an opposite tendency. The names of eminent libraries in the list of subscribers, formed a strong recommendation, and probably contributed to its extension No such inducement can now exist, and in addition to which there is the loss of profit on the copies which they were accustomed to take.

It is *a direct tax upon industry*. Nothing can be more unprincipled than this anomalous taxation of literary property. No other class than the literary was ever proposed to be so taxed. There is, indeed, no instance in which any art, trade, or profession, was ever subjected to such an imposition.

It is also an odious *restraint upon the press*. We are told by the highest authorities that they anxiously desire to promote the just liberty of the press, but then their "just liberty" has a peculiar definition, and whatever is unpalatable is branded with the name of licentiousness; but apart from these differences of opinion on the limits to be set to free discussion, we conceive that the present state of the law of copyright, and the library impost, is a direct invasion of that great palladium of our rights,—a FREE PRESS ; for it cannot be said to be free whilst its publications are subjected to such grievous restraints and exactions, from which other productions are wholly exempt. It is, in effect, instead of rendering it free, *tolerating only* its existence at a certain price, and under certain odious and oppressive restraints.

It is curious in the course of the discussions on this subject, to observe the expedients to which the opponents of justice have necessarily been driven. They reason in a circle of injustice and impolicy. The inventors of novel principles in machinery, or improvements and new applications of old ones, possess an exclusive property for a short term only. Then it is said, that literary works ought not to be better protected than those which are scientific. This we may grant, but we say they are *neither* of them sufficiently protected. The injustice inflicted upon the one class is not mitigated by its imposition on the other. In taking the account, however, of the evils endured, both by authors and scientific inventors, it must be stated that the latter are not compellable to present eleven copies or specimens of their mechanical inventions or improvements. To make the cases precisely correspondent, in the measure of injustice, the man of scientific genius should present the Royal Society, the Society of Arts, and other institutions in the metropolis or the provinces, with eleven specimens of every instrument or engine, however expensive. And we ask what would be thought by the British public of the modesty of that man, who should venture to propose an enactment, to the effect that eleven of all future implements and machinery, from a penknife to a steam-engine, should be deposited in Somerset-House? We presume he would be set down as a curious specimen of the knave and madman, who ought neither to be trusted, nor left at large.

It would be too much to say that no invention, nor any improvement, will take place, if these restrictions and acts of injustice are continued; for we well know that genius is irrepressible, and will force its triumphant way, in spite of and amidst every obstacle; yet we also know that the liberal feelings of the public are decidedly in favour of affording ample justice to men of learning, ingenuity, and talent; and it is not enough to say, that literary men still devote their days and nights to intellectual labor, notwithstanding the disadvantages by which they are surrounded. We feel assured that the laws must be altered, whenever their impolicy and injusticy are sufficiently made known by those who are without the walls of parliament, because at last it must be taken up by those who are within them, if they wish to promote and maintain that influence and character, which ought to belong to the members of an enlightened senate, the representatives of a free and intelligent people.

The law in its present state is a disgrace to the country. It is an anomaly in our legislative system. Let men of letters be placed, at least, on equal terms with the commonest artizan. We think the tax on the " raw material " of paper might be diminished; but if that cannot be done, surely the manufactured article of books should be free from impost. Every principle of political economy demands it, and the more especially, when it is recollected that the tax is not imposed for the benefit of the state or the community, but in favour only of chartered bodies, whose wealth and immunities are already sufficiently abundant.

If our literature be equal to that of the continental states, let us imitate their example : let us cease to injure and really encourage those to whom we are indebted for our eminence. If it be inferior, let us lose no time in removing every impediment from its way, and introducing every means that can facilitate its improvement, and promote its rise : let not Great Britain be the country in which literary property is burthened more oppressively, in a six-fold degree, than any other nation of the civilized world ; rather let her abolish the imposition altogether, and surpass even the republics of the new world, as she undoubtedly might the monarchies of the old.

N O T E S,

COMPRISING

A U T H O R I T I E S

REGARDING

THE LIMITATION OF COPYRIGHT,

AND

THE LIBRARY TAX.

———◆———

ARRANGED CHRONOLOGICALLY.

———◆———

𝕹𝖔𝖙𝖊𝖘.

In support of the views which have been taken of the injustice and impolicy of the laws, we deem it material to introduce some statements and reasonings taken from different sources, all of which importantly tend to confirm the positions in the text.

In making the selections for this purpose, we shall arrange them, in conformity with the general plan of the work, 1st. into the authorities which relate to the *extension of the term* of copyright, and 2dly, those on the subject of the *Library Tax.*

1. ON EXTENDING THE DURATION OF COPY-RIGHT.

Milton, 1644.

Among the glosses which were used to colour this ordinance against unlicensed printing, and make it pass, was *the just retaining of each man his several copy ; which, God forbid, should be gainsaid.*

For that part which *preserves justly every man's copy to himselfe,* or provides for the poor, I touch not, only wish they be not made pretences to abuse and persecute honest and painfull men, who offend not in either of these particulars.

Carte, 1735.

It cannot be amiss to obviate an objection founded on a mistaken notion, as if this privilege for old copies concerned only the booksellers ; whereas, in fact, many authors are greatly concerned in it. Mr. Anstis and Mr. Browne Willis have printed their very laborious collections at their own expense, and still retain the property thereof. It would be hard to let these gentlemen undergo the mortification of seeing their works (like those of Sir W. Temple) pirated and printed in the same letter and paper as Tom Thumb, besides the loss they would suffer through the hinderance given to the sale of their books, great numbers of which still lie upon their hands, and will do so for ever if they may be printed in weekly parcels, an evil which can never be effectually prevented but by securing the property of old copies as well as new, thereby depriving pirates at once of all their materials. The property of many books still remains in the heirs of the authors. Sir W. Dugdale left by his will the copy of the *Baronage of England,* and the right of reprinting the same (the best and most useful of all his works, and which points out more records serviceable to gentlemen, and relating to their estates, than all the books yet published in England) to his grandson Mr. W. Dugdale, whose son, Mr. John Dugdale, hath, in consideration of a sum of money, by a legal conveyance, assigned the same to me. In order to a new edition and continuation of that work, whick Sir W. before his death had carried on to 1691, I have made various searches, and put myself to considerable expense, and particularly I have now by me receipts for sixty guineas, which I have paid for transcripts of Pipe Rolls relating to antient barons from King Stephen to Edward II. and as there are many mistakes in the marginal references, &c. in that work, they must be all examined anew with the records from which they were taken, the labour and expense whereof must be immense, and unfit for any body to undergo without a full security for his property in that old copy. It doth not lessen the unhappiness of authors to be wounded through the sides of booksellers, or out of prejudice to this last set of men (who, after all, have fairly purchased what right they have in such copies, and lose by some what they gained by others;) but it is certain that more authors are concerned in this privilege to old copies than is generally imagined, and were there fewer, they might still hope for such a privilege, if it be reasonable, in this case, to follow the Roman maxim in another—*that it is better to save one citizen, than destroy an hundred enemies.*

BISHOP WARBURTON, 1747.(¹)

It seemeth to me an odd circumstance, that, amidst the justest and safest establishment of *property,* which the best form of Government is capable of procuring, there should yet be one species of it belonging to an order of men, who have been generally esteemed the greatest ornament, and certainly are not the least support of civil policy, to which little or no regard hath been hitherto paid. I mean the *right of property in authors* to their works. And surely, if there

(1) In a collection of law tracts in the British Museum, there is *A Letter from an Author to a Member of Parliament, concerning Literary Property,* on which the following memorandum is made in the hand-writing of Mr. Hargrave:---" This pamphlet is " said to have been written by Dr. Warburton, now Bishop of Gloucester.---F.H."

be degrees of *right*, that of authors seemeth to have the advantage over most others; their property being in the truest sense their *own*, as acquired by a long and painful exercise of that very faculty which denominateth us *men*. And if there be degrees of *security* for its enjoyment, here again they appear to have the fairest claim, as *fortune* hath long been in a confederacy with *ignorance*, to stop up their way, to every other kind of acquisition.

History, indeed, informeth us, that there was a time, when men in public stations thought it the duty of their office to encourage letters; and when those rewards, which the wisdom of the legislature had established for the learned in that profession deemed more immediately useful to society, were carefully distributed amongst the most deserving. While this system lasted, authors had the less occasion to be anxious about literary property, which was, perhaps, the reason why the settlement of it was so long neglected, that at length it became a question, whether they had any property at all.

But this fond regard to learning being only an indulgence to its infant age; a favor, which in these happy times of its maturity many reasons of state have induced the public wisdom to withdraw; *letters* are now left like *virtue*, to be their own reward. We may surely then be permitted to expect that so slender a pittance should at least be well secured from rapine and depredation.

The great temptation to invade this property is while the demand for it is great and frequent, which is generally on the first publication of a book, and some few years afterwards.---While this demand continues, the proprietor hath need of all additional sanctions to oppose to the force of the temptation. But when, in course of years, the demand abates, and with it the temptation, the common legal security of natural rights is then sufficient to keep offenders in order.

Sir THOMAS CLARKE, Master of the Rolls, 1761.

It is not necessary to determine, whether authors had a property in their works before the statute of Queen Anne. *If they had not, it was a reproach to the law.*

Lord MANSFIELD, Mr. Justice BLACKSTONE, Mr. Justice WILLES, Mr. Justice ASTON, &c., 1769.

In the commencement of the Historical View([1]), we have presented an outline of the luminous and powerful arguments by which these distinguished personages adjudged, in accordance with the principle of the common law—founded on reason and justice, experience and moral fitness—that the authors of literary compositions should have the exclusive right of publication in all time to come. We refer, therefore, to those parts of the work for the statement of the grounds on which that conclusion was established.

(1) Section I. and II. page 1 to 10.

The authorities thus referred to, are of the highest legal eminence. It may be important, however, on a question involving the interests of literature, as well as the principles of law, not to depend on professional authority alone, but to consult other writers who have investigated the nature and consequences of the present system. We shall therefore, in addition to some further legal opinions, avail ourselves of the learning and research displayed in various works of eminence; and our selections will consist, either of the lucid detail of essential facts, or the eloquent expression of important opinions.

Lord Monboddo, 1774.

That every author has a property in his own manuscript has not been denied; and it has been admitted, that in consequence of this property, he may, as the law now stands, print it if he pleases, and so far reap the fruits of his property. Let us then suppose that the author, instead of multiplying copies by the press, makes several in writing, and that he gives the use of one of these copies to a friend. This happened in the case of Lord Clarendon's History, and it was there adjudged, that the person who got the use of the copy had not a right to print it, though it did not appear that when he got it, he was laid under any restraint or limitation as to the use of it. It is true indeed, that the person in that case got the use of the MS. for nothing. But would it have altered the case if Lord Clarendon's heir in consideration of the expence or trouble, of transcribing the MS. had made him pay something for the use of it? Or suppose, that instead of transcribing it he had taken the more expeditious way of taking copies of it by the press? It appears, therefore, that by giving the use either of MS. or book, for hire or without hire, I do not give the liberty of printing or reprinting it, even where no such condition was mentioned.

I hold it to be part of the contract of emption, when a book is sold that it shall not be multiplied. In the case of a printed book, it is not only understood that the purchaser shall not reprint it, but it is expressed. For the title page bears that it is *printed* either *for* the author, or for some bookseller to whom he has assigned the copy, the meaning of which cannot be, that the author or the bookseller has a right to the copies already printed (for as they are in his possession such advertisement is altogether unnecessary) but to intimate that he has the sole right of printing: so that the selling a book with such a title is in effect covenanting that the purchaser shall not reprint it.

Mr. Dunning, 1774.

The statute of Anne, which professed to encourage learned men, was thus far realized, that so soon as protection to copyright was permanently afforded to the Courts of Justice, the price for its transfer increased. The supposed *additional security* given by the act, immediately enhanced the value of copyright. After the repeated injunctions which were granted in Chancery, it seems that payments were made for copyright of an amount previously unparalleled. The instances of the sums paid for the historical works of *Hume* and *Robertson* are a sufficient proof of the important effects which follow the due protection of this kind of property.

The decision which took place in the Court of King's Bench, in the year 1769, produced a still more remarkable effect on the interests of authors. The price paid for *Dr. Hawkesworth's Voyages*, was still larger than in the former instances, and it is evident from the comcomparative superiority of the historical works referred to, that the increase of remuneration was occasioned by the better understood nature of the property([1]).

We must consider the times which we examine, and the nature of the property in question. In ages wherein civility had made but small progress it would be absurd to look for litigations of a property so little valued and so seldom disputed. The want of precedents in such a case proves nothing. There are many unquestionable common law rights for which no precedent can be found so far back as Richard II. The nature of the property shews at first sight, that it would be in vain to look back for decisions in its favor, even supposing that from other circumstances the existence of it was unquestionable.

The Solicitor General WEDDERRURN, 1774.

Adverting to the application of the printers in *Prynne's* time to suppress the patents for printing the bible, he says, " that celebrated, lawyer declared that the most solid objection against the printers was the *inherent common law-right* of an author to multiply copies. This he observes, is one strong proof, that in the worst of times the *jus naturale* respecting literary property was not forgot. He adds, licences in general prove, not that the common-law right did not exist, but were the universal fetters of the press, at the times in which authors were obliged to obtain them.

Authors, both from principles of natural justice and the interest of society, have the best right to the profits, accruing from a publication of their own ideas, and it is absurd to imagine, that either a sale, a loan, or a gift of a book, carries with it an implied right of multiplying copies : so much paper and print is sold, lent, or given, and an unlimited perusal is warranted from such sale, loan, or gift ; but it cannot be conceived that when five shillings are paid for a book, the seller means to transfer a right of gaining one hundred pounds : very man must feel the contrary, and confess the absurdity of such an argument.

---

(1) We have presented the substance of this part of Mr. Dunning's speech in the case of Donaldson v. Becket. It is a sufficient answer to the assertion that booksellers alone would be benefited by an extension of the term. It would be equally advantageous to authors, and indeed it is manifest that nothing but justice can ever be generally beneficial to any class of persons.

Mr. Hargrave, 1774.

On the practicability of ascertaining the right of literary property.

I might urge that facts are conceded sufficient to render the discussion of this point wholly unnecessary; that it has been the practice to appropriate the right of printing books in all countries, ever since the invention of printing ; that it subsists in some form in every part of Europe ; that in foreign countries it is enjoyed under grants of privilege from the sovereign; that in our own country it is admitted to be legally exercised in perpetuity by the crown and its grantees over particular books ; and even the legislature has protected such a right over books in general for a term of years, and has repeatedly called it a property, and those in whom it is vested proprietors. These facts, however inconsistent they may seem, and really are with the argument against the practicability of asserting the claim of literary property cannot be denied; but this is not the proper place for urging them. I shall therefore for the present wave the authority of examples, and shall reason wholly from the nature of the subject in which the property is claimed.

The subject of the property is a written composition ; and that one written composition may be distinguished from another is a truth too evident to be much argued upon. Every man has a mode of combining and expressing his ideas peculiar to himself. The same doctrines, the same opinions never came from two persons, or even from the same person at different times, cloathed wholly in the same language. A strong resemblance of style, of sentiment, of plan and disposition, will frequently be found ; but there is such an infinite variety in the modes of thinking and writing, as well in the extent and connection of ideas, as in the use and arrangement of words, that a literary work really original, like the human face, will always have some singularities, some lines, some features, to characterize it, and to fix and establish its identity : and to assert the contrary with respect to either, would be justly deemed equally opposite to reason and universal experience. Besides, though it should be allowable to suppose that there may be cases, in which, on a comparison of two literary productions, no such distinction could be made between them, as in a competition for originality to decide whether both were really original or which was the original, and which the copy ; still the observation of the possibility of distinguishing in all other instances, and the arrangement in its application to them would still have the same force.

Whether publication destroys an Author's property.

It is asked, how an author, after publishing his work can confine it to himself, and exclude the world from participating of the sentiments it contains ? This objection depends on this supposition, that the exclusive right claimed from an author is to the ideas and knowledge communicated in a litterary composition. An attempt to appropriate to the author and his assigns, the perpetual use of the ideas contained in a written composition, might well be deemed so absurd and impracticable, as to deserve to be treated in a Court of Justice with equal contempt and indignation; and it would be a disgrace to argue in favor of such a claim. But the claim of literary property is not of this ridiculous and unreasonable kind; and to represent it as such, however it may serve the purposes of declamation, or of wit and humour, is a fallacy too gross to be successfully disguised. What the author claims, is merely to have the sole right of printing his own own works. As to the ideas conveyed, every author, when he publishes necessarily gives the full use of them to the world at large. To communicate and sell knowledge to the public, and at the same time to stipulate that none but the author or his bookseller shall make use of it, is an idea, which avarice herself has not yet suggested. But imputing this absurdity to the claim of literary property, is mere imagination; and so must be deemed, until it can be demonstrated that the printing a book cannot be appropriated without, at the same time appropriating the use of the knowledge contained in it; or in other words, that the use of the ideas communicated by an author cannot be common to all, unless the right of printing his works be also common. If the impossibility of proving such a proposition be not self-evident, I am sure, that there is not any argument I am furnished with, which would avail to evince the contrary.

On the expediency of confining the right of printing particular books to certain persons.

It is apprehended by many, that if there were not any such thing as property in the printing of books, the art of printing would be more beneficial to the public in general, as well as to those who practice the art, or are connected with it in particular. But the truth is, that the opinion, however popular it may be, is without the least foundation. How would making the right of printing every book common, be advantageous to those concerned in printing or manufacturing books, or in bookselling? Every impression of a work is attended with such great expences, that nothing less than securing the sale of a large number of copies within a certain time can bring back the money expended with a reasonable allowance for interest or profit. But is this to be effected, if immediately after the impression of a book by one man, all others are to be left at liberty to make and bend impressions of the same work? A second, by printing with an inferior type, on an inferior paper, is enabled to undersell the printer of the first impression, and defeats him of the benefit of it, either by preventing the sale of it within due time, or perhaps by totally stopping it. The second printer is exposed to the same kind of hostility; and a third person, by printing in a manner still worse, still more inferior, ruins the second; a fourth, the third; and so on it would be in progression, till experience of the disadvantages of a rivalship so general would convince all concerned, mediately or immediately, in the trade of printing, that it must be ruinous to carry it on, without an appropriation of copies to secure a reasonable profit on the sale of each impression.

Having thus explained the disadvantages, which would accrue to those concerned in printing, if copies were common, I will now ask, how making them so could produce the least benefit to the public in in general? Would lessening, or rather annihilating the profits of printing, tend to encourage persons to be adventurers in the trade of printing? Would it make books cheaper? So long indeed as the least legal idea of property in copies remains, most persons will probably hold it both dishonorable and unsafe to pirate editions; and so long only can the few, who now distinguish themselves by trafficking in that way, afford to undersell the real proprietors. Such persons at present enjoy all the fruits of a concurrent property without paying any price of it; and therefore it is not to be wondered at, that they should undersell those who have paid a full and valuable consideration for the purchase of their copies. But if the right of printing books should once be declared common by a judicial opinion, the advantage which enables particular persons to undersell those who claim the property, would cease; pirating would then become general; and perhaps those who now practice it would themselves be sacrificers to their own success in the cause they support. Whilst the question of literary property is in a suspended state, they have the harvest to themselves; but if they should gain their cause, like other Samsons, they would be crushed by the fall of the building they are pulling down.

On the supposed resemblance between the Inventor of a machine and the Author of a Book.

In my opinion, the principal distinction is, that in one case the claim really is to an appropriation of ideas; but in the other, the claim leaves the use of the ideas common to the whole world.

Lord LYTTLETON, 1774.

I own I have no acquaintance with the quirks and quibbles of the law. I speak to the matter merely as a question of Equity; I cannot enter into delusive refined metaphysical argument about tangibility, the materiality, or the corporeal substance of literary property; it is sufficient for me that it is allowed such a property exists: Authors I presume will not be denied a free participation of the common rights of mankind, and their property is surely as sacred and as deserving of protection as that of any other subjects. It is of infinite importance to every country that the arts and sciences should be cultivated and encouraged. Where men of letters are best protected, the people in general will be most enlightened, and where the minds of men are enlarged, where their understandings are equally matured in perception and in judgment, there the arts and sciences will take their residence. The arts and sciences had their origin in Italy, from thence they fled to a remote corner of Asia, at length they returned companions of the all conquering arms of the Roman Republic, and at last they were happily seated in this free country. I am of opinion that there are at present but two monarchs in Europe who are encouragers of the arts and sciences, and are themselves men of letters, the King of Prussia and the King of England. It hath been urged that authors write for fame only ; that glory is the best reward, and that immortality of renown i an ample recompence for their labors ; they therefore do not stoop to claim a further right than that of a first communication of their ideas to the public. This is in a confined sense a proper and a noble observation, but it will not hold generally. I beg your Lordships to remember that genius is peculiar to no climate; it belongs to no country; it is more frequently found in the cottage than in the palace ; it rather crawls on the face of the earth than soars aloft ; when it does mount its flight should not be impeded. To damp the wing of genius is, in my mind highly impolitic, higly reprehensible, nay, somewhat criminal. If authors be allowed a perpetuity, it is a lasting encouragement ; making the right of multiplying copies a matter common to all, is like extending the course of a river so greatly as finally to dry up its sources.

Mrs. Catherine Macaulay, 1774.

The Romans even in their degenerate days, had that high sense of merit in general, and of services rendered the public, that according to Pliny and other writers, in proportion to a man's character for literary abilities and virtues, in proportion to his power of rendering himself useful to his country and fellow citizens, and in proportion to his exertion of this power, he was sure of meeting from the generous hands of individuals an equal reward.

Pliny, if I remember right, in speaking of his own success in life, and that of one of his cotemporaries, mentions the leaving legacies to learned and good men, as a practice common and familiar. We were of the same age, said he ; we entered into life together, and we had the same number of legacies bequeathed us. This being the custom among the Romans, with what ardor must it inspire every youthful breast, to deserve such grateful, such useful returns of bounty !

An Englishman persuades himself he is acting with propriety, when he bequeathes the whole of his estate to a blockhead he despises in the fiftieth degree of relationship, though he leaves behind him many worthy ingenious friends, whom a small legacy would help out of very intricate circumstances.

That watchful guard selfishness, is a never failing check to any generous sally of the mind, or to any benevolent inclination in the human breast ; and the means of obtaining wealth from the good opinion of his country or his friends being thus barred from a man, whom fortune has denied to favor, yet of merit, of genius, and of virtue sufficient to instruct and enlighten mankind.—If such a man be deprived of the necessary lucrative advantage by the right of property in his own writings, is he to starve, or live in penury, whilst he is exerting, perhaps vain endeavors to serve a people who do not desire his services? Supposing this man has a wife and children, ought he, for the mere whistling of a name, to exert those talents in

literary compositions, which were much better employed in some
mechanical business, or some trade, that would support his family?
Will not such a man, if he have the tender feelings of a husband and a
father,—if indeed he have the conscience of a religious or a moral man;
will he not check every incentive arising from vanity, which would
tempt him, for the purchase of an ill bought fame, to expose to poverty
and contempt those who, by the law of religion and nature, he is
bound to cherish and protect

The author's and booksellers interests are inseparable. If booksellers ask sufficient prices for their books, authors will insist on a
sufficent price for copyright; but when books are sold as drugs,
authors must lower their demands.

Archbishop Tillotson died in mean circumstances, and if it had not
been for a copy of his sermons sold to the booksellers, his family
might have been under the necessity of perhaps applying in vain for
relief to their country.

DR. ENFIELD, 1774.

The right of authors to the exclusive possession of their own
works is founded in nature; and unless any sufficient cause appears
for depriving them of it, ought to be secured and guarded by law.
To grant them this security, is neither impracticable in the nature of
the thing, nor inconsistent with the interests of the public. The inconveniences which are apprehended from a perpetual exclusive right,
are trifling, and in a great measure imaginary. The advantages which
would arise from the encouragement which such security would give
to philosophical and literary pursuits, are obvious and important.
Since no good reason can be assigned, why authors should be deprived of their right of property, they have a just claim upon government for protection and security in the enjoyment of this right. The
interests of the public, instead of opposing, concur with this claim.
On the same principles, therefore, that a perpetual right to any other
kind of estate, real or personal, is secured to individuals, an author
may reasonably expect that his property in his own work should be
secured to him and his posterity. Such security is by no means at
present enjoyed. The provision which hath been already made for a
temporary security, in the statute of Queen Anne, and the favorable
attention which is at present paid to this subject by the legislature,
do, however, afford encouragement to hope, that authors will at
length obtain a legal grant of perpetual copyright; a grant which
they have sufficient ground to request. When authors desire permission to communicate their thoughts to the public with freedom,
on every subject which is of importance to individuals or society, and
the secure possession of the fruits of their own genius and labor, they
ask nothing of government, but what every Englishman hath a
right to expect from it, *liberty and property.*

MONTHLY REVIEW, 1774.

We shall suggest a few hints relative to Judge Yates's labored attack upon copyright. Almost all his reasonings proceed upon abstract definitions of property. Now if the maxim be just, that nothing can be an object of property which has not a corporeal substance, then no man can truly say *his soul is his own.* He has no property in the knowledge he has gained, the title he inherits from his ancestors, or the good name he has acquired: slander only robs him of a nonentity, and therefore ought not to be punished by law.

Every man's ideas are doubtless his own, and not the less so because another person may have happened to fall into the same train of thinking with himself. But this is not the property which an author claims; it is a property in a literary composition, the identity of which consists in the same thoughts ranged in the same order and expressed in the same words.

This object of property is not, indeed, visible or tangible, but it is not therefore the less real. A man who has composed a poem, though he has never committed it to writing, has a clear idea of the identity of the work, and justly calls it his own. If property can arise by labor, the poem is his, and the copyright really exists, though it is not visible, nor has any substance to retain it.

When he sells copies of his work, he does not necessarily part with his original right of multiplying copies: this being a thing entirely distinct from a printed copy, cannot be given up without his consent; and this consent ought not to be taken for granted without some explicit declaration. When an author sends his work into the world, he gives the purchaser a natural *power* to reprint it, and in this sense " suffers the bird to escape; " but this cannot imply a *right* of reprinting, unless such a premium is given him, as he shall acknowledge to be a sufficient compensation for the profits arising from the exclusive sale of his work.

All that is advanced concerning an author's claim to an adequate recompense is trifling, till it be made apparent that he has no property in his works after publication. If he have a right of sale arising from property, why should he ask a reward? or why should the use of the right be branded with the opprobrious appellation of a monopoly.

QUARTERLY REVIEW, 1819.

Upon what principle, with what justice, or under what pretext of public good are men of letters deprived of a perpetual property in the produce of their own labors, when all other persons enjoy it as their indefeasible right—a right beyond the power of any earthly authority to take away? Is it because their labour is so light, the endowments which it requires so common, the attainments so cheaply and easily acquired, and the present remuneration so adequate, so ample, and so certain?

The last descendants of Milton died in poverty. The descendants of Shakspeare are living in poverty, and in the lowest rank of life. Is this just to the individuals? Is it grateful to the memory of those who are the pride and boast of their country? Is it honorable or becoming to us, as a nation, holding (the better part of us, assuredly, and the majority affecting to hold) the names of Shakspeare and Milton in veneration? To have placed the descendants of these men in respectability and comfort; in that sphere of life where, with a full provision for our natural wants, free scope is given for the growth of our intellectual and immortal part, simple justice was all that was required,—only that they should have possessed the perpetual copyright of their ancestor's works,—only that they should not have been deprived of their proper and natural inheritance.

It has been stated in evidence that copyright, in three cases out of four, is of no value a few years after publication: at the end of fourteen years scarcely in one case out of fifty, or even out of a hundred. Books of great immediate popularity have their run, and come to a dead stop. The hardship is upon those which win their way slowly and difficultly, but keep the field at last. And it will not appear wonderful, that this should generally have been the case with books of the highest merit, if we consider what obstacles to the success of a work may be opposed by the circumstances and obscurity of the author, when he presents himself as a candidate for fame, by the humour or the fashion of the times, the taste of the public, (more likely to be erroneous than right at all times,) and the incompetence or personal malevolence of some unprincipled critic, who may take upon himself to guide the public opinion, and who, if he feel in his own heart that the fame of the man whom he hates is invulnerable, endeavours the more desperately to wound him in his fortunes. And if the copyright (as by the existing law) is to depart from the author's family at his death, or at the end of twenty-eight years, from the first publication of his work, if he die before the expiration of that term, his representatives, in such a case, are deprived of the property, just when it is beginning to prove a valuable inheritance.

The decision which time pronounces upon the reputation of authors, and upon the permanent rank which they are to hold, is unerring and final. Restore to them that perpetuity in the copyright of their works, of which the law has deprived them, and the reward of literary labor will ultimately be in just proportion to its deserts. If no inconvenience to literature arises from the perpetuity which has been restored to the Universities, (and it is not pretended that any has arisen,) neither is there any to be apprehended from restoring the same common and natural right of individuals, who stand more in need of it.

However slight the hope may be of obtaining any speedy redress for this injustice, there is some satisfaction in thus solemnly protesting against it; and believing, as we do, that if society continue to advance, no injustice will long be permitted to exist after it is clearly understood, we cannot but believe that a time must come when the wrongs of literature will be acknowledged, and the literary men of other generations be delivered from the hardship to which their predecessors have been subjected by no act or error of their own.

PHILOMATHIC JOURNAL, 1825.

Man has a natural right to the fruits of his own labour. That which he calls into existence by the exercise of his limbs or faculties is as much his own as the limbs and faculties themselves. Who else, indeed, can claim any right to it? Why should a stranger possess himself of the beneficial produce of the labour of another? Would not every one feel this to be unjust in his own case? The labour of one man cannot be the labour of another. The produce is the reward of the labour, and ought to remain with him who has laboured, unless he consent to part with it by compact or donation. If this be true with regard to *bodily* labour, must it not be so with regard to that which is *mental?* Are the operations of a man's mind not his own? Is the result of those operations not his own? And shall not the beneficial recompense be his own also? The property which a man has in the produce of his own mind is founded in the very constitution of nature. It has a more solid foundation than property of any other kind. It has a great advantage over property gained by occupancy, which was at first common, and required some act to render it the property of an individual. This was *originally* the author's; it never was common, and never ought to become so, but with the full consent of the natural proprietor.

Literary property, then, has its origin in reason and justice. The right of property of course implies the sole right of using and disposing of it; and this right is, in fact, acknowledged by the law, so long as the author refrains from publishing his manuscript. He may withhold it altogether if he will, and his descendants may retain it in their possession for ever, and no one can compel them to publication; nor can any one lawfully publish it without their consent. What difference can the fact of publication make, or rather what difference *ought* it to make? It has been said, that an author, by publishing his work, abandons the possession of it,—an assertion almost too idle to deserve notice. A man who lends his horse does not abandon his right in him. Because, for a time, his corporal possession has ceased, we do not conclude that he never intends to resume his property. But then it has been said, that the author *cannot* reclaim that which he has parted with. The reader has absolutely purchased the book, and has a right to do what he will with it. The reader has indeed purchased a certain copy of a work, and the author cannot demand it back. It is impossible for him to repossess himself of the ideas which he has imparted to the mind of the reader; and, if possible, he would have no right to do it; because the reader has honestly bought and paid for them: of all the knowledge that the book contains, he may avail himself for improvement or delight. But, because he has a right to the full use and enjoyment of his own copy, can it be inferred that he has therefore a right to multiply copies for his own pecuniary emolument? A man who has a right of walking in the garden of another, may exercise this right according to the conditions upon which he holds it. He may walk in the garden for his health or pleasure: he may possibly be entitled to introduce his friends; but the garden is not his, and he must not dispose of the produce of the trees for his own advantage, or in any other way injure the pecuniary interests of the proprietor. A man who has a spring of water upon his ground, may give or sell water to his neighbours; but, by so doing, he does not dispossess himself of the spring. The houses in the metropolis, and other large towns, are supplied with water by public companies. Upon condition of the payment of a certain sum, the occupants of the houses are entitled to as much water as they can consume; but they must not make it a source of profit. Although they may use as much water as they will, they must not sell the smallest portion. A man who has a ticket of admission to a theatre, has a right to enter the theatre; he has a right to all the entertainment which is there to be met with. If the ticket be a transferable one, he may lend or let it for hire; but he must not multiply tickets, and vend them for his own profit. He who has access to the garden of another; he who has the privilege of fetching water from a spring, or has it delivered at his house; he who has admission to a place of amusement, and all other persons in similar circumstances, must enjoy their benefits and advantages according to the terms upon which they were granted by the proprietor who had originally the sole right of using and disposing of them. We must look at *his* intention. We must not conclude, that he has parted with more than he evidently intended to part with. To suppose that, without some cause, a man will abandon his property, is unreasonable. To determine, in the teeth of evidence, to the contrary, that he *has* done so, is unjust. Now, when a man writes, prints, publishes, and sells a book, so far from intending to abandon the pecuniary emoluments arising from its publication, he manifests a directly contrary intention. He does not give his book away. He does not charge the mere cost of the paper and print. He charges something beyond this, which is the reward of his labour of literary composition. It is he who has laboured. It is he who is entitled to the reward of the labour. It is he who, by demanding this reward, asserts his right to it. The same act cannot be the assertion of a right, and the abandonment of it. The act of publication for money *is* an assertion of the right of property; therefore, it is not an abandonment.

Again, publication is not merely a declaration of the intention of the author to appropriate the profits of the work to himself, but it is the only means of making it profitable at all. Until published, the world can derive from it no intellectual improvement, the author no pecuniary advantage. Publication is the necessary act to make the work useful to mankind, and beneficial to the owner. To discourage learned and ingenious men from benefitting the public by their works, is impolitic and unwise. To construe the necessary act by which alone a literary work can be rendered profitable, to be destructive of the right of the author, is not only harsh and cruel, but unreasonable.

Previous to publication, the work is the property of the author, and of course he is entitled to its profits. But it can only be made profitable by publication. If publication, then, be a forfeiture of the right of the author in his own production, the very act which is necessary to render the property a source of profit, divests him who is entitled to the profits of his right to enjoy them; which is absurd.

It was thought necessary to urge thus much, to prove that a man had a natural right to the profits arising from the productions of his mind, and that this right was not abandoned by publication. These points being established, it follows, that literary property is not *created* by the law, but *restrained* and *limited*. The right to this species of property is a *natural* right; and as no natural right should be abridged without good cause, it behoved the advocates for the present law to show that good cause existed for its enactment.

Now, what is the pretence usually set up to justify the law in its non-protection of the rights of literary men? It is this, that if copyright were made perpetual, authors, or their representatives, would fix an unreasonable price upon books, and the public would thus be deprived of the benefit of cheap editions of valuable works. There is no reason to suppose that this would be the case. A literary proprietor would find, as the bookselling trade now do, that his interest would be more promoted by a small profit, upon a rapid and extensive sale, than by a larger profit upon the slow sale of a smaller number. Besides, if he were so far blind to his own interest as to fix such a price as should nearly withdraw his work from circulation, the public could rarely be injured. Works of imagination might, indeed, be thus suppressed, but here the evil would end. All historians must relate the same facts. The phenomena of nature are open to all enquirers. The principles of art are not the inheritance of a single individual, but are possessed by numbers. If, therefore, the imbecile cupidity of authors or publishers suppressed certain works of history or science, others, as good, would make their appearance, and by being sold at a moderate price, would obtain universal circulation. Even if the want could not be readily supplied, the evil is not irremediable. The proprietor would not be allowed to demand for his books a price that was altogether unreasonable. He who offers his goods for sale, must be contented with a market-price. He may demand the highest market-price, but he has no right to more. In this principle is the protection of the public from imposition: and even if the worst came that possibly could, and the proprietor were to refuse to reprint his book, when necessary, the fact of its having been a certain number of years out of print, might, without injustice, be regarded as an abandonment of the property, which would then become common. No one would be able to recover damages for infringement of copyright, without the verdict of a jury; and he who seeks redress for an injury done to his property, must be prepared to shew that he has taken reasonable care of it.

The objection to the rights of literary property, which has just been answered, proceeds, it should be observed, not upon fact, but upon vague and unwarranted suspicion. In effect, it says, "we dare not

Q

trust you with your rights, because we suspect that you would make
an ill use of them." Why *should* this be suspected? No good reason can be assigned why the descendants of literary men should be
less honest or less liberal than other persons. Surely, then, the objection is of a most ungracious character.

If it be desirable to encourage literature in a state, the easiest,
as well as the most equitable, way of doing it, is by securing the rights
of literary property. An author has sometimes been compared with
the inventor of an ingenious machine. The latter must secure the
property of his invention by a patent, and it can be thus secured only
for a limited number of years. It has been argued, that an author
stands in the same situation as the inventor of a machine, and is only
entitled to the same protection. Now, in the first place, the ingenious
mechanic has a better chance of immediate success. If his machine
tend to shorten labor, or to perform it with greater accuracy, its
effect will be immediately perceived, and within the limited term
secured by a patent, he will, most probably, be remunerated. With
regard to literary works, (more particularly when the subject is a
heavy one,) this probability does not exist. Secondly, the cases
are not parallel; because the imitation of a machine is not the
original machine itself, but only one resembling it. The wood,
metal, or other materials constitute the machine. There is nothing
else necessary to its existence. The second machine is, therefore,
not the same as the first. It is a perfect imitation of it, and that
is all. Whereas the pirated book is the identical production of the
author. It is the very same *in substance* with the genuine book;
because its doctrines, sentiments, and language are its *substantial* and
essential parts. The paper and ink are only *accidents*. They constitute the vehicle of conveyance from the mind of the author to the
mind of the reader; but they are not of the *substance* of the thing
conveyed. Lastly; is it quite certain that ingenious mechanics are,
under the existing law, sufficiently protected? If they are not, is it
meant to defend one wrong by another? Men will be industrious
when the fruits of their industry are secured to them; but, when this
is not the case, why should they toil? Why should any one devote
himself to any great literary labor, which will require the sacrifice
of the better part of his life, when the reward of his labor must cease
with his life, and he can preserve no portion of it for his family?
Will he not be tempted to apply himself to the production of works
of temporary interest, which require little or no mental exertion, and
which will immediately become a source of emolument? The tendency of the law is, therefore, injurious to sound literature, by dis-
couraging men from undertaking works of great dignity or lasting
utility, and seducing them by the prospect of gain to become mere
manufacturers of the trashy production of the day.—Works of
standard merit not only require immense labor in their production,
but they make their way slowly in the world. Years generally elapse
before they will even repay the expences of publication; and, when
their value begins to be known and appreciated,—when their reputation is extending, and they are about to become as valuable in a

commercial as in an intellectual point of view, the law steps in to snatch from the children the bread for which the father has labored, and to consign to penury the posterity of him who has given his days and nights to his fellow men, in administering to their most refined pleasures, and promoting their noblest interests. This is not a representation of the mere possible effect of the law. Again and again has it occurred, that the families of literary men have languished in indigence, while others have been enjoying the profits which in nature, reason, and justice should have been theirs. About the middle of the last century, the grand-daughter of Milton was so far reduced, that Dr. Johnson solicited and obtained from Garrick a charitable benefit for her at Drury Lane Theatre. Within a very few years, a member of the family of Shakspeare was working as a day-laborer, in M'Adamizing the roads of Warwickshire. Are these things as they should be? Is it right that the natural representatives of men of genius should be left to starve, while strangers are amassing fortunes from works, upon which neither they or their fathers have labored? The lives of literary men are too often passed amidst disappointment, and penury, and sorrow. Would it not be a consolation to them to reflect, that though the reward of their labors was postponed, and in their own persons they should never enjoy it, yet that posterity would do them justice, and would not only soothe their memory with fame, but repay their descendants with wealth? Would it not add to the gratification of him who enriched his library with a copy of Shakspeare, or of Milton, to know that he was contributing to the benefit of the families of the illustrious men, whose names are the proudest in the annals of their country's glory?

In France, the term of copyright is fifty years. In Germany, it is perpetual. In those countries there is no want of books. On the contrary, they abound. Dr. Johnson observed long ago, that the French had a book upon every subject. In Germany, this is even more extensively the fact. It is not found, either, that the proprietors put upon their works a prohibitory price. Books are, in those countries, remarkably cheap. A comparison of the state of literature in France and Germany, with the state of the law, will strikingly illustrate the truth of the homely adage, that "honesty is the best policy."

While authors in this country have been deprived by the statute law of the full property of their works, they have been called upon to contribute to the public convenience by presenting a considerable number of copies to public libraries. In large and expensive works, this is a heavy drawback upon their profits. It may possibly make the entire difference between gaining and losing. It is, at any rate, both unjust and cruel, at the same time, and by the same act, to impose a heavy tax, and to diminish the means of paying it.

Let the laws relating to literary property then be amended. If it be not thought advisable to render copyright perpetual, let the term be considerably extended. Let not the *literary* laborer be the only one excluded from the full enjoyment of the beneficial produce of labor. Rarely, indeed, can he enjoy it himself; but let him bequeath it as an estate to those he loves, and when *he* shall no longer be sensi-

Q 2

ble of our attention or our neglect, let us pay his children, and his children's children, the debt of gratitude which we owe to him.

LIBRARY OF USEFUL KNOWLEDGE, 1828.

Commencement of Printing.

The art was commenced soon after the murder of Henry VI., and carried on during the remainder of the reign of Edward IV., and the reigns of Edward V. and Richard III., when the minds of those most likely and able to encourage printing were seldom free from alarm for their own safety, their time much occupied, and their means necessarily reduced by the distracted and wasted state of the country, and when little attention or money could be spared for literature. England at this period was much behind France. Caxton was obliged to have recourse to the French language for most of the works which he printed.

It is supposed that Caxton returned to England about the year 1472, and brought with him the unsold copies of the translation of Recueill. His first patron was Thomas Milling, Bishop of Hereford, who held the abbotship of St. Peter's, Westminster, *in commendam.* Caxton took up his residence, and established his printing-office, either in the immediate neighbourhood of the abbey, or in one of the chapels attached to it.

That Caxton introduced the art of printing into England, and first practised it here, was never doubted till the year 1642 : a dispute arose at this time between the Company of Stationers and some persons, respecting a patent for printing ; the case was formally argued; and in the course of the pleadings, Caxton was proved, incontestably, to have been the first printer in England. Soon after the Restoration, a book was discovered in the public library at Cambridge, the date of which was Oxford, 1468. The probability is, however, that the date of this book is incorrect, and that it should have been 1478, not 1468; this is inferred from its being printed with separate fusile metal types, very neat and beautiful, from the regularity of the page and the appearance of signatures ; and, moreover, from the fact, that no other production issued from the Oxford press till eleven years after 1468, it being highly improbable that a press connected with a University should have continued so long unemployed.

Between the years 1471, when Caxton began to print, and the year 1540, the English press, though conducted by industrious, and some of them learned printers, produced very few classics. "Boethius de Consolatione," in Latin and English, three editions of "Æsop," "Terence," the "Bucolics" of Virgil twice, and "Tully's Offices," were the only classics printed. From Cambridge no classical work appeared; and the University of Oxford produced only the first book of "Cicero's Epistles ;" and that at the expense of Wolsey.

II. *ON THE LIBRARY TAX.*

The comments of writers on the subject of the library tax are principally to be met with subsequently to the year 1812. The additional remedy, in the shape of fine and forfeiture, for pirating copyright, was confined by the statute to *books registered* at Stationers' Hall ; we find therefore no complaint of the exaction where the protection of the penalty was sought for. When, however, it was determined that copies of all books, whether registered for the sake of the protecting penalties, or not, must be delivered, a general feeling was very naturally excited against the exaction.

Mr. SHARON TURNER, 1813.

As the delivery of copies cannot be contended for, as a matter of right, independent of the statute, the expediency of the delivery must rest on one of the following grounds : either that it is unjust to take away from the libraries a benefit which they have so long enjoyed ; or that it is useful to the public that it should be continued.

On the first of these arguments it may be observed that this is not a benefit which these libraries have actually enjoyed. They have, from the time the act of Anne passed to the present day, received copies of no books but such as the proprietors chose to register ; they have never received copies of those which were not registered.

The registered books for at least forty or fifty years were but a small proportion of those which were actually published. Therefore the question really is not whether the libraries shall be divested of a benefit which they have long enjoyed, but whether literature shall be subjected to a burthen which it has never yet borne.

It cannot be unjust to divest them of a more theoretical right, grounded solely on an enactment which was not founded on any right, rather than to intrench on that sacred right of property which appertains to all individuals ; for in considering this subject no one ought to lose sight of the important principle that the rights of private property are sacred, and ought never to be intruded upon without the last necessity. The *salus publica* is an imperious dictator, to which every well regulated mind will cheerfully bow : but no consideration less than the necessity of supporting the general welfare can sanction the intrusion upon individual property. Unless this is upheld as a firm and sacred principle in legislation, all personal security is endangered, and one of the best foundations of public prosperity is shaken.—If this principle ought ever to be maintained in one case more strictly than in another, it should be in that property, and towards those individuals who have most signally benefited society. In this respect the author yields to none. England, as it is, compared with England as it was, before literature was cherished in it, demonstrates the blessings which it owes to its intellectual benefactors.

But in taking eleven copies of every work compulsorily from its author or proprietor, his right of property is directly invaded; it is invaded as completely as if it were to be enacted that a silversmith should give to these public bodies eleven silver candlesticks. So long as the act of Anne was construed to enforce a delivery of those copies only which the owner chose to register, the objection would not so fully attach. The proprietor had then an option—of that he is now deprived, and therefore the compulsory delivery of eleven copies becomes a direct infringement on that right of property which ought never to be violated, unless the welfare of the nation requires the sacrifice.

Does the *salus publica* make this violation necessary? Does it exact this sacrifice?

Let the extent of this sacrifice be first considered. The act of Anne directs the best paper copies to be delivered. Now the actual amount of eleven best paper copies of the following eleven works would, at their selling price, be £5,698: 1s.

	£	s.	d.
11 Daniel's Oriental Scenery, 6 series, 200 guineas -	2,310	0	0
11 Lord Valentia's Travels, 3 vols. largest paper, 50 guineas (N.B. only 50 of such printed) -	577	10	0
11 Salt's Views, 26 guineas - - - - -	300	6	0
11 Bloomfield's Norfolk, 11 vols. 4to. 22 guineas (N.B. only 120 copies printed; 2 copies only printed on large paper, worth 100 guineas each) -	254	2	0
11 British Gallery of Engravings, large paper - -	1,065	13	6
11 Costumes of the World, 7 vols. - - -	532	2	6
11 Dryden's Works, 18 vols. - - - - -	138	12	0
11 Sir R. Hoare's Ancient Wiltshire (only 60 printed)-	207	18	0
11 Giraldus, 2 vols. 4to. - - - - -	127	1	0
11 Perry's Conchology - - - - -	184	16	0
	£5,698	1	0

Numerous lists might be added to these. We will only mention a few striking individual cases.

A new edition of Wood's Athenæ Oxonienses is preparing with additions. The price of each copy of this, on the best paper, will be seventy-two guineas. If the editor be compelled to give away eleven copies of this work, it will be a loss to him of £830.

A new edition of Dugdale's Monasticon is preparing with additions. The subscription price of this on the best paper is 130 guineas for each set. This will be a very expensive work to the reverend gentleman who has undertaken it, from the number of plates which it will contain. If he should be compelled to give eleven copies of this, it will be a loss to him of £1,500.

The Rev. T. F. Dibden is well known to be publishing a new edition of Ames's Typography, with many valuable additions, the fruit of his active and unwearied researches. This work will be completed in six volumes, of which the price is six guineas each volume for the best paper. The loss to him, if he must give eleven copies, will be above £400.

Eleven copies of Mr. Nichols's History of Leicestershire would be to him a loss of £288 : 15s.

Eleven copies of his "Bibliotheca Topographica Britannica," ten volumes quarto (of which in the whole only 250 copies were printed, and all on small paper), £231.

Eleven copies of Mr. Gough's Sepulchral Monuments (only 250 printed), £277.

Several works are now in the press that will cost from fifty to seventy guineas each, of which the value of eleven copies will be from £500 to £700.

These individual cases (and a greater number of others precisely similar at this moment exist, and might be mentioned) are not the cases of gentlemen with large fortunes publishing books. Indeed, instances are rare of gentlemen of fortune risking any part of that in expensive publications. These, and such like, are the cases of public spirited authors, who, with a laudable zeal for literature, and an honorable desire of an honorable remuneration from the public for their labors, undertake these arduous, troublesome, and expensive works. But shall they not be protected from attacks which tend so directly to take from them a large portion of the profit which they are entitled to expect?

Thus stands the case as to large paper copies, and it is probable that every one will feel that the delivery of these ought to cease.

We will now state the case on the delivery of eleven *common paper* copies.

One most respectable publisher took the trouble to make an accurate calculation of the sum to which the delivery of eleven copies, on common paper, of all the books he had published for the last three years would have amounted, and he found that the amount would have been £1,436 : 9s. 3d. Another highly respectable publisher has stated, that on the average of his publications for the last ten or twelve years, the eleven copies would have been to him a taxation of above £300 a-year, exclusive of works in which he was but a partner. If there had been time to have collected from every publisher the amount of the sacrifice which he would have made by the delivery of eleven copies of all books published by him, the aggregate of the whole would have surprised the reader. But from these two instances the total amount of eleven copies of every work, even on common paper, that is published in Great Britain and Ireland, may be conjectured; and it may be fairly asked, if a taxation so heavy as this ought to be imposed on the authors and owners of literary property?

A few instances will show how heavy the burthen will be on the common paper copies. The delivering of eleven copies of the following fifteen works, on common paper, would have cost the publishers £2,699 : 8s. at their selling price.

	£	s.	d.
Johnson's Poets, 21 vols. 8vo. by Chalmers - -	275	0	0
British Essayists, 45 vols. 18mo. - - - -	115	10	0
——— Novelists, 50 vols. 18mo. - - - -	138	12	0
Bowles' Pope's Works, 10 vols. 8vo. - - -	57	15	0
Wakefield's Pope's Homer, 9 vols. 8vo. - - -	44	11	0
Dryden's Works, by Scott, 18 vols. 8vo. - - -	103	19	0
Swift's Works, by Nichols, 19 vols. 8vo. - - -	99	0	0
Camden's Britannia, 4 vols. folio. - - - -	184	16	0
Miller's Gardeners' Dictionary, 2 vols. 8vo. folio.- -	161	14	0
Buffon's Natural History, 20 vols. 8vo. - - -	132	0	0
Aiken's Biography, 10 vols. 4to. - - - - -	173	5	0
Inchbald's Theatre, farces and modern Theatre,42vols.18mo.	121	16	6
Somers's Tracts, 10 vols. 4to. - - - - -	346	10	0
Harleian Miscellany, 10 vols. 4to. - - - -	381	3	0
State Trials, 21 vols. royal 8vo. - - - - -	363	16	6
	£2,699	8	0

Those gentlemen who have attended to the nature of the publications that perpetually issue from the British press, will know that this list might be made very extensive. So that it is clear that to emancipate literature from the delivery only of the best paper copies, will not be a sufficient relief. Unless Parliament also extend the relief to the common paper copies, the burthen will still be severe, and will frequently operate to prevent the publication of many works, on which the chance of their sale is uncertain.

Sir EGERTON BRYDGES, Bart. M.P. 1818.

I am bound to ask (though some of the public bodies may affect to repel the question indignantly) what do they do with this indiscriminate mixture of expensive and useful works and contemptible trash ? Where do they deposite them ? Do they keep them in order ? And do they bind them ? *If they do,* would not the funds expended in paying the binder, the house room, and the librarians for thus dealing with the mass of rubbish, be more generously and more usefully expended in paying some small portion of the price of the valuable works ? *If they do not,* what becomes of the alleged color of their claim—that of public use ?

The copyright act, as now put into force, is the most perfect instrument of collecting and disseminating all the mischiefs flowing out of an abuse of the liberty of the press, which human ingenuity has ever yet contrived. Thus is brought together in each of eleven public libraries dispersed in the three great portions of the empire all that is silly and ignorant, all that is seditious, all that is lascivious and obscene, all that is irreligious and atheistical, to attract the curiosity, and mislead the judgment and passions, of those for whose cultivation of solid learning and useful knowledge these gratuitous supplies are pretended to be enforced. Nothing short of such a law could have brought many of these contemptible, disgusting, and contagious publications out of the obscurity in which they would otherwise soon have perished. Here they remain registered in catalogues preserved on shelves and protected for posterity, with all the care and trustiness of public property.

How are they to be separated from the valuable matter with which they are intermixed? To whom is such a discretion to be confided? If once they are allowed to make waste of what they do not want, where is it to end? Abuse will creep upon abuse: from waste it will come to gift or sale!

But if every thing be kept, the room, the trouble, and the expense will soon become overwhelming. Already the libraries begin to complain heavily of the inconvenience.

In thirty years the united catalogues of the books thus claimed by the eleven libraries will amount to ten folio volumes of 600 pages each, eighty-two articles in a page. The whole number of articles will not be less than *half a million*.

_____

Evidence before the Committee of the House of Commons, 1818.

Mr. OWEN REES.

Have the goodness to inform the Committee what sum has the delivery of the eleven copies, under the copyright act, cost your house since July, 1811? I presume you mean from the date of the passing of the act in 1814. From the nearest calculation we are enabled to make, the actual cost of the books delivered upon the whole, since the passing of the act, is about £3,000.

Have you, in consequence of the burthen of this delivery, declined printing any works which you would otherwise have undertaken? Yes; we have declined printing some works, particularly a work of Non-descript Plants, by Baron Humboldt, from South America; being obliged to deliver the eleven copies, has always weighed very strongly with us in declining other works.

Have the libraries demanded all books promiscuously printed, or have they made any selection? Every book entered at Stationers' Hall has been sent to them. No selection has ever been made; nine copies of all books have been demanded, and eleven of all, with the exception of novels and music, which have not been demanded by two of the libraries.

What duty do you pay upon paper? The duty for paper used for printing is from 20 to 25 per cent. on the value of the paper.

Was it not usual, before the passing of this act, for the public libraries to subscribe to, and frequently to purchase, learned and very expensive works; and did not authors calculate on the Universities as probable purchasers of the work they were about to bring forward? They certainly have looked to the Universities as subscribers or purchasers of these books; and upon examination I find it was the custom of some of the libraries, who can claim books under the act, to subscribe to expensive works, and that within fourteen years after the passing of the act of Anne.

Have not some valuable books been discontinued from want of sufficient subscribers? Yes, there have been important works, which have been abandoned for want of sufficient encouragement:—

    Rev. Mr. Bourchier's Dictionary of Obsolete and Provincial Words.
    Dr. Murray's (the Editor of Bruce's Travels) History of Languages.
    Translations of Matthew Paris, and other Latin Historians. William of Malmesbury only published. One more has been translated, but not published.
    An extensive British Biography, arranged in Periods. A considerable portion of this work has been written by some of the first writers of the present day.
    The collected Works of Sir Isaac Newton.
    Hearne's (the Antiquary) Works.
    Collections of the Irish Historians.
    Bawdwen's Translation of the Doomsday-Book, after the Translation was finished, and one volume and a half printed.

What do you apprehend to be the effect of the delivery of these copies to the public libraries? The effect I conceive to be that they interfere with the sale of books from persons who would otherwise be purchasers, having access to the libraries, and being enabled to borrow the books, some of them being circulating libraries, as is the case with the Advocates' Library at Edinburgh, and the Aberdeen Library. From Aberdeen, I have had complaints from booksellers that they find their trade considerably injured by such books being in circulation, and that formerly they supplied the King's College with books to a considerable amount; that their accounts at present are a mere trifle, and that some of their books have been sold to a circulating library.

Can you state in any given period what you have paid for advertising books? In the last twelve months we have paid for advertising in newspapers alone £4,638 : 7s. 8d.

Do you know what proportion of that goes to Government? I should conceive about £1,500 of that goes to Government.

In point of fact, according to the act in 1814 having been passed, have you not been obliged to deliver some very expensive works of old English literature, which otherwise would not have been demandable? We have.

Has not that demand had an effect, among other reasons, of inducing you not to embark in other reprints of the same nature? It has.

Mr. RICHARD TAYLOR.

What description of books do you apprehend to be principally affected by the delivery of the eleven copies to the public libraries? State the different kinds of books that you think are most affected by this law. I think that all the most important works, which furnish the materials for the advancement in the sciences, are those by which the least is gained ; or I should say, rather the most is lost by those who undertake them; such as records of experiments in chemistry and other branches of physics. Astronomical observations, such works as Bradley's Observations, and Dr. Maskelyne's, if they had been published at private expense, must have been published at a loss; because the demand for them is very limited, and the expense of printing would be very great. Bradley's Astronomical Observations are published in two volumes, folio, and Dr. Maskelyne's, in four or five volumes. I should observe, that all table and figure work costs twice as much as common printing, on account of the greater trouble in composing such work. Such works as these furnish all the materials from which the science of astronomy can be advanced. All these works are of infinite value to science, and cost the authors an immense deal of labor, as they are frequently the result of their observations during a great portion of their lives. Elementary, or popular works of astronomy, may be objects of gain to the booksellers ; but no book-seller could be induced to publish the astronomical observations of any gentleman, who might have an observatory of his own, and who might have been making observations for many years. Of mathe-matical works, the most profound are the least likely to attain a considerable sale. A gentleman, whom I have known for many years as one of the most munificent patrons of science, who has expended perhaps more than any man in publishing, and enabling others to publish, valuable mathematical treatises, I mean Baron Maseres, the Cursitor-Baron of the Exchequer, once told me that the produce of the whole sale of his *Scriptores Logarithmici*, (which is a collection of the most valuable mathematical tracts, reprinted at his expense) did not pay for the binding of the presentation-copies which he gave away.

Mr. JOHN CLARKE.

Have you lately declined the publication of any law-books with the improvement of notes ? I have.

What are they ? One of them was Mr. Anstruther's Reports.

Any others ? Not immediately that I recollect. I have made re-prints of law-books, without the addition of notes or improvements.

Why did you decline the publication of them with improvements? Because if I had added the notes, I should have been necessarily obliged to deliver the eleven copies to the public libraries.

If you merely published the reprint of any book without addition or improvement, you would not be liable to deliver the copies to the Universities ? I should not, having delivered them before.

Should you decline republishing a book with notes for that reason ? I should in some instances.

Mr. ROBERT BALDWIN.

What do you apprehend to have been the effect of the regulation for the delivery of the eleven copies to the public libraries, upon the bookselling trade in general ? I think it has been a heavy loss to the bookselling trade, and, in some instances, it has operated to check the publication of books, and particularly to prevent additions and improvements to old editions of books.

In the demand made by the public libraries to the bookseller, has any regard been paid, either to the utility of the respective books demanded, or to the books previously delivered by the publisher? None at all; they have been taken indsicriminately. I should suppose that if a sum of money was allotted to the Universities to purchase books, they would not purchase one in ten of what are published, perhaps not one in twenty.

Do you think that the depositing of the eleven copies in these public libraries, has any tendency to take away private purchasers? Certainly, I think it must.

Does it not, in your opinion, supply gratuitously many people who would otherwise be purchasers? I should think it would.

Do you conceive the evil is to be at all counteracted by any supposed notoriety given to those publications, by the depositing of such copies in the public libraries? Not by any means.

Do you conceive that your publications acquire any advantage by any such supposed notoriety? We do not consider the supposition of notoriety arising from the depositing of the books, to be well founded, or productive of any advantage; if we did, we should send the books to the public libraries without any compulsion.

Mr. JOHN MURRAY.

Did you not publish the Costumes of various Countries? Yes.

Was that an expensive work? It was very expensive.

Should you now hesitate in the publication of such a work, knowing that you would be compelled to deliver eleven copies to the eleven public libraries? Certainly I would.

Were you not concerned in the publication of the Harleian Miscellany, Lord Somers' Tracts, and Piers Ploughman's Visions? Yes.

Would you, knowing that you are compelled to deliver eleven copies of all works, be disposed to engage in the publication of such books? In the publication of Piers Ploughman's Visions, I think I should not have engaged in it, if I had to deliver the eleven copies; but as to the other two books, it might, perhaps, be matter of consideration.

But would the delivery of those eleven copies make you hesitate? Certainly; the number to be printed being so limited, even of those, and the expense of the Harleian Miscellany and Lord Somers' Tracts so great, I think I should hesitate.

The wholesale price of these eleven copies would amount to a very large sum? It would be a very serious object.

What may be the amount of the books which you may have delivered at Stationers' Hall since the passing of the Act of 1814? The amount of the sale price to the public is about £1,700, and as those books had a very swift sale, I consider that I am the loser of that sum, deducting 25 per cent., which would be the sum at which the greatest part of those works would have been sold, I would deduct about £420, the whole loss then would be about £1,275.

Do you not consider the compulsory delivery of eleven copies of every book that is published, as a very heavy tax on those who speculate in the publication of books, in addition to the very high duty on paper and advertisements ? Very much indeed.

In making the demand, do the libraries omit the reprints of such works as they may already have in their libraries, or is their demand a sweeping one of every book entered at Stationers' Hall, whether it be a reprint, or an entirely new book ? According to my observation, they make a sweeping demand of every book.

Did you not publish Mr. Duppa's Life of Michael Angelo ? Yes.

Was not that a work in which the delivery of the eleven copies would have been a great injury and inconvenience to you ? Yes.

You also published D'Israeli's Character of James the First ? Yes.

What number of that book did you publish ? I published 250.

After the sale of the whole of that edition, were you not obliged to buy up or collect some copies of that work, to make up the eleven to be delivered to the public libraries ? I was.

Upon the whole, you consider the gratuitous delivery of eleven copies to the public libraries as a great grievance ? Yes.

Mr. WILLIAM DANIEL.

Has the act, directing the delivery of eleven copies to the public libraries, had any effect upon any publications which you have made, or which you had intended to make ? Checking many.

Will you be so good as to state what effect it had upon you individually ? It has prevented the continuation of a large folio work, intituled Oriental Scenery. It has prevented also a reduced edition of an African work, another of Ceylon, " A Series of Scenes and Figures, illustrative of the Customs of India, and of Persons and Animals peculiar to that Country." I believe these are the chief works which the act has checked me in proceeding with.

Mr. WILLIAM BERNARD COOKE.

Are you not publishing a work upon the ruins of Pompeii ? I am.

What would be the price of a complete copy of that work ? A complete copy would be sixteen guineas, and the price of the copies upon India paper 32 guineas.

Is that the retail price? Yes ; the retail price to the public.

Then what will be the amount of eleven copies at the retail price ? £201 : 12s., because the finest copies are claimed by the British Museum.

If the act of 1814 had not passed, should you have expected any of the libraries to have been subscribers to the work ? I certainly should, because the British Museum had purchased the first edition of the Thames, and have discontinued purchasing any other work since.

Has the delivery of the eleven copies, in your opinion, operated to discourage such publications ? Most certainly.

Had you any hesitation in undertaking the work of Pompeii ? I certainly had, in consequence of those eleven copies.

Mr. Joseph Harding.

Are you a bookseller? Yes.

And a partner in the house of Lackington, Hughes, Harding, Mavor, and Jones, in Finsbury-square? Yes.

Are you at present engaged in the publication of any works of considerable expense? Yes.

What works are you publishing of that description? We are publishing an edition of Dugdale's Monasticon Anglicanum, in four or five folio volumes; Dugdale's History of St. Paul's Cathedral; Portraits of Illustrious Personages of Great Britain, in two folio volumes, with 120 Portraits and Memoirs; Ormerod's History of Cheshire; Wood's Athenæ Oxoniensis, in six volumes quarto; they are the principal works we are publishing at this time.

What will the delivery of eleven copies of these works amount to? The delivery of eleven copies of these works will amount to £2,198 : 14s.

Can you state *the comparative prices of English books printed in London, and the same books printed abroad?* I have the prices of some English books, printed on the Continent which may throw light upon that question: Gibbon's Miscellaneous Works, with his memoirs, printed at Basle in seven volumes octavo, are sold retail for twenty-five francs, which amounts to about a guinea. The price of the London edition of the same book in five volumes octavo, is £3 : 5s.; Hume's History of England, from the Invasion of Julius Cæsar to the Revolution in 1688, published in twelve volumes octavo, is sold at forty-five francs retail price, which is about thirty-eight shillings; the price in London is £3 : 12s. small paper, and £5 : 12s. if printed on large paper; Robertson's History of Scotland, published in three octavo volumes, is printed, and sells for twelve francs, about ten shillings, the price of the London edition in three octavo volumes is £1 : 1s.; Roscoe's History of the Medici Family, published in four volumes octavo, is sold for sixteen francs, about 13s. 4d., the London price is £1 : 11s. 6d.; Pope's Works, with notes by Warton, published in nine octavo volumes, are sold for twenty-five francs, about a guinea, the London price in ten volumes octavo is five guineas; the price of Johnson and Stevens's Shakspeare, published in twenty-three volumes octavo, with sixty plates, is sixty francs, about £2 : 10s., the London edition, published in twenty-one volumes octavo, without any plates at all, is sold at twelve guineas on small paper, and on large paper for eighteen guineas.

Have you declined publishing any works from the pressure of delivering eleven copies, besides Mr. Ruding's "History of the Coinage?" Yes, we have.

Is there any inconvenience in stating what they are? We have declined republishing Alexander Barclay's "Ship of Fools," a folio volume of great rarity and high price. Our probable demand would not have been more than for one hundred copies, at the price of twelve guineas each. The delivery of eleven copies to the public libraries decided us against entering into the speculation. There is another work which we have declined printing, materially from the pressure of the eleven copies, which is a work of great value: it is "A Series of

Views relating to the Architectural Antiquities of Normandy," by Mr. Cotman of Yarmouth; it is a work peculiarly interesting to antiquaries and to architects, but to few other classes of society.

Mr. JOHN MARTIN.

Are you not engaged in the publication of Mr. Dodwell's Scenes and Monuments of Greece? We are.

What would be the price of a complete copy of that work? About thirty guineas.

Should you expect any of the eleven libraries to be subscribers to this work, if the copies were not delivered in pursuance of this legal obligation? I should expect they would. I see by a reference to a book on the same subject, Mr. Mills's "Magna Græcia," that there are entered amongst the subscribers, the University libraries of Cambridge; Trinity College, Dublin; and several other colleges.

Does the placing eleven copies in these eleven libraries in your opinion benefit or injure the sale of the work? I should conceive that any work so expensive as this would be materially injured by such delivery. It would have an injurious tendency.

If the law which requires the delivery of eleven copies to the public libraries continues, do you propose to publish the work without letter-press? If that provision for the delivery continues, we shall publish it without letter-press.

Was any and what application made to you on the part of the French Government to have this work to publish at Paris? The proposition was made to the author when he was in Paris; and on his return home, the work was shown, at the request of the French Institute, to the French Princes, to the Officers of the French Government, &c., and by them an offer was made to publish the plates in four volumes folio, each volume to contain one hundred plates, with accompanying letter-press; but the author wishing it to be published in this country, declined the proposition.

Would it have been more beneficial to the author to have published at Paris? I should conceive it would certainly.

Mr. CHARLES STOTHARD.

You are publishing the Monumental Effigies of Great Britain? Yes.

The price is twenty-eight guineas the large paper, and twenty-guineas the small? Yes.

Do you publish the work on your own account? Certainly.

Do you conceive that the delivery of the eleven copies to the public libraries is a great grievance? A very great one indeed, for I believe that if I had known it when I commenced the work, I should not have begun it.

Do you conceive, that subject to the delivery of the eleven copies that work could have been published by a bookseller? No, certainly not, nor at its present price. Indeed at its present price it is impossible, when the work is completed, that I can sell it at that price. In order to sell it, I must raise it one quarter above its present price.

Mr. Samuel Lysons.

For twenty-five years I have been preparing for publication an extensive work on the Roman Antiquities of England, entitled " Reliquiæ Britannico Romanæ," consisting of more than 160 plates in folio, many of them forty inches by twenty-three, on which work I have already expended £6,000. From the nature of this work, which requires that the greater part of the plates should be colored to render them intelligible, it is not probable that more than a hundred copies will ever be completed; and if the whole of that number should be sold at fifty guineas a copy, I should not reimburse my expenses. In the two first volumes of this work already published, I have given a short letter-press description of the plates; but finding under the last Act of Parliament for the encouragement of learning, my continuing to give such printed explanations would subject me to the heavy tax of eleven copies of my work for the public libraries, and deprive me of several of my purchasers, some of those libraries having bought my two first volumes, I have determined to omit any letter-press, and have engraved my title pages and list of plates. I am convinced that few books of antiquities or natural history, consist-ing chiefly of plates, which are attended with a very heavy expense, and especially those which require to be colored, can be published in this country with letter-press, if the editors are thereby liable to be taxed with the delivery of the eleven copies for the public libraries; and that the publishers will be under the necessity either of omitting any printed description, or having them printed on the continent, where much would be saved in the article of paper alone, the price of the larger sorts of which in this country is extremely high, in conse-quence of the heavy duty on them.

You are Keeper of the Records of the Tower of London, and greatly acquainted with works of English History in every department; do you consider that the eleven copies demandable by the public libra-ries are a great discouragement to such persons as would otherwise adventure the publication of ancient English documents? I can hardly venture an opinion upon that; generally speaking, it is a very great discouragement to literature; to books of a certain expense, or to books of which very many large impressions are printed, and that are like to have an extensive sale, it might be of very little importance; but certainly in large quarto volumes attended with heavy expenses, and which take many years before their expenses are repaid, the giving up eleven copies in the first instance is certainly a very heavy taxation.

Mr. Samuel Brooke.

What is your line of business? Printing and publishing.

In what peculiar line? Particularly in the law line.

Have you experienced any inconvenience or injury from the pro-visions of the Copyright Act? I am very much aggrieved by the necessity of delivering eleven copies of the works which I publish, principally law works, on which it falls very hard.

In what manner do you conceive law works are particularly affected by the delivery of the eleven copies? The temporary nature of their matter makes it necessary to confine their editions to a comparatively small number of copies, and the expences of printing and editing are so great, that the deduction of eleven copies is a very serious evil as attaching to every new edition.

Mr. ROBERT HARDING EVANS.

In very expensive works, particularly of scientific illustration, can you speak to the operation of the act of 1814? I conceive it to be a very heavy and very grievous imposition upon the bookseller, and such as is not levied by any other country in Europe.

Have you found from your own experience that, that act, has operated to the discouragement of any literary production to which you refer? Certainly it has prevented the printing and publishing of several editions of the classics, which were about to be printed at the time the act passed, but which were laid aside by the booksellers in consequence.

Specify a few of those books to which you allude that happened to be within your recollection? For instance, Damm's " Lexicon to Homer and Pindar," and a reprint of " Brotier Tacitus." These were laid aside.

In making a contract with the author of a book, would the eleven copies that are to be delivered to the public libraries be taken into the account, and charged against the author. Suppose you were to reprint an old book, such as "Corpus Rerum Anglicanum," should you take the eleven copies into account and charge them against the author? Certainly I should take it into the account; and [I should conceive, that literature would be injured by the operation of this obligation, because the author must participate in that loss.

Mr. THOMAS FISHER, 1817.

Observing myself publicly called upon to explain, why, a publication, which was commenced in the year 1808, upon paintings discovered at Stratford-upon-Avon, in Warwickshire, has not yet been completed in the manner then proposed, I feel it to be a duty which I owe to the public to afford the required explanation.

The work in question, was undertaken at a period, when the practical interpretation of the Copyright Act of the 8th year of Queen Anne had, *for exactly a century preceding*, left authors and publishers at liberty to judge for themselves, how far the protection held out in that act, was desirable to them at the price they were called on to pay for it, *viz. eleven* copies; and, according to the decision of their own judgment, it was optional with them, either to register their works under the provisions of this and a subsequent act, and thus to sacrifice eleven copies, or to omit such registration, and leave their works open to piracy.

Estimating, from the character of my work, its probable circulation at a very small number, and considering the laborious manner in which every copy was to be finished in colors ; convinced also, of

R

the impossibility of any profitable piracy under these circumstances (and I conceive nothing but the hope of profit will induce piracy), I resolved on executing an impression of only 120 copies of the paintings at a *polyautographic* press ; by the eventual sale of which impression, chiefly amongst students in antiquity, I expected to obtain a very small remuneration for my labor.

For the accomplishment of my design, I had obtained access to materials, original and interesting, beyond the general run of topographical publications; and, in the confidence of success, I certainly did intimate a purpose of completing the work, by the addition of copperplates and *copious letter-press*, thereby intending a memoir of the ancient fraternity or Guild of Holy Cross at Stratford-upon Avon, at whose cost these paintings were executed, to be compiled from the authentic records of the Corporation.

But, unfortunately, while the materials for the fourth part were in a state of considerable progress, a question was brought under legal discussion, arising out of an *unconditional* claim, made by one of eleven privileged bodies, to receive from the proprietors of all works, without *purchase,* and without *exception,* one copy of every literary performance, even although it might not be deemed expedient by the author to claim the protection of the Act of Queen Anne for the copyright.

Mr. Brougham's arguments against this claim in the Court of King's Bench appeared to me at the time, and have ever since appeared to me, just and convincing ; those of the opposite party had this obvious defect, that they led to a result prejudicial to that literature which the Act of Queen Anne, in its preamble, expressly professed to befriend. A decision, however, was obtained, favorable to the claim ; on the legal validity of which there could be no question, whatever doubts might exist as to its accuracy.

Under these altered circumstances, I conceive myself justified in declining either to involve myself in the predicament of attempting to evade the law, which is repugnant to my feelings—or of submitting to an unreasonable loss of property, which I have a right to avoid,— or, as a remaining alternative, to involve myself in legal disputes with powerful and wealthy bodies, who, *with ample funds, and a host of legal retainers,* have, by an extraordinary plea of *poverty,* obtained the sanction of the legislature to their claim.

To the yet unpublished plates of my Stratford-upon-Avon, the subscribers will be welcome, as soon as I can put them together ; and I am not yet so far advanced in life, but that I entertain a hope of being enabled to complete my original design, when the legislature shall have perceived, as it unquestionably must in a very few years perceive, the prejudicial consequences to literature and science of the law as it now stands.

REPORT OF THE COMMITTEE OF THE HOUSE OF COMMONS, 1818.

In no other country, as far as the Committee have been able to procure information, is any demand of this kind carried to a similar extent ;—in America, Prussia, Saxony, and Bavaria, one copy only is required to be deposited; in France and Austria, two; and in the Netherlands, three; but in several of these countries the delivery is not necessary, unless copyright is intended to be claimed. They are of opinion, that one copy should be delivered in future to the British Museum ; and that in lieu of the others, a fixed allowance be granted to such of the other public libraries as may be thought expedient. Upon an average, it appears that the price of one copy of every book entered at Stationers' Hall would be about £500. If it should not be thought expedient by the House to comply with this recommendation, they think it desirable that the number of libraries entitled to the claim should be restricted to those of Oxford, Cambridge, Edinburgh, and Dublin Universities, and the British Museum. They advise, also, that books of prints, wherein the letter-press shall not exceed a certain very small proportion to each plate, shall be exempted from delivery, except to the Museum, with an exception of all books of mathematics ; that all books, in respect of which claims to copyright shall be expressly and effectually abandoned, be also exempted; and that the obligation imposed on printers, to retain one copy of each work printed by them, shall cease, and the copy of the Museum be made evidence in lieu of it.

QUARTERLY REVIEW, 1819.

It is argued that the bookseller may and will increase the price of a book in consideration of the tax. The reply to this is, that books are already too dear—so dear, that their sale in a foreign market is diminished by this cause to a very great degree, almost indeed destroyed. And this is one reason why our literature is so little known on the continent. Such works as happen to have a reputation there, are printed there, and sold for less than half the selling price of the same works in England. The Americans continually complain of the dearness of our books, and it operates in their country to lessen the sale of those which they do not print for themselves. With the tax upon advertisements, with the duty upon paper from 20 to 25 per cent., books are necessarily dear, and they can bear no additional tax. It must be also remembered that every English book printed abroad is a loss to the revenue of so much duty on paper. Hence, whatever tends to induce publishers to print English works on the continent, is an injury to the country at large.

The most amusing part is, that the advocates of the Universities take credit for promoting the interests of literature, and especially for having originally suggested an extension of copyright in favor of authors or their assigns. They are indeed notable friends to authors, and have treated them as lovingly as Isaac Walton's Piscator instructs his pupil to handle the frog:—"Put your hook into his mouth, which you may easily do from the middle of April till August, and then the frog's mouth grows up, and he continues so for at least six months without eating, but is sustained; none but he whose name is Wonderful, knows how. I say, put your hook through his mouth and out at his gills, and then with a fine needle and silk, sew the upper part of his leg with only one stitch to the arming-wire of your hook, and in so doing, use him as though you loved him." But unlike the frog, the author cannot subsist for six months without eating; and there is also another point of dissimilitude, that as his mouth does not grow up, he is sometimes able to express his sense of the loving usage which he receives.

———

PAMPHLETEER, 1821.

I will first remark on the original idea, that the *eleven* copies to the libraries is for the encouragement of literature. If this were granted, it would be an argument for the extension of the gift to *all* the public libraries, in which case it would surely better become Government to furnish them at the public expense; and not, as at present, render the tax so partial, that it has checked, and must often check, the publication of many works of taste and importance.

It is urged, that the privilege is merely a quid pro quo, i.e. the security of the copyright. Surely literature should not be the only shackled patent; for copyright is another term for patent. Who, indeed, would have invented a steam-engine, if he had been obliged, *before* he could sell *one*, to give *thirteen* to public buildings?—(for the large paper copy to the British Museum, and one to the printer, make the number *thirteen*.) As well might coals and candles be thus *given* to the libraries for the encouragement of literature. At all events, the stationer should be obliged to furnish the paper gratis, and Government should allow the draw back on the duty.

It has been argued in favor of the claim, that it was enacted and exacted in former times; but to this I should answer, that before the diffusion of literature became general, an apprehension might exist, that works of merit and information might be lost; that in the mode of printing which prevailed at that time---crowded pages and on common paper—the expense was trifling: but inconsiderable as it was then, the good sense of the directors of the libraries had induced them to forego and abandon the claim.

It cannot be urged that the public pay for it, because it is not certain that the other 487, out of the 500, will sell; if it were, the author, *so* situated, would be indemnified: but it will readily occur, that in such a case, the price of 487 must be raised, and consequently the sale become more slow and precarious. Besides, the answer to that argument is easy,—the thirteen copies should only be taken AFTER the sale of the 487, by which means authors would lose less, and the libraries preserve their privilege. To confirm this position, it might be added, if the book is worth any thing, it will be certain of sale, and they of their copies; if otherwise, it will not be worth a place on their shelves.

There are, however, great objections to this increase of price, necessarily incurred by this gift, or rather extortion.—1st. That our continental rivals are enabled to undersell us in our own market, even without the weight of this additional tax, in consequence of the high duty on paper, metal, rags, leather, &c. used in the manufacture of a book:—ex. gr. *Porsoni Adversaria, P. Knight's Prolegomena,* and the *School Gradus,* reprinted on the continent, are sold cheaper in this country, with all the burthen of the import tax, than our own editions—besides most of our popular English authors.—2nd. That poor authors, who are most to be considered, are miserably discouraged, since publishers reject much of their labors, owing to the operation of the act.—3rd. That the revenue itself suffers in a variety of ways by this check to publication, from decreased consumption of paper, &c., and the consequent diminution of employment to artists and mechanics. Indeed, I am sure that the present loss to the revenue would amply enable Government to grant 300*l.* per annum to each of these libraries; which would more than purchase all the useful books published in the year, for I believe 400*l.* would pay for a copy of every work printed within each year. The duty on the paper alone, of a work value one hundred guineas, would repay Government for such a grant to these libraries.—But it is well known that they are sufficiently rich to supply themselves with the works they want.

It is notorious that the minor productions sent to the Universities are not immediately shelved, but *lent through* the University, to one after another. This, no doubt, encourages the *reading* of many works; but as the reading *so* obtained *cannot* increase the sale, what chance of remuneration is left to the author? If it were supposed that persons would, by seeing such works, become purchasers, then the act should rather oblige the libraries to buy, or, at any rate, only have the books lent them for a certain time; which might thus induce the libraries to purchase, in order to keep them, after having discovered their value.

———

NEW MONTHLY MAGAZINE, 1826.

Among the serious inconveniences, or rather losses, which the public sustains from the present oppressive enactment of presenting eleven copies of all published books to certain public and private libraries, we may instance two recent works, which consist only of a series of engravings, without any letter-press, and which are thus published to obviate this literary tax—*Illustrations of the Pavilion at Brighton;* one of these is an expensive production of prints, beautifully drawn, engraved, and colored, but without a line of historical or descriptive information accompanying them. Thus the stranger, viewing them, may *fancy* the engravings the chimera of the architect's and painter's fancy, *or* the " country palace" of its monarch. Should he be told this is the fact---that it has been crowded with princes, lords, and ladies, and is now deserted, he will be more than commonly inquisitive to learn something of its history---when and by whom it was designed, built, and fitted up.—On this, and on all other points, he is left to ruminate, and probably draw erroneous conclusions, for no information is afforded; and we are credibly informed, that the *King's architect*, who has just published these prints, was induced to avoid giving any letter-press to save himself from the unjust tax of presenting eleven copies of a twenty guinea volume, or throwing away 220 guineas in copies, but one of which (namely, that to the British Museum) is purely devoted *pro bono publico*—the only excuse which could sanction such an appropriation and sacrifice of private property. Robson's *Picturesque Views of all the English Cities* (one number of which has just appeared, containing a very interesting and beautiful series of engravings), is another example of the workings of this oppressive act. In the prospectus, the editor, who has been a staunch and zealous defender of " the rights of literature," says, " The reader will see that it is not proposed to give letter-press with these plates." Historical and descriptive accounts of the cities" treated and illustrated in a novel style," will be published ; but this will form a separate and distinct work, in order to obviate the very *unjust, oppressive, and vexatious tax* of giving eleven copies of an expensive series of illustrations to public and wealthy institutions, which ought to *encourage* art as well as literature,—which have ample funds of their own, and the benefits of which are of a private and exclusive nature ; for it cannot be denied, that even the advantages of Oxford and Cambridge are sealed against one half the population of England, that is to say, against all who dissent from the established church, and they form a fair half of her population, to say nothing of nine-tenths of the population of Ireland, which consists of catholics and protestant dissenters — Scotland alone having Universities open to all her population.

TABLE

OF

CASES

CITED OR REFERRED TO,

AND

WORKS OR SUBJECTS LITIGATED.

I N D E X.

LITERARY PROPERTY,
    definition of, 1.
LYSONS, Mr. Samuel
    his evidence on the library tax, 240.
LYTTLETON, Lord,
    his opinions on the rights of authors, 218.

MACAULEY, Mrs. Catherine,
    her opinions on the rights of authors, 219.
MAGAZINES,
    See *Reviews*, 126.
MANSFIELD, Lord,
    his opinion on the rights of authors, 1, 8, 9.
MANUSCRIPTS,
    copyright in, 74.
    unpublished works in general, 74.
    pirating, 137.
    of deceased persons, 140.
    private letters, literary and general, 141.
MARTIN, Mr John,
    his evidence on the library tax, 239.
MAPS, CHARTS, &c.
    copyright in, 79.
    pirating, 162.
MILTON,
    his opinion on copyright, 211.
MODELS. See *Sculpture*, 84.
MONBODDO, Lord,
    his opinion on the rights of authors, 214.
MONTHLY REVIEW
    on the rights of authors, 221.
MORALS,
    works excluded from injury to public, 89.
MURRAY, Mr. John,
    his evidence on the library tax, 236.
MUSIC,
    property in, 76.
    the transfer, 174.
    acquiescence in the publication, 174.
    partial consent, 175.

Netherlands,
    the tax for public libraries, xii.
NEW EDITION,
    copyright in the notes to an old work, 76.
    pirating, 128.

S

J. EVANS, PRINTER, 91, BARTHOLOMEW CLOSE, LONDON.

ERRATA.

Page xviii,   line 9, for *o* read *of* literary.

6,   25, for *underwritten* read *unwritten*.

11,   80, for *process* read *progress*.

71,   7, for *where* read *were*.

120,   Note (1) for 55 read 65.

173,   2, for *implied* read *impliedly*.

182,   last line, insert "*is* said."

187,   2, for *mere* read *merely*.

196,   37, for *Augustine* read *Augustan*.

206,   30, for *injusticy* read *injustice*.

For EU product safety concerns, contact us at Calle de José Abascal, 56–1°,
28003 Madrid, Spain or eugpsr@cambridge.org.

 www.ingramcontent.com/pod-product-compliance
Ingram Content Group UK Ltd.
Pitfield, Milton Keynes, MK11 3LW, UK
UKHW010347140625
459647UK00010B/883